MADE TO PLAY HOUSE

MADE TO PLAY HOUSE

Dolls and the Commercialization of American

Girlhood, 1830–1930

MIRIAM FORMANEK-BRUNELL

The Johns Hopkins University Press
Baltimore and London

The original edition of this book was published with assistance from the foundation established in memory of Philip Hamilton McMillan of the Class of 1894, Yale College.

Johns Hopkins Paperbacks edition, 1998
2 4 6 8 9 7 5 3 1

The Johns Hopkins University Press
2715 North Charles Street
Baltimore, Maryland 21218-4363
www.press.jhu.edu

Designed by Sonia L. Scanlon
Set in Garamond type by Tseng Information Systems

Photograph on title page by Schecter Lee.
Photographs on pages 56, 84, 96, 105, 143, 147, 149, 177, 178, and 183 by Ruth Formanek.
Photograph of Grace Storey Putnam on p. 158 reprinted with the permission of Charles Scribner's Sons, an imprint of Macmillan Publishing Company, from *Dolls through Three Centuries* By Eleanor Saint George. Copyright 1951 Charles Scribner's Sons; copyright renewed ©1979

Library of Congress Cataloging-in-Publication Data
Formanek-Brunell, Miriam.
Made to play house : dolls and the commercialization of American girlhood, 1830–1930 / Miriam Formanek-Brunell.
p.   cm.
Originally published : New Haven : Yale University Press, c1993.
Includes bibliographical references and index.
ISBN 0-8018-6062-8 (pbk. : alk. paper)
1. Doll industry—Social aspects—United States—History.
I. Title.
HD9993.D653U63   1998
338.4´76887221´0973—dc21   98-27077
                                                                                                                      CIP

A catalog record for this book is available from the British Library.

In memory of Selma W. Greenberg

CONTENTS

Contents

ACKNOWLEDGMENTS

My interest in the history of dolls first began when I was an undergraduate in a women's history seminar, and the professor asked us to consider the variety of nontraditional sources that could be used to study the history of women. My sister and I had just returned from the Philadelphia Children's Museum, where the antique dolls seemed to convey something about gender, race, and class. Dolls, I thought, then doubted my own notion. It suddenly occurred to me that I did not really have any idea what dolls could tell us, and not even to what precisely in history they referred. Nevertheless, I spent the next decade trying to understand the relation between dolls and American culture with the help of several mentors. I am deeply grateful to Barbara Berg, who posed the question that launched this project, and to John Gillis, whose fascination with childhood, the family, and rituals inspired me during difficult times, especially after the death of my first doctoral adviser, Warren Susman. It was my good fortune to then study with T. J. Jackson Lears, whose warm friendship and outstanding scholarship have provided me with insight and a sense of irony.

The project also benefited from the observations of many conference participants and commentators, especially at the seventh Berkshire Conference on the History of Women, the 1987 International Conference on Women's History at the University of Amsterdam, the 1986 National Women's Studies Association at the University of Illinois, "The Material Culture of Gender: The Gender of Material Culture" conference sponsored by the Winterthur Museum and Gardens in 1989, and the 1992 American Studies Association conference. I want especially to thank those who encouraged me to think beyond girls' acceptance of dolls and to consider their resistance to them.

The research for this book could not have been completed without the help of numerous people at various institutions. Mrs. Eileen Ryan arranged for me to leaf through volumes of *Playthings* magazine for weeks at a time. Both Margaret Whitton and Judy Emerson, her successor at the

Margaret Woodbury Strong Museum, directed me toward useful sources on women in the doll industry. At the Smithsonian's National Museum of American History, Rodris Roth, curator of the division of domestic life, generously shared her dolls, expertise, and time with me. The Smithsonian's librarians kindly held back the flood of overdue notices sent by the Library of Congress. I also wish to thank the examiners at the United States Patent Office for their patience.

I am especially indebted to descendants of the dollmakers who shared not only their family records but their friendship as well. Paul and Dorothy O'Neill were generous hosts and excellent tour guides. Bob and Olga Chase shared rare family documents and memories as did the late Beatrice Behrman (Madame Alexander). Mrs. Gwen Stevenson provided copies of rare photographs and articles about Alabama dollmaker Ella Smith. Phyllis Levenson shared an unpublished autobiography which gave me insights no other source could. I am grateful to Marilyn Donovan for sharing portions of the diary written by her grandmother, Grace Storey Putnam, and to Dottie Baker for her assistance in facilitating this arrangement. Finally, I am indebted to Dorothy and Evelyn Jane Coleman for the vast amounts of information they have accumulated in their published works that opened up many new avenues for research.

My work could not have been completed without financial assistance from various foundations and institutions. I am grateful for a Woodrow Wilson Foundation Predoctoral Fellowship in Women's Studies and a Smithsonian Institution Predoctoral Fellowship. A research grant from the New Jersey Historical Society enabled me to pursue regional interests. A 1992 National Endowment for the Humanities Summer Stipend allowed me to focus on the commercial artist Rose O'Neill, and a Faculty Research Award from Wellesley College enabled me to employ my research assistant, Marcella Pereira.

In addition, this book could not have been written without the support of friends, especially Lisa Tiersten and Martha Hodes. April Masten edited chapter 2 as if it were her own. Paul Borcier, formerly of the Rhode Island Historical Society, is not only a fine editor but also an outstanding curator. I benefited from the insights of Paula Petrik, Elliott West, Bernard Mergen, Kenneth Ames, Diane Buck, Katherine Martinez, David Nasaw,

Virginia Yans, Martha Howell, and Susan Reverby, who all read portions of the manuscript. Charles Grench, my editor, showed confidence in this project when it was little more than a proposal and was patient with me as it became more substantial. Noreen O'Connor copyedited the manuscript with an eye and an ear for clarity.

Without the devotion of Ingrid N. Kondos and the patience of Laura Schlossberg, Melissa Hardin, and other baby sitters, revising the book would have been much more difficult. I am especially grateful to Carolyn S. Ellman, who guided my understanding of myself as a historian of gender and childhood. I want to thank my family, especially my mother, Ruth Formanek, whose encouragement, scholarship, and editing have been an inspiration to me. My six nieces and nephew have provided me with lots of ideas about dolls, what they mean, and how to play with them. My little boy, Perry, brought toys into my office and joy into my life. Finally, I want to thank my husband, Claude, for his thoughtful editing, unfailing support, and true love.

MADE TO PLAY HOUSE

INTRODUCTION

Have dolls always promoted self-fulfillment in girls? How do dolls shape the gender identities of girls? Although collectors have been dolls' most conscientious historical researchers, they have seldom posed such questions. While useful in the identification of a doll's national origin or material make-up, doll encyclopedias typically overlook the forces that shape the doll play of girls and boys, the consumer behavior of parents, and the motivations of inventors and manufacturers of dolls.[1]

Similar to the inattentiveness of collectors to historical context is the skepticism of many historians about the study of the history of girls' culture. And, until recently, feminist scholars dismissively interpreted dolls as representative of a patriarchal culture and girls as passive consumers. Because our basic assumptions about dolls have gone unchallenged, dolls continue to be misunderstood in many ways: as trivial artifacts of a commercialized girls' culture; as representations of femininity and maternity; as generators of only maternal feelings and domestic concerns and, as such, obstacles to the development of girls as individuals; as creations of socially conservative dollmakers; and as products of a dominant national culture.

These assumptions have led us to overlook the significance of struggles between women and men for the cultural control of dolls. Informed by recent theoretical debates within the "new" histories of women and consumer culture, this book traces the ways in which dolls—far from passively accepted—were the objects of struggle. On the one hand, businessmen created dolls they marketed as symbols of an idealized feminine domesticity; on the other, women dollmakers manufactured toys that embodied more malleable notions of girlhood and boyhood. That businesswomen reappropriated dolls to suit their social agenda challenges the assumption that all doll manufacturers promoted a uniform notion of gender.[2]

Drawing upon such sources as diaries, autobiographies, newspapers, catalogues, advertisements, photographs, trade journals, juvenile literature, stereographs, and popular magazines, this study documents how American men and women doll manufacturers created remarkably different kinds of dolls that were also distinct from those made by Europeans.[3] Although many feminist scholars now consider the notion of "women's culture" to have distorted our picture of the past, American men and women who manufactured dolls did, in fact, live in different symbolic worlds. The differences in values, attitudes, ideas, and perceptions between businesswomen and businessmen can be gleaned from a "reading" of the ideas embedded in the mundane material objects they invented and then manufactured. Cultural anthropologists, folklorists, and historians who use a material-culture methodology have shown how the objects of ordinary life are readable "texts." As early as 1909 doll collector Laura Starr suggested that "history could be taught by means of dolls. The future historian will have no difficulty in reconstructing our age if he finds merely a few toys in dusty garrets or museums." This study, which also relies on numerous dolls and doll patents issued between 1850 and 1930, takes up Starr's challenge to chart the history of American girlhood and its relation to commercial culture "by means of dolls."[4] Though popularly conceived of as impassive and mute, dolls provide a rich source of information about Americans—women, men, girls, and boys—who were often at odds over issues of gender.[5]

The gender-based traditions that emerged in Victorian America shed light on the differences among dollmakers and the dolls they manufactured. For both men and women, a gender-specific upbringing shaped aesthetics; women drew upon a genteel arts background while men gained experience from mechanics and a trade-oriented tradition. The dolls women produced expressed an orientation to the senses (e.g., being soft to the touch), a preference for individual craftsmanship, and a consideration of the players rather than just the product. In contrast, male dollmakers preferred mechanization, "realism," and "scientific management."

The concerns that motivated American male and female dollmakers were as different as the dolls they designed and manufactured. In the late nineteenth century, middle-class wives contributed to the mothers' magazines that inspired them to make dolls. *Babyhood* magazine was among a number of popular periodicals that extolled the virtues of antebellum rag dolls and disparaged European dolls made of breakable bisque. Middle-class mothers took doll manufacturers to task and rejected their products. Instead of encouraging their daughters to imitate the affectations of American or continental elites with their elegantly dressed china dolls, they promoted cloth dolls that nurtured their emotional growth and ethical development. Unlike Gilded Age dolls that fostered conspicuous consumption, ritual, and display, hand-crafted dolls of the Progressive Era encapsulated the values of "scientific motherhood" espoused by urban and middle-class professionals.

Unlike male dollmakers, women who turned their dollmaking hobby into a career of doll production often lacked previous business experience. Women were far more likely to launch dollmaking ventures with sisters or other female kin with whom they shared the skills and sensibilities of their gendered culture. Conversely, male dollmakers who had previous business experience established partnerships with brothers, sons, and business associates. The differences between businessmen and businesswomen are also evident from an examination of their practices on the shop floor. Late-nineteenth-century female doll producers relied upon other women, with whom they often shared the experience of actually making dolls. In backyard cottages, women combined aspects of feminine, middle-class Victorianism with a premodern workers' culture. These "material maternalists" paid attention to work place safety and promoted congeniality between workers and owners. But the doll workers in the factories of American businessmen performed sex-stereotyped, routinized jobs. Denied union representation, striking doll workers disrupted production.

The differences between the women and men who made dolls was most apparent during the early years of the twentieth century. Dolls produced by such businesswomen as Mary Foote and Martha Chase were endorsed by reform organizations, the settlement house movement, and professional associations of nurses and doctors (including the American Medical Association). At the same time, however, some exploitive businessmen hired children to make dolls in unsanitary and unsafe tenements, paying them by the piece. Thus they incurred the wrath of the National Child Labor Committee and the National Consumer's League. While businesswomen emphasized social reform, the male-dominated Doll Manufacturers of America created Children's Day, a commercial holiday that combined the *image* of social reform with the *reality* of a consumer culture.

Different understandings of girls and their needs also explains, the differences between dolls made by American women and those produced by men. Initially, male Yankee inventors and German-born immigrants drew upon gender-specific skills and sensibilities to construct mechanical dolls for American girls they little understood. According to nineteenth-century male inventors (who rarely mentioned children in their patent applications), dolls entertained and amused. Female inventors, on the other hand, guided by a different conception of American girlhood, cited the *needs* of children as the basis for their inventions. In their patents, women claimed that children needed safe, portable, and durable dolls to teach them about relationships. Women drew upon their childcare experiences, often using their own children as models, while men did not. Progressive Era female entrepreneurs also applied contemporary notions of "scientific motherhood" to the dolls they produced to help working-class children.

Maternalistic dollmakers of the late nineteenth century not only urged their sons to play with dolls but also made dolls in their likeness. By the early twentieth century, "New Women" commercial artists (new entrants into the work force) generated designs of boy dolls, though they did so as employees of businessmen, who forced designers to modify their models. Businessmen who manufactured Kewpie dolls feminized the androgynous Kewpie boys Rose O'Neill had initially created as cartoon characters.

Although both men and women doll manufacturers urged girls to play with the dolls they produced, they disagreed on just what that activity entailed. Businessmen urged "little mothers" to shop for the doll babies they "loved." To Martha Chase and her contemporaries, playing with dolls taught both middle- and working-class children the importance of health and hygiene in the home. And to this Rose O'Neill added an interest in social hygiene. Her Kewpie boys imitated Progressive Era "social housekeepers" who saw the city as one big home in need of a good cleaning. Instead of finding humor in the violence of slum poverty (as did Richard Outcault's mischievous "Yellow Kid" comic-strip character), the affectionate Kewpies mothered the neglected and adopted the unwanted in working-class neighborhoods.

Whatever meaning dolls had to grownups, playing with dolls meant something entirely different to girls, who often confounded adult expectations. Playing house with dolls may have taught skills useful for household production in the antebellum, but most girls preferred outdoor games instead. In the Gilded Age dolls served to teach girls how to represent the bourgeois home to the world beyond through visiting and other social rituals. Girls resisted, however, by staging frequent doll funerals. In the early years of the twentieth century, immigrant girls of working-class families who regularly cared for younger siblings felt burdened enough by real child-care responsibilities. Middle-class girls in the suburbs and in small American towns preferred roller skating to playing with dolls. Thus, while some girls played with dolls in ways that parents and producers had hoped they would, many others challenged adult intentions to determine the meaning of dolls in their own lives.

some girls played house in the ways their parents hoped they would, many others in the period from 1830 to 1930 challenged adult prescriptions for play as they determined the meaning of dolls in their own lives.

Doll play and girls' socialization today is understood as much by what themes and values were submerged (and partially lost) in the struggle for dolls as by what prevailed. Thus, this history of dolls is significant not only for comprehending the past but also for understanding the construction of gender in the present. Overlooking the evidence of girls' resistance to codified doll games, scholars of sex-role stereotyping have argued that girls today suffer as a result of the centrality of doll play. By excluding other games and toys, doll play, they argue, inhibits conceptual development, encourages passivity, teaches girls to conform to cultural norms, and makes them overly concerned with socially acceptable behavior. Dolls have offered an important tool for socialization, but it is important to realize that their influence has also been diverse in nature and their effects related to the social context. The role dolls have played in socialization has changed over time, interacting with the shifting practices of childrearing and sex roles. Dolls played a far less central role in socialization in the early nineteenth century, for example, than they did toward its end, when doll play became solitary and fantasy-oriented to increasingly isolated girls. Yet as this study suggests, the outcome could have been different.

In 1909 doll collector Laura Starr suggested that "history could be taught by means of dolls. The future historian will have no difficulty in reconstructing our age if he finds merely a few toys in dusty garrets or museums."[5] In this study, which also relies on numerous dolls and doll patents issued between 1850 and 1930, I take up Starr's challenge to chart the history of American girlhood and its relation to commercial culture "by means of dolls."[6]

CHAPTER ONE

The Politics
of Dollhood in Nineteenth-
Century America

"Of doll haters I have known quite a few," wrote a contributor to *Babyhood* magazine about the "hoydenish" little girls she had observed swatting their dolls.[1] The observations of this Gilded Age writer stand in sharp contrast to the more pervasive image of the angelic Victorian girl who was, in the words of one nineteenth-century poet, "sugar and spice and all things nice." In this chapter, I challenge the widespread assumption that attributes minimal agency to girls whom we *still* assume slavishly played in socially prescribed ways.

We begin in antebellum America, where the political ideology, class values, and cultural and economic forces of the young nation shaped new attitudes about dolls, play, and girlhood. Mothers, informed by the new domestic advisers, instructed their daughters to be "useful" within the matrix of the family. Dolls, of which there were few, served as training in everything *but* emotional development and expression. Daughters of the evolving middle class made cloth dolls to develop sewing skills that integrated leisure with instruction in domestic economy. Outdoor play, education, and a schedule of daily, weekly (punctuated by the Sabbath), and seasonal responsibilities limited the role that dolls played in girlhood.

In broad terms, utilitarian purposes of dolls and of girls, however, became increasingly obsolete in the Gilded Age as simplicity yielded to splendor among girls of urban middle-class families. Girls' lives, like those of their parents, were affected by the shift from household production to conspicuous consumption. Children's magazines, books, poems, songs, and stereographs revealed that girls were encouraged by adults to develop strong emotional bonds with their numerous dolls, to indulge in fantasy, and to display their elaborately dressed imported European dolls at such ritual occasions as tea parties and social calls.

Although adults, especially parents, perceived dolls as useful vehicles in feminine socialization, this rehearsal for adult womanhood met resistance as it had earlier in the century. At least some daughters with a different agenda from their parents used dolls for purposes other than training in the emotional and practical skills of mothering. Girls' funereal doll play, for example, revealed far more evidence of resistance than of accommodation to newly formulated prescriptions and proscriptions. Memoirs, autobiographies, biographies, oral histories, and the expressive "language" of play reveal that girls—and boys—challenged parental authority, restrictive social customs, and gender roles. Girls in the process of constructing their own notion of girlhood engaged their parents in a preconscious political struggle to define, decide, and determine the meaning of dolls in their own lives and as representations of their own culture.

Dolls and their clothing, argued Catharine Beecher and Harriet Beecher Stowe in *The American Woman's Home* (1869), provide girls with "another resource . . . to the exercise of mechanical skills." Girls should be "trained to be healthful and industrious." Earlier in the nineteenth cen-

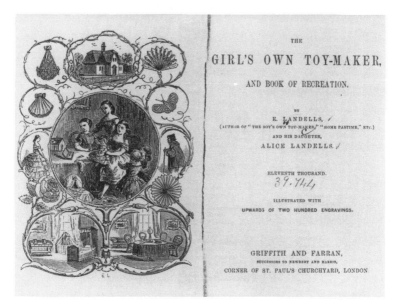

1. Although antebellum advice manuals often included philosophical and practical information about the role of dolls in the domestic economy for middle-class mothers, recreation manuals provided their daughters with practical information for "productive" doll play. Reproduced courtesy of the Library of Congress.

tury, advice books, "ladies'" magazines, and other printed sources similarly urged mothers to apply Christian principles to the regulation of the bourgeois family, which only recently had become the mothers' domain. Thus, they were to direct their children's play toward useful ends. Printed material that offered practical advice and philosophical explanations to middle-class mothers standardized methods of antebellum childrearing. In the prescriptive literature published starting in the 1820s, middle-class girls and their mothers were kept informed of genteel manners, bourgeois values, and domestic training.[2]

Girls were urged toward usefulness in their play as natural training in the republican values they would need as future wives and mothers of citizens (fig. 1). New attitudes about girls' play were shaped in part by the political ideology of the young nation. Experts advised mothers to use "gentle nurture" to teach their children to be self-governing and to exercise "self-control" while at play. Eliza Leslie, author of the *Girls' Book,* suggested, as did other prescriptive writers, that making dolls rather than indulging a love of dress and finery would prevent degeneration into godless anarchy. In her moral tracts, Mary Sewell exhorted mothers to inculcate "habitual restraint" by structuring play periods with "habitual regularity."[3]

"In this land of precarious fortunes, every girl should know how to be 'useful,'" wrote Lydia Maria Child, one of the best-known writers of the period. A girl's vocation, to which dolls contributed, was to be a domestic one shaped in response to the world beyond the Victorian hearth. A canon of domesticity contrasted the safety of the home, where women presided, to the restlessness, competition, selfishness, and alienation of the masculine world beyond. Although the reality of slipping down the economic ladder was obscured by the mythology of the self-made man whose life of hard work, moderation, and temperance promised untold rewards, young ladies were nevertheless forewarned to make themselves useful should misfortune strike.[4] *Mothers' Monthly Journal,* one of the leading maternal association periodicals, advised its broad readership that dressing dolls provided "a semblance of the sober activities of business." Making dolls, nurturing the family, and taking care of household duties constituted a girl's informal apprenticeship for being a wife and mother. According to such experts as Maria Edgeworth, who "firmly believed in the utility of toys," sewing dolls and doll clothing stressed a pragmatic contribution to the domestic economy of the antebellum household. Popular "ladies'" magazines often included directions for making pen-wiper dolls (to clean nibs), sewing dolls (whose pockets held thimbles and other items), and pincushion dolls.[5]

It was from their mothers, who were newly endowed with both the capacity and the social responsibility to determine the fate of their children, that girls were to learn their lessons, both practical and moral. Although the widespread availability of cloth meant that women no longer had to weave the household's supply of fabric, family comfort still depended on skillful use of the needle. Catharine Beecher, who felt "blessed with the example of a most ingenious and industrious mother," suggested that

> When a little girl begins to sew, her mother can promise her a small bed and pillow, as soon as she has sewed a patch quilt for them; and then a bedstead, as soon as she has sewed the sheets and cases for pillows; and then a large doll to dress, as soon as she has made the undergarments; and thus go on till the whole contents of the baby-house are earned by the needle and skill of its little owner. Thus, the task of learning to sew will become a pleasure; and every new toy will be earned by useful exertion.

In their treatise on household management, the nineteenth-century architects of domesticity boasted that they "had not only learned before the age of twelve to make dolls, of various sorts and sizes, but to cut and fit and sew every article that belongs to a doll's wardrobe."[6]

In the absence of mothers, other female kin such as Lucy Larcom's "adopted aunt" provided instruction in how to knot thread and sew clothing for rag dolls (fig. 2). A doll character in one children's story recalled that "there were hours and hours when she [her owner] had to sit quietly beside grandmother, and sew her stint."[7]

In addition to adult women, older sisters often helped younger ones create homemade dolls. "I once knew a little girl who had twelve dolls," wrote Lydia Maria Child. "Some of them were given her; but the greater part she herself made from rags, and her elder sister painted their lips and eyes." One of Lucy Larcom's older sisters outlined faces on her dolls with pen and ink.[8]

Despite the practical suggestions provided to mothers by experts and in turn passed along to girls, the hours during which toys were expected to absorb their attention were limited by genuine household responsibilities.[9] Few matched the ideal as represented in the numerous extant canvases—showing girls leisurely holding dolls—painted by itinerants for socially conscious, middle-class parents (fig. 3). Though the texture of girls' lives was changing, childhood was still neither as precisely demarcated nor as prolonged in the early 1800s as it would be by the end

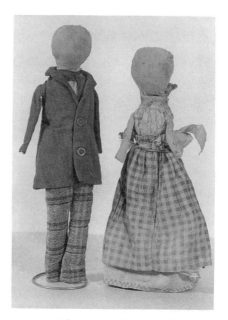

2. Girls in antebellum America
preferred homemade rag dolls to
expensive imported dolls. Photo by
Richard Merrill, courtesy of the
Essex Institute Collections, Peabody
& Essex Museum, Salem, Mass.

of the century. Instead, a mother of a large rural family was likely to be assisted by the elder children, especially her daughters, as soon as they were able, despite decreasing household productivity and the increasing availability of commercial goods. Thus, the number of hours a girl spent in play would have been circumscribed by immediate familial obligations. Though minding younger siblings combined amusement with training, it was a weighty responsibility nonetheless.

Time spent in doll play was also limited by school attendance, which required an increasing number of girls to spend a portion of their day

3. Portrait of Sarah Spenser by H. Walton, 1842. In a display
of their newly acquired social status, many middle-class parents
hired itinerant artists to paint portraits of their daughters holding
dolls resembling fashionable ladies which were intended for
neither soothing nor cuddling. Reproduced courtesy of the
Abby Aldrich Rockefeller Folk Art Center, Williamsburg, Va.

in decidedly nonleisure activities, and by Sabbath observance. In a children's story from the 1850s, retribution was visited upon two girls who skipped school in order to play with their dolls. Similarly, on Sundays, which were "not like any other day," girls were expected to pray, not play. All middle-class Christian children were expected to observe the Sabbath like adults, even those who were not very religious. "We did not play games nor read the same books," on Sunday as on other days, recalled one girl from the 1850s, and church services and Sunday school seemed to last forever.[10] Consequently, girls were less likely to devote much of their time to doll play.

Though the number of toys had increased since the colonial period, there were still few dolls around in the average middle-class household in the 1850s, a fact of doll demography that would change dramatically only after the Civil War. "Life for children was simple in the extreme [as] there were no array[s] of costly toys," recalled one New England woman in her autobiography. "[My sister and I] had the regulation rag doll with long curls and club feet, very ugly but dear to our hearts," and no others. Harriet Robinson, who grew up a New England mill girl, "had no toys, except a few homemade articles of our own. I had but a single doll, a wooden-jointed thing, with red cheeks and staring black eyes."[11]

Because of the scarcity and cost of dolls, parents and relatives tended to treasure those they purchased far more than did their daughters, granddaughters, and nieces. One father in Petersburg, Virginia, included the two large dolls he had bought for his daughter in his will. With little regard for a doll's economic value, however, girls like Lucy Larcom rejected the "London doll that lay in waxen state in an upper drawer at home." To her, this "fine lady did not wish to be played with but only to be looked at and admired." Larcom, instead, preferred the "absurd creatures of her own invention." Antebellum writer Eliza Leslie similarly observed that cloth dolls "remain longer in favor with their young owners, and continue to give them more real satisfaction, than the handsomest wax doll that can be purchased."[12]

Yet many girls who lived in rural areas preferred to spend their time outdoors instead, largely forgoing the pleasures of even cloth dolls. Lucy

Larcom played on farms and in fields, rivers, quarries, and cemeteries; Emily Wilson and Frances Willard (who later led the national temperance movement) preferred skating, sledding, and running to playing with dolls. Carol Ryrie Brink's fictionalized stories about her great-grandmother depict Caddie Woodlawn as an active girl. According to Karin Calvert, girls were more likely to recall rolling hoops, tossing snowballs, and jumping rope to playing with dolls. Hiding in the attic, Harriet Robinson secretly played high-low-jack with the playing cards her brother had made. Little girls lived "as unfettered and vigorous an outdoor life as their brothers." [13]

After the Civil War, doll play absorbed and channeled a number of interrelated changes in the lives of American girls: increased affluence, new consumer outlets, smaller family size, and greater emphasis on imitation of adult social rituals and the formalized play it encouraged. In the country but especially in cities, middle-class girls born in the postwar years amassed quantities of dolls unknown to the previous generation. In contrast to the four decades preceding the Civil War, dolls sold well and widely after 1865 as the traditional moral, utilitarian, and even political functions of dolls were gradually replaced with "needs" based on new middle-class notions.

A rising personal income meant that most middle-class Americans could become consumers of articles formerly available only to the rich whom they admired along with the Europeans that the rich emulated. Nevertheless, buying imported dolls still required a solid bank account. In 1890, when the annual income of an industrial worker was $486, a French jointed kid doll with a composition head cost between $3 and $30. As a result, the majority of dolls remained prohibitively expensive for working-class families. In one doll story, a poor seamstress was unable to purchase a wax doll because she "could not afford to spend her money that way." Her little girl asks, "Does she cost a great deal, mamma?" Her mother answers, "It would be a great deal for us—she costs $10, Lucy." [14]

A revolution in European doll production enabled jobbers, manufacturers' agents, importers, and distributors to channel European toys to

American retail stores where mothers and fathers purchased great quantities of dolls made out of china or bisque with open mouths and little teeth or some with closed mouths.[15] Some of the most expensive French fashion dolls in the 1870s and 1880s arrived with fully packed trunks, often tripling the price of the doll alone. French and German dolls—with hourglass figures and *bébés,* idealized and romanticized representations of European bourgeois girlhood—flooded U.S. markets at a time when most Americans began to enjoy increasing affluence.

For those living far from urban centers with financial resources, mail-order catalogues brought the opportunity to shop at home and share in the consumer-goods market for dolls. Seven years after Richard Sears began advertising watches to the rural market, Sears, Roebuck broadened its wares to include dolls. Wholesale suppliers like Butler Brothers provided the small merchant of the rural midwest with dolls and other items.[16]

Beginning in 1865, department stores including R. H. Macy, Jordan Marsh, and Marshall Field dazzled shoppers as spectacular "palaces of consumption." By 1875, Macy's stock featured dolls and other toys in addition to dry goods and home furnishings. While Macy's was the first to establish a toy department, others soon followed its lead. "Most of us adults can recall the time when the toy shop exhibited but a slim stock," commented one observer. But in the years after the Civil War, toy shops, some of which issued illustrated catalogues, increased in number and size. "Enter one of our big toy shops now and there is really an *embarrass de richesses,*" noted one contemporary observer. In fact, "the first impression of the visitor to the big toy shop is . . . apt to be one of bewilderment."[17]

Toy stores also catered to a clientele of urban middle-class women, most of whom did not work outside the home and for whom shopping for self, friends, and family was becoming a central activity. According to an 1881 *Harper's Bazaar,* dolls and other toys were "chosen by mothers with a view to giving their girls correct ideas of symmetry and beauty." In stories from the late nineteenth century, nurturing female shopkeepers patiently assisted leisured female customers. In "A Doll's Story," a jointed bisque doll recalls seeing from inside her glass display case "mostly

4. Toy stores, which became far more numerous after the Civil
War, catered to a clientele of middle-class women for whom
shopping had become a central activity. By the 1880s, dolls like
those pictured in this 1883 drawing in a *Doll's Dressmaker* looked
far more like idealized European girls of the bourgeoisie than had
previous generations of adult-looking dolls. Reproduced courtesy
of the Library of Congress.

mothers and young children—sometimes nurses with small children"[18]
(fig. 4).

Women were the largest group of consumers, but fathers also purchased dolls—some of which said "Papa"—for their daughters at each
birthday or homecoming. Bourgeois fathers began at midcentury giving
gifts to their children at Christmas, instead of to their employees or to

the poor as previously had been the case. One fortunate middle-class daughter of German immigrants recalled that she received gifts only on Christmas and for her birthday typically in an abundance suitable for several children.[19]

In doll stories, "papas with weary heads" committed to a business ethos were frequently too preoccupied to notice a sick or a sad daughter. Fathers were increasingly separated from the family during the day, especially those who commuted from the sprouting suburbs. Sons might have been more acutely affected by their diminished opportunities to assist fathers, but the relationship of fathers to their daughters was influenced as well. Gift-giving could solace an alienated father and reinforce his belief that he was fulfilling his role as provider. As a result, "most fathers," observed a writer for *Doll's Dressmaker,* "are inclined to overindulge their daughters." In one story, Pearl's father "bought me a beautiful bedstead," narrated a doll character, "round which were hung some elegant blue silk curtains." In *A Doll's Journey,* a story written by Louisa May Alcott, one sister reassured another that "papa will give you a new doll." [20]

Generous gift giving, whether on Christmas or at other times of the year, had been a recent consequence of a number of factors, including the increasing emotional distance between parents and children. Busy parents with fewer children provided their daughters with the companionship of dolls, thereby lengthening childhood and prolonging their "dollhood." Middle-class women had become not only increasingly isolated from production but also from their children. Mothers' contact with their children became circumscribed shortly after birth. By the late 1890s, leading pediatrician Luther Emmett Holt observed that "at least three children out of every four born into the homes of the well-to-do-classes" were not fed at the breast. Instead, fashion and etiquette, shopping, and visiting dominated the life of the matron. Fashion magazines, as one indicator, far outnumbered mothers' magazines. Many children probably saw more of "nanny" than their mothers and fathers.[21]

Girls living in urban and newly created suburban areas were given far less productive work, fewer responsibilities, and fewer siblings to look after. Middle-class mothers had successfully limited their number of children, spaced them farther apart, and ceased childbearing earlier than had previous generations. As a result, fewer brothers and sisters to watch increased the amount of time for play but decreased the number of friends and kin with whom to share it. Instead, girls were given many more toys, books, magazines, clothing, and furniture made especially for them. As a single child of well-to-do parents, Margaret Woodbury Strong adored the numerous dolls she received—now the foundation of the museum in Rochester, New York, that bears her name.[22]

In the decades that followed the Civil War, gradually dolls began to serve a more modern and symbolic function than a utilitarian one. Doll play in the postwar era emphasized the display of high fashion rather than the sewing skills emphasized earlier. In one story from the period, Pearl adores the doll she sees in Mrs. Lieb's toy shop though she hesitates to purchase it because it is undressed. "You know, dear mother," she says in a whisper, "how badly I sew." The emphasis on sewing for dolls had become obsolete by the 1880s. Instead, organized doll play developed rules that became nearly as formalized as those recently devised for baseball. Pastimes that had made previous generations of well-to-do Protestants uneasy now became increasingly accepted. As with production and consumption, amusement in general became a more structured activity.[23]

This organized amusement came to be located in the nursery, which for the middle-class was the arena where (similar to organized sports), values, attitudes, and standards of behavior were imparted. Changes in the family, childhood, and and new marital ideals had given rise to the middle-class nursery by the second half of the nineteenth century, differentiating households as well as the space between family members. The nursery—where the large numbers of dolls, their accoutrements, and other toys could be kept—became indispensable. Although Victorian houses were spacious, they were cluttered with possessions too precious to risk around children at play. In the autonomous space of the nursery described by J. M. Barrie in *Peter Pan,* children lived apart from parents and the rest of the household. A room of adorable miniature adult furniture became a standard feature especially of the spacious upper middle-class Victorian home. Some chairs were stenciled with affectionate names like "My Pet," and miniature tea tables painted to represent marble imitated adult lavishness.[24]

Adults expected girls to imitate the new rituals of high society with their largely imported dolls in their nurseries. Elaborately dressed dolls were thought useful in the instruction of social conventions such as housewarmings. Far more common, however, were dolls' tea parties, frequently depicted in stereographs, tradecards, and books like *The Dolls' Tea Party*. Adults proudly noted that "the children's doll parties of to-day are counterparts of grown-up people's receptions."[25]

In addition to tea parties, girls were urged to imitate another adult social ritual of polite society in the Gilded Age, that of visiting. Dolls could be purchased wearing "a stylish visiting dress, and also accompanied by a trunkful of clothes ready for all the demands of fashionable occasions" (fig. 5). Miniature calling cards, which were a measure of family standing to neighbors and friends, imitated the mother's *carte de visite* for girls who paid formal visits with their dolls. Now instead of singing, "here we go round the mulberry bush," girls were encouraged to sing, "this is the way we carry them . . . when we go visiting." Popular magazines like *The Delineator* advertised instructions for making visiting dresses and even "a stately toilette for Miss Dolly to wear on the promenade." "With their companions or dolls you will hear them imitating the discussion [on fashion] . . . that they daily hear in the parlor or nursery from their mother," observed Mrs. H. W. Beecher in 1873.[26]

Not all the feelings and issues which doll play accommodated were superficial and sweet. Of all the newly constructed middle-class rituals girls were urged to imitate, doll funerals were by far the most common. In a change from sparse and somber colonial funereal customs, late nineteenth-century Americans (following Queen Victoria's lead) romanticized grief and burial practices. Mourning was demarcated by shades of black dresses, stationery, and other mourning accoutrements. According to Harvey Green, "visiting ill or dying relatives and friends was an expected and socially required part of women's sphere, part of the broad set of nurturing responsibilities with which she was charged." To middle-class parents in the second half of the nineteenth century, that children devised imaginary and miniaturized funerals was not seen as evidence of a morbid preoccupation with death. As a result, adults encouraged rather than discouraged the doll death ceremonies their daughters conducted.

5. Gilded Age French fashion dolls with elaborate wardrobes
of exquisite clothing and suitable accoutrements like calling cards
enabled girls to rehearse social rituals such a visiting. Photo by
Mark Sexton, courtesy of the Wenham Museum, Wenham, Mass.

Mourning clothes were even packed in the trunks of French dolls in the 1870s and 1880s (fig. 6). Fathers constructed doll-sized coffins for their daughters' dolls instead of what we consider the more usual dollhouses.[27]

The process of learning about the meanings of grief began early in life, as the etiquette of mourning became an integral part of a girl's up-

6. Fashion dolls dressed in mourning attire demonstrated that doll funerals were a social ritual that middle-class parents expected their daughters to master. Photo courtesy of the Strong Museum, Rochester, N.Y., ©1993.

bringing. Young students in private schools learning the decorative arts created countless embroidered mourning pieces filled with new iconographic symbols such as willow trees and morning glories. Even the fictional Rebecca of Sunnybrook Farm routinely staged deaths and funerals with her rural friends. As the ritualization of mourning increased during the course of the century—all maintained within the feminine sphere—it is no wonder that parents encouraged funeral ceremonies meant to properly sanctify the "bodies" and protect the "souls" of those poor, deceased dolls.[28]

Short stories about dying dolls were included in the popular fiction for children and provided them with new ideas about how they should play with dolls. By contrast, earlier in the century so few stories about dolls had been written that one disappointed doll in a story from the 1840s remarked, "I never heard any stories about dolls, and what they thought, or what happened to them!" In the years after the Civil War, however, a conspicuous doll culture unfolded in widely available children's books and popular magazines. Beginning in the late 1860s, colorfully illustrated and miniature books were printed for girls (and their dolls). Nursery shelves were lined with books about dolls, books *for* them such as *The Dolls' Own Book,* which went through numerous editions, and even books *by* dolls. Stories such as "Dolly's Experience, Told by Herself" or doll memoirs were ostensibly written by doll authors.[29]

It was the fictional literature of "doll culture" that broached the more powerful feelings of love and violence. Doll fiction provided girls with both an outlet and a way of playing with their dolls so as to grapple with serious needs. Unlike the antebellum literature for children that stressed the development of skills and morals, doll fiction of the Gilded Age emphasized the exploration of self, interpersonal relationships, and fantasy. Despite the innumerable images of girls washing their dolls and doll clothing, grooming had not yet become a primary justification for doll play because most dolls made out of horsehair or wood shavings had little chance of surviving a good dunking. Instead, it was through her relationship to her female dolls—also portrayed as passive, pretty, enigmatic, domestic, dainty, mute, vain, and delicate—that a girl learned about the essence of "true love" and how to distinguish it from more superficial feelings. While the more elaborate dolls were often portrayed as shallow, one bisque sophisticate observed, "Oh, it's nice to be grand and all that, I suppose/But of late I'm beginning to reap/The Knowledge that happiness isn't fine clothes/And that beauty is only skin deep."[30] Although hopelessly unfashionable, rag dolls were most likely to have insight about interpersonal relationships.

> Lillian Grace is a fine city girl
> I'm but a queer "country cousin,"
> I have one dress of coarse cotton stuff,
> She has silk gowns by the dozen.
> She is so pretty, and dainty and gay
> I am so homely and funny;
> I cost a trifle, I'm but a rag doll,
> She costs a whole heap of money,
> She came from France in a big handsome box,
> I, from a country bazaar,
> Things are more precious I've often been told
> That travel so long and so far.
> Yet it is strange, but Oh! it is true
> We belong to the same little mother
> And though she loves Lillian Grace very much
> It is queer, but somehow or other,
> I have a spot in her dear loving heart
> That Lillian Grace cannot enter;
> She has a hold in the outermost rim,
> But I have a place in the center . . .
> And all the silk dresses and other fine things,
> Though they do look so fair to the eye,
> Are not worth a thought since they cannot win love.
> O a happy rag dollie am I![31]

The portrayal of love between a doll and a girl, which often straddled the boundaries between maternal love and romantic love, was reciprocal, communicative, and passionate. By the early 1890s, the growing importance of mothering and child study had influenced popular ideas about

7. In post-Civil War juvenile fiction,
"mischievous" boys like these in this
1880 illustration in *Chatterbox* often
inflicted injury on doll victims.
Photo courtesy of the
Library of Congress.

doll play for girls. *Doll's Dressmaker* (a monthly magazine first published in New York City in 1891) reprinted images of girls with their bevies of dolls, which conveyed a new maternal fecundity out of step with actual demographic changes (families were getting smaller) but in step with more scientific notions about mothering. Thereafter, in numerous images girls cradled bébés with maternal sentimentality while contemporaries rhetorically asked, "Is it not the harmless, childish joy that develops and educates the young girl's maternal instinct, and in so doing helps to elevate her to the pinnacle of true womanhood?" [32]

Elsewhere, fictional characters encouraged the pursuit of feminine submission to masculine dominance. In fact, girls' dolls were often portrayed as hapless victims of mischievous boys who taunted girls and tortured dolls (fig. 7). The incorrigible boy was familiar in fiction, art, cartoons, advertisements, and the enormously popular stereographs of the period. One doll in a story recalled that her "little mistress" had a book entitled *Mischievous Tommy,* "about a troublesome, rude boy" who had disgusting manners. As Mary Lynn Stevens Heininger and others have noted, the mischief and manipulation by the boys in *Tom Sawyer* and *Peck's Bad Boy* fulfilled the expectation of stereotypical masculine behavior. Such was the case in another popular story in which a girl named Gladys is portrayed as defenseless against her scheming, scissors-wielding brother who cuts "a great patch of hair out of the poor doll's head."[33]

In addition to bad boys, other threats restricted the boundaries of safety for dolls and, hence, their owners. In numerous stories, birds, cows, and monkeys like "Naughty Jacko" stole, pecked, gnawed, and kicked defenseless dolls unable and unwilling to resist. In *The Dolls' Surprise Party,* a roving mother pig and her piglets attack a group of dolls enjoying their picnic. Although most stories attributed powerful emotional responses to dolls and thus to girls, in fiction both often sat helplessly with "wooden legs" while antagonists hounded them.[34]

Home provided little safety for two dolls in a Beatrix Potter tale in which "two bad mice" destroy their domestic security. In this 1904 children's story, two working-class mice (a foul-tempered husband and his thieving wife, Hunca Munca), ransack the house of two wooden dolls absent from the nursery. Returning from their stroll, the dolls are shocked into victimized passivity. One doll merely "sat upon the upset kitchen stove and stared," while the other "leant against the kitchen dresser and smiled—but neither of them made any remark." Doll policemen and nurses (brought into play by the girl whose dollhouse has been burglarized) set mouse traps. To make a short story even shorter, the repentant mouse husband pays for everything he broke and "very early every morning—before anybody is awake—Hunca Munca comes with her dust pan and her broom to sweep the Dollies' house!"[35]

Stories did not completely siphon off the underlying aggression. Dolls were not necessarily safer in the hands of little girls. In *Little Women,* "one forlorn fragment of *dollanity* had belonged to Jo; and, having led a tempestuous life, was left a wreck in the rag-bag." The top of the doll's

8. Stereographs, a new form of parlor entertainment, showed
girls displaying aggression toward dolls. Photo courtesy of the
Library of Congress.

head was gone, as were her arms and legs. George Eliot's fictional heroine in *The Mill on the Floss,* nine-year-old Maggie Tulliver, expressed her
rage by hammering nails into her wooden doll's head, beating it against a
wall, and grinding it against a rough brick. In numerous American stereo-
graphic images that became a parlor staple by the turn of the century,
girls used more typical domestic implements, cutting their dolls with
scissors or forcing them through clothes wringers. Like other "Conduct
Stereos," these pictures were probably intended to dramatize proper
feminine manners and behavior through humor (fig. 8).[36]

Although a juvenile mass culture was imposed from above by parents
and other adults with their own intentions, what about the interactions
of girls—and boys, for that matter—with dolls and other toys? Abuse of
dolls at the hands of their owners alerts us that adult prescriptions for
proper play were often not what girls had in mind. In the last decades of
the century stereographs and other images suggest a middle-class ideal
of girls, overflowing with metaphors of abundance, yet we know far more
about adult expectations than we do about childhood reality. Prescriptive literature tells us little about how ordinary girls actually behaved.

Did girls identify with the dolls they heard about in stories? Did they confide in the dolls they cradled in studio portraits? Did they actually prefer dolls to other toys and activities? Were girls who played with dolls more gentle and nurturing than boys or girls who preferred more active play?

There is no disputing that girls in late nineteenth-century America liked dolls, but not just any doll. According to one study, girls preferred dolls made of wax, paper, rag, and china over those made of rubber, kid, wood, tin, or celluloid. Among the favorite dolls were those made of cloth. Emily Kimbrough disliked the fashionable doll her grandmother gave her but adored her Topsy-turvey rag doll. Adults were often at a loss to understand why their daughters preferred ragged and "countrified" dolls to brightly colored and elaborately dressed ones.[37]

Among rag dolls, black ones were a favorite among white children, observed one contemporary shopper. Both Mary Hunt and her friend favored black dolls over white ones. "My little girl has two such [rag] dolls," commented a mother, "one white and the other black, but her affections are centered on the colored woman . . . never going to bed without Dinah in her arms, and crying for 'di' if the nurse had forgotten to put it in her crib" (fig. 9). African-American women played an increasingly significant role in the rearing of middle-class children. Suggesting a relationship born of affection, one four-year-old girl fed everything that tasted good to her black rag doll.[38]

Despite their uniform fictional portrayal as adversaries, boys were also among doll lovers. One contributor to a mother's magazine reported that her son treated the doll he loved with "the greatest care and tenderness." Nor did boys like this one shed their dolls along with their diapers. G. Stanley Hall found that 76 percent of the boys he studied played with dolls to age 12. Not surprising, then, are the numerous examples of boys especially fond of doll play. A boy doll (c. 1875) named "Theodore" became a "chum" to a little boy for eight years. A man who participated in a 1987 doll oral history project recognized a painted cloth boy doll as one similar to his childhood toy.[39]

Boys, like girls, sang to and rocked the dolls they endowed with emotional, intellectual, physiological, moral, political ("democrat"), and religious qualities. They "fed" dolls milk, bread, buttons, or pickles when they were "hungry," occasionally breaking tiny teeth and heads in order to do so. Children succored dolls sick with measles or brain fever with remedies like tapioca and paper pills or dissolved candy. According to one ten year-old girl, "My doll Liz had a headache, so I put on her micado and read her some of Longfellow's *Hiawatha,* as she wanted me to." [40]

9. Dorothea Castelhun, pictured in 1899 affectionately gazing at her homemade black rag doll, was one of many girls who often preferred their "Dinah" rag dolls to fragile dolls with bisque heads. Photo courtesy of Frieda Marion.

Girls and boys often played with their dolls in socially prescribed ways. While girls pretended to be little mothers to their dolls, boys often assumed authoritative public roles such as doctor, preacher, and undertaker to sick, dying, and dead dolls. One eight-year-old doll dentist used toothpicks as dental tools. Another boy shot his doll full of holes with a bow and arrow so that he could dress its wounds. Boys' play also included doll crucifixions and executions. Unlike the girl characters in doll stories, however, girls did not always mind. "When my brother proved my doll had no brains by slicing off her head, I felt I had been deluded; I watched him with stoicism and took no more interest in dolls."[41]

Examples of girls like this one—who either always or eventually preferred other activities to doll play—are also numerous (fig. 10). Present expectations that dolls are for girls and not for boys are confounded by the fact that less than one quarter of the girls in T. R. Croswell's study of 2,000 children in Massachusetts considered dolls to be their "favorite" toy. Eleanor Abbott (granddaughter of Jacob Abbott, author of the *Rollo* series) preferred paper dolls, toy soldiers, or fights with her brother to her dolls. As before the Civil War, school-aged girls still largely preferred sledding, jumping rope, or playing tag, hide-and-seek, or any other game to playing with dolls. "In my own immediate family," recalled an aunt, "a canvass through three generations of women shows only two doll-lovers out of fifteen little girls, the rest decidedly preferring rough and tumble, active play in the open air." Someone asked "Wouldn't you rather play with dolls?" of a girl playing horse and driver with her friend. "We'd rather run," replied the pair.[42]

Although Karin Calvert found few girls' diaries from the late nineteenth century that even mentioned dolls, they nevertheless played a prominent role in the lives of many. Surprisingly, however, girls' play behavior was not always submissive nor instinctively maternal; evidence reveals that doll players pushed at the margins of acceptable feminine and genteel behavior. A wide variety of sources suggests that in their doll play, numerous "hoydenish little girls" expressed anger and aggression nearly as frequently as love and affection. "Of doll-haters, I have known a few," wrote the contributor to *Babyhood* magazine in 1905. Punishments were often particularly brutal. One thirteen-year-old girl broke her doll

"A FAIR EXCHANGE IS NO ROBBERY."

10. Although many girls and boys often played with dolls in socially prescribed ways, they were also just as likely to transgress gender role norms. Illustration from *Doll's Dressmaker,* 1894, courtesy of the Library of Congress.

by knocking it against a window for crying. A four-year-old girl disciplined her doll by forcing it to eat dirt, stones, and coal.[43]

Although parents believed doll funerals could be assimilated to proper forms of femininity, girls were often more interested in the unfeminine events that led to these solemn rituals. In the numerous doll funerals that appear with startling consistency in doll stories, memoirs, and questionnaires, it was not the passive grieving that provided doll players with pleasure. Doll funerals probably appealed to girls in part because the domestification of heaven (along with the beautification of cemeteries where families found rest and recreation) made the afterlife sound fun. For others, the staging of doll funerals was an expression of aggressive feelings and hostile fantasies. George Eliot remembered that she "only broke those [dolls] . . . that could not stand the test of being undressed, or that proclaimed their unfleshy substance by falling and breaking their noses."[44] According to an article in the *Pittsburgh Post,* a five-year-old girl purposely broke her doll, then declared with satisfaction, "it was dead." Girls like this one changed the emphasis from ritualized funerals to cathartic executions. Using available kitchen utensils she dug a grave in the backyard and then invited other little girls to do the same. "I have vivid memories of harrowing games with Mary Gordon," wrote Ethel Spencer in her turn-of-the-century memoir, "during which our children [dolls] became desperately ill and died." Though this gruesome scenario bordered on the unacceptable by the end of the nineteenth century, their fascination for girls was not at all unusual. "Funerals were especially popular, with Becky [doll] ever the willing victim," confided one doll player. "No day was too short for a funeral, just so they [my friends] all got home for supper."[45]

For some, a doll's worth was determined by its ability to subvert convention, mock materialism, and undermine restrictions. For example, doll parties, considered entirely too sedate by some girls, were transformed into invigorating activities unlikely to win the approval of adults. Some girls preferred exhilarating "indoor coastings"—sliding down the stairs while sitting on a tea tray—to dull tea parties. Zona Gale and a friend wreaked havoc on their tea party by smashing their unsuspecting dolls to bits. Gale, who became a writer and a feminist, had consciously determined to live life unencumbered by sex roles.[46]

Through their doll play, girls also seemed to enjoy the challenges they posed to patriarchal authority. One autobiographer recalled deliberately sewing clothes for her doll on Sundays, "quite as on other days," until finally sobered by the warning that "every stitch she sewed on Sunday, she would have to rip out with her teeth when she got to Purgatory." Undaunted, she decided to learn how to rip out the stitches that way before she got there. The task, however, proved to be such a difficult one that she gave up sewing on Sundays until her mother purchased a Wilcox and Gibbs chain-stitch sewing machine. "After that, I did all my Sunday sewing on the sewing machine, feeling it would only be an additional pleasure to rip it out [with her teeth] in Purgatory, and with a deep satisfaction at having gotten the best of the Devil."[47]

Girls who played with dolls in late nineteenth-century America sometimes developed a sense of self that was anything but submissive. Sarah Bixby, who was raised in southern California, skinned, dressed, and boiled rabbit meat for her doll, Isabel. In one story, Lydia smacks a roving pig with her wooden doll, formerly an outcast among her doll peers but thereafter their heroine. Late nineteenth-century autobiographies similarly reveal that, contrary to the prescribed version, girls whose dolls fell victim to aggressive animals or belligerent boys defended themselves and their dolls instead of seeking male protection. One young girl "burst out" and "flew at" her friend, Harry (who bullied and teased), after he bit a hole in her favorite doll. She "grabbed him by the shoulders, . . . ready to fight to the death for [her] rights, [when] he burst into cries for help . . . I shall never forget my surprise and triumph as I realized that I conquered—conquered in spite of being small, with a strength I could always command. I only had to set [myself] free, to let her come, outside, and she could do anything."[48]

By the turn of the century, dolls with their own wardrobes, literature, and ideology had altered the nature of doll play. Girls born and raised in middle-class antebellum households had few dolls, and those they had were mostly of their own making as prescribed and instructed by a literature directed at mothers and daughters. Making dolls and playing with them had fostered skills useful to character development, self-government, and a domestic economy. In the years after the Civil War, as European imported dolls proliferated and became more splendid, the meaning of dolls in girls' lives changed. Doll stories provided companionship and the seed of fantasies, which brought girls beyond the confines of the material world. Girls were encouraged to display the store-bought dolls they received on holidays and from indulgent relatives. The productive and "useful" activities of their mothers' generation had left the dollhouse as it had the American household, gradually replaced by new values and skills revolving around status (and kin). Previous generations had learned useful household skills, but girls in the Gilded Age were encouraged to play with their china and bisque dolls in ways that increasingly aped the conspicuous display of consumer goods and social status epitomized by the European bourgeoisie their parents emulated.

Although postwar popular culture differed dramatically from the antebellum period, girls revealed obvious continuities over the course of the century. If they played with dolls at all, they rejected elaborate dolls for coarse ones, favored black rag dolls over white ones, resisted rote prescriptions of play rituals by substituting their own earthy versions, and often preferred active "physical culture" to passive doll culture. At times, boys also challenged sex-role stereotyping and at other times reinforced it. Those girls who resisted patriarchal prescriptions in their play displayed confidence, not conformity. Their play, like language, revealed girls' agency in the construction of their own upbringing.[49]

While occasionally victorious in their struggles with parents, girls faced other contenders who claimed it as their right to shape dolls both literally and figuratively. In the years after the Civil War, American businessmen, with no prior experience in dollmaking but eager to make a profit, turned their attention to doll invention and production. How businessmen perceived an American girlhood and how they conceived of the role that dolls would play in girls' lives would have profound consequences for the nature of nineteenth-century doll invention.

CHAPTER TWO

Masculinity, Technology, and the Doll Economy, 1860–1908

In 1899 inventor Vincent Lake of Pleasantville, New Jersey, was poised for success—he had just patented his new typographic machine. By the time his invention was ready to be installed, however, it had been rendered obsolete by a competitor—the Linotype, which used a more sophisticated and efficient process. Though he was stranded with his outmoded prototype, the determined Lake persevered by directing his knowledge of machines away from the masculine world of printing. He designed, of all things, a doll. But his creation little resembled the exquisite, fragile imported bisque doll that he might have bought for his daughter. Rather, Lake's invention, a steel-springed "All Steel Doll" (fig. 11), was the epitome

11. The seemingly indestructible
"All Steel Doll" epitomized the male
world of business in which
American dolls were produced.
Reproduced from *Playthings,* 1904,
by permission.

of the American male world of business and production from which
he came.[1]

Did other doll inventors like Lake develop new techniques or entertain alternative sensibilities to produce dolls? Were they responding to an
unfulfilled need expressed by girls for types of dolls not otherwise available? How did these dolls and doll production influence later generations
of dolls? Despite the novelty of Lake's invention, dollmakers using conventional methods of industrial production in a backwater industry seem
less significant to historians than do industrial innovators. Yet by the end
of the nineteenth century, men with origins as diverse as carriage manufacturers and typesetters would end up as doll manufacturers. Yankee
as well as foreign-born businessmen applied their extensive experience
as printers, carriage builders, clock makers, pulley-belt makers, carriage
trimmers, bonnet-frame makers, printers, and machinists to the production of dolls. Businessmen established partnerships with sons and associ-

ates, created new materials, and perfected existing ones. More often than not, male inventors created doll parts and relied on a network of business relationships to construct a whole doll. Dolls, mechanical or machine-like in construction, were produced in factories, circumventing traditional skills like whittling and sewing previously used in making dolls.

Ultimately, male inventors produced allegedly "indestructible" dolls based on the machines they admired. With the breaking down of the doctrine of separate spheres after the Civil War, women began to enter the world previously dominated by men. Conversely, men began to enter the world of women. But still shaped by the dominant construction of manhood, male inventors were more interested in how a doll worked and looked. By introducing movement and voice, businessmen removed the doll they created from the child's imagination and control. Conceiving of it as an autonomous object, men strove to give the doll a semblance of a life of its own, but only succeeded in creating a "thing" with little connection to girls who, as a result, rarely played with them. Related only to the abstraction of play, the dolls were products of attempts to transform pulleys into profits.

In 1866, seventeen-year-old Albert Schoenhut immigrated from Wurttemberg, Germany, to America, where he joined George Borgfeldt and other young men with business training and ambition.[2] These men arrived during the years when one third of the 3.3 million European immigrants to America were German-born. Although many were poverty-stricken peasants, displaced artisans, devastated farmers, or political refugees, many teenage boys had worked as apprentices. According to John Cawelti, immigration "helped make America a country of devotees of success by sending to her shores men who believed in their right and their need to better their condition."[3]

In America, young men like Schoenhut, who arrived with business experience and skills, found places for themselves in a male world in which established German immigrant businessmen provided salaried employment. Immigrant employers with shared gender, class, and ethnic affiliations extended a hand to others most like themselves. The German-speaking Albert Schoenhut, who settled in Philadelphia, was employed to make rocking horses by a firm where many of the employees shared a cultural background. Another common arrangement was for the already employed brothers of newly arrived immigrants to arrange white-collar jobs for their brothers, thereby minimizing the impact of dislocation and maximizing opportunities for success. Marcell Kahle, who worked at Strasburger, Pfeiffer & Company, was joined in 1873 by his brother, Joseph. Similarly, when Frederick Schwarz (founder of F. A. O. Schwarz) immigrated to America from Herford, Westphalia, he joined his older brother, Henry, a partner at a fancy goods store in Baltimore. Two more Schwarz brothers followed, each one establishing his place among other middle-class young men in American commerce.

Industry and business were increasingly specialized during the first half of the nineteenth century in cities like Philadelphia, Baltimore, and New York. Generalized merchants of the eighteenth century gave way to importers, exporters, and wholesalers. The large warehouses in "downtown" commercial districts offered importers, wholesalers, distributors, and assemblers abundant space for their increasing stock. The relocation of doll importers, wholesalers, and jobbers from the midwest and elsewhere to the New York metropolitan area would make it the heart of the American doll industry by the turn of the century.[4]

Young men of American birth also migrated to urban centers to make their fortune. Despite their national differences, both those who immigrated and those who migrated shared much in common. In northeastern and midwestern cities, European immigrants and young men of American birth were likely to have similar mentalities, shaped by experiences scripted by larger social and economic forces. Edward Imeson Horsman, a teenager of American birth (who was later to be a dominant figure in the doll industry), entered an importing business as a clerk for two dollars a week. The halcyon days of clerking were ending, however, especially in the post–Civil War period when the circumscribed responsibilities of clerking no longer provided an auspicious launch to a business career nor offered prospects for advancement.[5] This probably frustrated those like Horsman who, by their mid-twenties, had hoped to accumulate sufficient capital to provide for a wife and family. Faced with the declining prospects for clerks, Horsman established himself at 21 as an entrepreneur of games and "home amusements," catering to a newly created market of middle-class families.

While Horsman appears to have had little help from other family members, more often immigrant brothers typically shared counters and coffers forming "family" businesses in which their wives and daughters seldom played a part. In the 1860s future doll entrepreneur Philip Goldsmith peddled notions in Milwaukee before moving to Chicago where he and his brother would establish a dry goods store. The company names of New York firms alone reveal the prevalence of brother partnerships.[6] In Philadelphia, German immigrant John Doll, Sr., was in the business of importing and wholesaling dolls with his brother George.

Despite ethnic differences, middle-class men of Western European and American birth inhabited social arenas separate from women.[7] Late nineteenth-century Victorians believed that women were more suited to the domestic fireplace than to the marketplace. Distinct character traits ascribed to men and women assigned each gender to a separate sphere. In the private realm where women could be wife or mother, they were expected to be gentle, nurturing, self-sacrificing, emotional, physically weak (but morally strong), pious, and pure.[8] Girls were raised to assume their maternal position in a home that was insulated from an unstable and competitive world.

Boys, on the other hand, were trained to be assertive and individualistic and to take their place in the public sphere with other men. The ideal they were to emulate was unemotional, rational, protective, even tough. Young men were encouraged to enter the world of business, make their fortune, and brave the economic cycles, bankruptcy, or unemployment. According to late nineteenth-century success manuals, initiative, aggressiveness, competitiveness, and forcefulness were the cardinal virtues of the self-made man. An ideology of masculine individualism was exemplified in the contemporary literature to which American men were exposed. Advice books written by Henry Ward Beecher (brother of the Beecher sisters) and others informed young men that economic success was determined by temperance and sobriety. For men, business "was a philosophy, a morality, and an atmosphere."[9] Young men were motivated by a work ethic that equated financial success with masculinity.

Despite their cultural differences, German immigrants and Yankees alike fueled the American doll industry as importers, wholesalers, and retailers flooding nurseries with imported dolls in the years between the Civil War and World War I. For Americans, dollmaking was not a life-long avocation handed down from generation to generation as was often the case in Germany, where the dollmaking industry dated back to the Middle Ages. Whether German-Americans or Yankees, those who would eventually turn their attention to the invention and production of dolls, however, had deep roots in business. George Hawkins of New York made "Excelsior Bonnet Frames." Franklyn Elijah Darrow owned a factory in Bristol, Connecticut, where he made rawhide pulley belts for machines. Albert Schoenhut's experience was more relevant: he had produced rocking horses for forty years. And Joel Addison Hartley Ellis, known locally as "Cab" Ellis, manufactured carriages, perambulators, and toys in Springfield, Vermont.[10]

When men turned to dollmaking, their creativity was shaped not only by business experience but by faith in progress as well. In this "age of invention," the explosion of technological achievement and industrial development was measurable by the volume of patents.[11] In late nineteenth-century America, invention was seen as a product not only of Yankee ingenuity but also of masculine resourcefulness. The public, commercial function of patenting is what made dollmaking, in part, an acceptable masculine pursuit. For "Cab" Ellis, employment at his uncle's side in Rochester, New York, equipped him with the mechanical training he needed. By age 19, Ellis had designed a "steam excavating machine" intended for railroad building, one of thirteen inventions he would patent.[12] These early forays into technology would help Ellis design the mechanical dolls' joints he would later produce. These were the methods, means, and networks American men like Ellis would use to make dolls.

In many ways, Ellis was typical. Drawing from their business experiences and technological know-how, male inventors made dolls that resembled the sturdy machines they admired more than the delicate porcelain dolls of European origin that dominated the American market in the years after the Civil War. It was not that dollmakers particularly liked to make dolls. Doll production usually was only a phase in long and diverse business careers. What these men liked best was inventing machines. The Webber Singing Doll, for example, which sang sentimental songs such as "Home, Sweet, Home," was even advertised by the Massachusetts Organ Company as a "most ingenious machine." No one represented the age of invention better than Thomas Alva Edison, who received more than one thousand patents at his Menlo Park laboratory. It had been Edison's aim to turn out "a minor invention every ten days and a big thing every six months or so." One of Edison's smaller projects had been to apply his newly invented phonograph to dolls. "My talking doll," Edison would claim enthusiastically, was as "nearly perfect as machinery can be." [13]

Many dollmakers, like other inventors, were inspired by the prospect of animating "things." Enoch Rise Morrison was the first in the United States to patent an "Autoperipatetikos," or walking doll. Duplicating human movement, rather than approximating the texture or appearance of the human body, was the chief aim for doll inventors. Clockwork "creeping" dolls crawled by means of two large protruding gears (fig. 12).[14]

Most dollmakers did not make whole mechanical dolls, but rather specialized in the mechanization of some aspect of the doll's anatomy. One Connecticut toymaker patented a "Fancy Doll" whose wax head, suspended in a wig-frame, swiveled on an axis revealing four faces, each with a different expression. A doll head that worked by means of a pulley system had "two opposite faces of different expressions" that could "be turned to the front by a mechanism while the hand-gear remains stationary and covers the opposite face." Other inventors devised mechanisms whereby dolls' eyes could open and close. A movable lower lip made another doll appear to smile.[15]

That most male inventors patented parts of doll bodies as if constructing parts of a machine has been partially obscured by the official record, which identifies their inventions as "dolls" rather than doll parts. Jacob Lacmann's 1871 patent for a "doll" was no more than a design for a lead-filled hand and forearm.[16]

Other inventors patented doll bodies. Charles Dotter patented a corseted doll's abdomen, as did Philip Goldsmith, who supplied Montgomery Ward with doll torsos in five sizes (fig. 13).[17]

Some male dollmakers devoted their work solely to the invention of doll joints. The patent that Henry Mason and mechanic Luke Taylor obtained for the "Construction of Dolls" in 1881 consisted of "a device for uniting the head of a doll to the body." Designed with little regard for the overall appearance, however, few dolls resembled either the female or even the human anatomy when undressed. For example, the leg joints on some dolls were placed over the thigh in such a way as to give the pubic

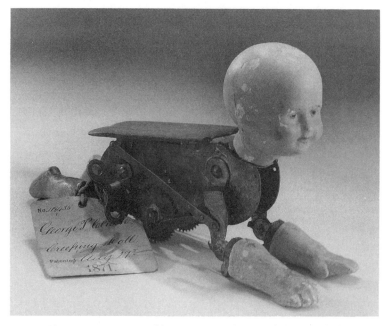

12. American inventors like George Pemberton Clarke, with little understanding of girls' play and imagination, patented mechanical dolls like the Natural Creeping Baby Doll, patented in 1871, that expressed their fascination with technology. Machine-like dolls, however, became the target of mothers, authors, and educators concerned about the encroachment of industrialization into the nursery. Photo courtesy of the National Museum of American History, Smithsonian Institution, Washington, D.C.

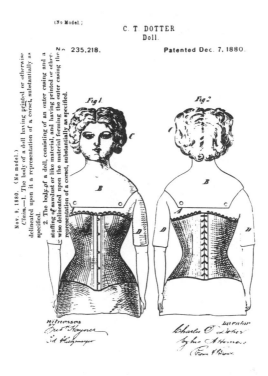

13. Charles T. Dotter was among
many male inventors who patented
doll components that fractionalized
and distorted the adult female
shape. U.S. Patent Office.

region a male "anatomy" (fig. 14).[18] Perhaps by making parts rather than
the whole doll, inventors mitigated threats to their masculine identity as
producers of feminine and frivolous objects. The evidence is inadequate
to draw a definite conclusion as to why, but their products suggest that
they felt more at ease with producing parts of women's bodies than with
intact wholes.

Because of this fractionalized production of doll parts, most inventors
had to establish a network of business relationships in order to produce

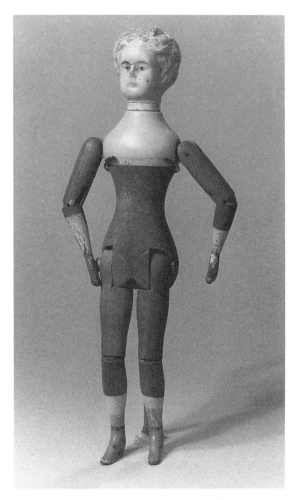

14. Concentrating on joints and
hinges, New England inventors
sacrificed anatomical realism to the
mechanics of mobility in the
wooden dolls with metal limbs they
created. Photo courtesy of the
Wenham Museum, Wenham, Mass.

a whole doll. In the late 1880s, Thomas Edison combined his patents with those of another inventor in order to produce a much improved version of his "Talking Doll" (despite the earlier claim of perfection). In New York, George Hawkins, who manufactured doll heads, attached them to bodies patented by inventor William Farr Goodwin. Similarly, Ludwig Greiner's papier-mâché doll heads were frequently attached to doll bodies made by Jacob Lacmann, whose "Manufactory" was advertised in Philadelphia business directories in the early 1860s.[19] Though he earnestly tried to make doll heads himself, Philip Goldsmith reluctantly attached his corseted doll bodies to heads produced by others.

This network also expanded overseas, where German businessmen manufactured and exported porcelain and china heads at lower costs than in the United States. In 1890, Thomas Edison's representatives surveyed the German dollmaking region for a manufacturer who could supply seventy thousand inexpensive bisque heads for American-made tin phonographic bodies (fig. 15). The German firm Simon & Halbig, one of several porcelain doll head factories that produced heads for Edison, supplied twelve thousand heads for $30,000, or about $2.50 each. Brooklyn-based doll producer Solomon Hoffman imported doll bodies from Germany—much to the chagrin of American manufacturers, who felt that they could make a better article.[20]

The European doll heads were likely to be attached to American doll bodies made of steel, pewter, wood, hard rubber, papier-mâché, and other sturdy materials. The Goodyear Rubber Company advertised three pages of hard rubber doll heads in its 1881 trade journal. By using durable substances male inventors resolved the dilemma of bisque dolls' fragility by making their dolls almost indestructible. Pewter hands and feet of wooden dolls were made by two different Vermont producers. Edison's "Talking Doll" was formed from six heavy pieces of metal. Recalling Lake's "All Steel" doll, one 1877 patent was granted for a doll made out of electroplated sheet metal (fig. 16).[21]

Male dollmakers used hard substances for reasons that were only partially explained by the needs of children for more durable toys. It was more likely that working with these materials provided an outlet for the skills the inventors themselves possessed. If raised in a rural household

15. Despite repeated improvements of the phonograph (left) and
the cylindrical record (right), Thomas Edison's "Talking Doll,"
with an imported bisque head and American-made metal body,
would suffer from numerous "grave and trifling" faults unsatisfac-
tory to both customers and stockholders. U.S. Department of the
Interior, National Park Service, Edison National Site, Edison, N.J.

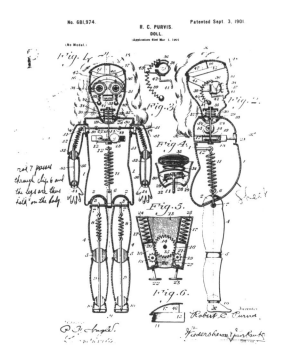

16. Male inventors, who used hard
substances like sheet metal to make
dolls like this one, were often more
concerned with imitating movement
than approximating the texture or
appearance of the human body.
U.S. Patent Office.

as was Joel Ellis, a boy was likely to be taught by male kin about the
properties of wood and metal, whereas his sister was taught about cotton and cloth.

Skills learned from previous employment further determined the
resources used to make dolls. Using tremendous pressure, Bruckner
steamed pieces of rawhide in molds to form the doll's features.[22] Drawing
on his bonnet-frame expertise, George Hawkins pressed gluey material

47

between two dies to shape his dolls' heads. When dried, the stiff heads kept their shape. The fractionalized, hard, mechanized dolls made by men were the products of skills, materials, and modes of production that had been evolving over generations as general solutions in the manufacture of industrial products. Dolls were swept into production lines along with buggies, clocks, and machine parts.

In part because boys were not taught sewing, male inventors often preferred cement and other adhesives to needle and thread. Doll inventor and manufacturer Albert Bruckner typically called for the use of cement and glue to bind the doll face to its head. Instead of sewing his rawhide dolls, Frank Darrow used "any suitable adhesive substance" available to circumvent the "irksomeness" of sewing dolls at his pulley belt factory. When the unavoidable need emerged, immigrant wives appear to have provided complementary sewing skills. With a few sewing machines and a loan of $1,000, Philip Goldsmith established a factory in Covington, Kentucky, assisted by his wife, Sophia, who, in addition to raising five children, made patterns and sewed clothing for the dolls. Wives dressed the dolls their husbands made because of their domestic experience. Sophia Goldsmith, for example, had already been a dressmaker. Like many wives who applied their domestic skills where and when they were needed, the wife of entrepreneur Charles Braitling helped make dolls' shoes for her husband's concern. Such production did not bring women into the public sphere, however, but reinforced their husbands' role as primary provider. This division of labor by gender tended to underscore the idea that designing dolls was the important function in the process of dollmaking, whereas making dolls' dresses was ancillary and feminine. Wives' or female workers' sewing skills were often summarily disparaged by dollmaking men, who made explicit the advantages of their methods over more drudging domestic methods used by dollmaking women.[23]

In addition to production, the aesthetics of dollmaking was being shaped by technology and business as many turn-of-the-century male producers applied photography and other technical innovations. "In 1901 while watching one of his friends working through the tedious process of stuffing and shaping the faces then used on rag dolls, [Albert Bruckner] conceived of the idea of giving form and expression to the faces by stamping out or embossing the features onto a mask." Bruckner drew upon his previous work with efficient industrial techniques while employed by the Gray Lithography Company.[24]

Dolls with lithographed faces captured the refined look of bisque dolls but at a very low cost to the producer. In this way those like E. I. Horsman, producer of "Babyland Rag Dolls," were able to make more "beautiful" versions of coarse-looking rag dolls popularized by women entrepreneurs. The appearance of rag dolls had broad implications as girls were being asked to identify with an adult male's idea of what a woman should look like.[25] Like women in photographs or paintings, these dolls, which looked as if they belonged to the nineteenth century more than the twentieth, became something to look at rather than touch (fig. 17). For Bruckner and his associate Rudolph Gruss, the "attractive face" of the doll and not its head (referred to as the "stuffed dummy-head of the doll") was the source of their satisfaction.

Most of these dolls reproduced three-dimensional "reality" as lifeless and flat. Although it photographed better in advertisements, the doll's face appeared as far more sophisticated than the rest of the doll's body, a confusion of dimensional effect in sacrifice to industrial efficiency. The hands and feet of the "Stella" rag doll, for example, ended in sharp seams which looked anything but "natural." Thus, photographic dolls that attempted to capture reality isolated it to one part of the doll, its face.

Thus, whether utilizing photographic or lithographic processes, male dollmakers eagerly sought alternatives to domestic skills as did entrepreneurs in other industries. For instance, by integrating the corset in the doll's body, Philip Goldsmith rid the process of one step: stitching an extra corset over the body. "My improvement," wrote Goldsmith, "dispenses with this additional material of the corset and the additional labor required to make [it] and put it on." Makers of cloth doll patterns eliminated entirely the need for sewing and hand-painting, jobs usually undertaken by skilled women workers. Doll blanks produced by Edgar Newell left the sewing to mothers and daughters, who purchased yards of fabric printed with doll patterns at dry goods stores. While many dollmakers were concerned with finding a way around stitching dolls together, Wolf Flechter circumvented the "strenuous" process of stuffing them. His in-

17. Utilizing the latest printing technology to make rag dolls more "beautiful" than those popularized by women and promoted in contemporary women's magazines, inventors utilized lithography and other industrial forms. Photo by Laurie Minor, courtesy of the National Museum of American History, Smithsonian Institution, Washington, D.C.

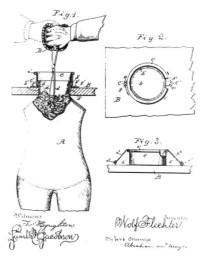

18. Doll producers relied upon
recent technological inventions such
as these "forceps" patented by Wolf
Flechter in 1877 in order to make
dolls and distance dolls from
workers. U.S. Patent Office.

vention, similar in appearance to forceps used with a difficult childbirth,
permitted operators to stuff dolls without handling the "fleecy or fibrous
material" which included cotton wool and "hair-filaments" (fig. 18).[26]
Flechter's technological device might have made working conditions
more healthful, but it also contributed to the mechanical takeover of the
production process which continued to distance the worker from the
task of dollmaking.

Flechter's "iron hands" invention was an example of how the per-
sistent and pervasive machine not only determined doll invention but
the nature of doll production as well. At Edison's New Jersey plant, "the

finest new tools and machinery were procured" to make dolls. "Great iron presses, some of them weighing five tons, were used, and steel dies for stamping out the different parts were constructed." Doll workers in one Vermont firm mass-produced wooden heads using one ton of hydraulic pressure. A four-sided planing machine rounded woodblock heads, while another machine made sharply pointed noses. Fine steel dies pressed features into doll faces. The machines that cored the wooden heads that Taylor invented were like those used in making shoe lasts. "The lathes used to make [Ellis] dolls were used extensively for turning shoe lasts, hat-blocks and other irregular forms," recalled Herbert Ellis about his father's Vermont toy firm. Braitling's doll shoes and stockings were produced by machines designed to turn out three hundred pairs of shoes an hour.[27]

The manly identity of doll entrepreneurs and their male workers was bolstered by using machines to make dolls. Because many machines still required strength, "Pride in physical prowess was . . . an important aspect of working-class masculinity."[28] In describing one doll factory in 1909, a writer for *Toys & Novelties* noted the

> great brawny fellows, these men, naked to the waist, wearing leathern aprons . . . There is a special machine for stamping out the hands . . . I stood in front of it, fascinated by the steady stream of queer, little hands that fell ceaselessly from the iron monster—it was awful, uncanny, hypnotizing. Indeed, the whole sight was grim and monstrous. The low factory rooms were misty with steam and lit by strange, red-glowing fires; always the steel machines pulsed and clanged; and through the mist sweaty giants of men went to and fro with heaps of little greenish arms and legs.[29]

The dolls men invented were produced on machines which, while buttressing the gender identity of the worker and entrepreneur, also eroded the skills of the former. In Edison's plant, as dolls were made into machines, so were doll workers who repeated one operation in the manufacturing process, developing little relationship to the end product to which their labor contributed a minute part.

At Edison's plant, men and women were allocated jobs according to their sex. Whether making cloth, porcelain, or wooden dolls, mass production was divided according to gender. In the factories owned by men, those aspects of dollmaking often associated with dexterity were assigned to women workers, while those requiring strength were left to the men. For example, while male workers produced miniature metal phonographs in Edison's plant, it was the women who recorded nursery rhymes onto wax records (fig. 19). "A large number of these girls are continually doing this work . . . and the jangle produced by a number of girls simultaneously repeating 'Mary had a Little Lamb,' 'Jack and Jill,' 'Little Bo-Peep,' and other interesting stories is beyond description," reported a writer for *Scientific American* in 1892. Sixty workers, one third of whom were women, labored at Joel Ellis's Vermont establishment, where pairs of wooden dolls were sawed apart at the hips by men who also bored, mortised, pressed, and sanded them. Meanwhile, women operatives removed "a slight burr" at the joining, assembled dolls, and dipped them in vats of paint.[30]

In doll factories that formerly served other industries (like a glass factory that Philip Goldsmith converted), male dollmakers used modern business methods. The modernization of doll manufacturing, as at the Edison plant, typified late nineteenth-century mass production where professional engineers applied the latest "scientific management" ideas to the production process. In Edison's plant, "Order and system reign in every department," observed a contemporary reporter on a tour of the facilities (fig. 20).[31]

Because dollmaking made use of machines, factories, and an industrial workforce, most sons could follow in their fathers' footsteps without fear of compromising their masculinity. The same fraternal business networking that encouraged the younger generation to pursue dollmaking could continue uninterrupted. Sharing the same repertoire of skills, Joel Ellis and his son, Hartley, patented a doll's joint. Dexter Martin manufactured wooden dolls with his son, Frank. Henry E. Taylor, who worked "mornings and nights . . . after school and during vacations," helped make dolls on the machines invented by his father, a mechanic. As Albert Schoenhut's six sons came of age, they sold the toys manufactured at their father's Philadelphia establishment (fig. 21).[82] By 1908, *Playthings,* the toy

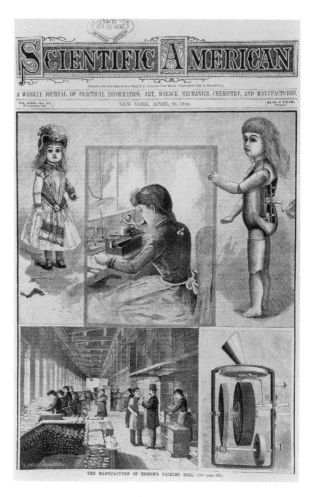

19. At the Edison plant, faith in technology determined that the
mechanical phonographic dolls were produced by machines.
Photo courtesy of the National Museum of American History,
Smithsonian Institution, Washington, D.C.

20. Rationalized factories like the Edison plant mass-produced the "Talking Doll" according to the principles of "scientific management" and the ideology of domesticity which relegated women workers to dressing assembled dolls. U.S. Department of the Interior, National Park Service, Edison National Site, Edison, N.J.

industry's trade journal, reported that Schoenhut's six sons all served in supervisory positions. Frederick Braitling launched his career at the age of 12, sweeping the floors of his father's doll shoe factory. First pushing a broom and then paper, Frederick rose steadily in the hierarchy as sons of entrepreneurs and professionals often did.[32]

Doll importers and distributors similarly brought their sons into their businesses as they came of age, as suggested by the enormous number of father-and-son firm names, like G. Frankel & Sons and P. Goldsmith & Sons. E. I. Horsman's son, E. J. Horsman, Jr., would become a junior partner in his father's firm. Gustavus Schwarz's son Henry joined the Philadelphia toy firm in 1894. "A son, Henry F. Schwarz, entered the business and became a partner while F. A. O. Schwarz was on the Square. When it moved to West Twenty-third Street, he began to assume more of his father's burdens."[33]

Occasionally, however, sons lacked enthusiasm. Following Philip Goldsmith's drowning while on vacation, his widow and sons were left to carry on the partnership of P. Goldsmith & Sons. But it was not long

21. "Mr. Albert Schoenhut and his Six Sons, Talking over the Doll Question for 1912." Sons rather than daughters (for whom paid employment was an unlikely option) often followed in the family business. Socialized by a Victorian culture that rigidly distinguished between masculine and feminine spheres, sons acquired the same values, sensibilities, and skills as their fathers. Reproduced from *Playthings,* by permission.

before the Goldsmith brothers sold off the stock and repaid creditors. Instead of making patented corset doll bodies, this first Americanized generation of young men utilized the skills and materials of the Goldsmith firm to make baseballs. "I learndt [sic] to sew baseballs so as to be able to instruct the girls," wrote Goldsmith's widow, Sophia. As a fitting icon to their future, the brothers erected a huge baseball on top of their new building when they moved the firm across the river from Covington, Kentucky, to Cincinnati, Ohio.[34]

There is no evidence that daughters ever joined their fathers or brothers even though doll businesses catered to girls. Horsman had three daughters, but only his son became his junior partner. Neither of Philip Goldsmith's two daughters worked in the "family" business although all of their brothers did.[35] Similarly, none of Charles Braitling's five daughters worked at the Bridgeport, Connecticut, firm their brother inherited. Business, regardless of its products or purposes, was considered by male dollmakers a masculine pursuit and unsuitable for their genteel daughters.

Moreover, male dollmakers rarely located doll production near the home, and those who did were unlikely to stay there. The close proximity between home and work enabled wives of immigrant craftsmen-producers like Sophia Goldsmith to participate in doll manufacturing.[36] Albert Schoenhut's wife similarly assisted in the workshop as long as it was situated behind their family home. It was probably when the firm relocated, expanded, and modernized, however, that Mrs. Schoenhut's participation ended. The increasingly industrialized nature of doll production precluded the possibility of most wives from participating.

With factories and offices removed from the home, late nineteenth-century middle-class urban fathers were likely to see far less of their children, ostensibly insulated from the harsh realities of the workplace. The same forces that created the middle-class domestic sphere, wherein daughters played and mothers presided, led fathers to seek employment away from the home they were expected to support and protect. Thus, they tended to have less contact with the girls for whom their dolls were actually intended.[37]

Changing ideologies of fatherhood and motherhood in part shaped doll invention. Men who made dolls considered fatherhood nonparticipatory. Male inventor/producers were as out of touch with their daughters as with the popular discourse in contemporary mothers' magazines which stressed the necessity to reform toys as well as childhood. Although male objectification of the doll also corresponded with a view of children as objects, feminine attitudes toward dolls paralleled an emerging ideology that emphasized the relationships between mother and child within a notion of "scientific motherhood." Inspired middle-class mothers (discussed in chapter 3) would praise cloth dolls and disparage mechanical ones for these very reasons.

Parenting styles and perceptions of children are revealed in the fact that in patents of doll parts male inventors rarely mention children, describing technical details instead. Only the exceptional inventor stressed "the value of dolls as a means of amusement for children," as opposed to the child's comfort or safety. Contemporaries even took note; a reporter for *Harper's Young People* commented that "Mr. Edison knew much more about phonographs than he did about children's nurseries" and that the tin doll looked more like a "miniature stove-pipe with the letter 'V' stuck on top of it."[38]

Because of the limited contact of fathers with their daughters, few men had any idea about what constituted a good doll for play. Had Edison watched small children playing with his "Talking Doll," he might have realized that the bisque head was too fragile, the metal body too dangerous, and the four-pound doll too heavy. Clearly, a heavy doll that slipped out of cradling arms was far more likely to injure the child than suffer any harm itself. On the other hand, if wooden and metal dolls were less likely to break, their mechanical workings were more inclined to break down. Edison corrected twenty-five "grave and trifling" faults in the talking dolls, but they still remained rather poor machines. Letters to his toy company complained of "loose works," dolls that would not talk, and those whose voices were too faint to be heard. Among the twenty dolls that one doll dealer in San Francisco received, "Two were broken and four wouldn't talk." One disgruntled customer complained, "The voices of the little monsters are exceedingly unpleasant to hear."[39]

Like Edison's invention, Morrison's mechanical doll suffered from both conceptual and structural problems. Because its hourglass figure was far too slender, his "lady doll" easily lost its balance when cranked into motion and cracked its fragile china head. When Connecticut cast iron and tin toymakers reintroduced Goodwin's patented walking doll, their catalogue acknowledged "former defects" in its design. The Webber Singing Doll failed to live up to its name when sheet music inside the doll body stuck to poorly constructed bellows.[40]

Dollmakers whose contact with girls was fleeting had little opportunity to observe children's ability to make dolls come "alive." Thus, dollmakers not only underestimated but also misunderstood girls' imaginations. One four-year-old girl did not like talking dolls because "the fixings in the stomach are not good for digestion."[41] In the turn-of-the-century British novel *The Child's Mind,* mechanical dolls amused parents far more than they entertained the daughter, who became a passive spectator as the doll claimed a life of its own—albeit a constricted one.

> The parents wound it up, and it ran across the floor towards the child. There was something threatening in its gait and almost diabolical in its noisy gesticulations, so that the child shrank from it as it hastened drunkenly in her direction. It came close to one of her feet, and she could have almost shrieked with terror, but ere it reached her, it fell over on its side in attempting the figure eight, and groaning out the last few minutes of its brief life. The mother pounced on it, and having resuscitated it with a key, set it off to the father's side at the other side of the room. It suffered, however, from locomotor ataxy, and failed to reach the father by many feet. It went wide to the right and staggered against the board, and then fell down, buzzing like an entrapped bee. The parents laughed hysterically but the child sat solemnly in the centre of her nursery floor, and did not even smile. Though she was glad that her parents were so happy, the ingenuity of the toy frightened her. She was too young as yet to understand how and why the thing moved and ran and shook its arms. For her there was an appalling reality in its movements, and when the angry buzzing against the skirting board at length ceased, she heaved a big sigh of relief.[42]

Mechanical dolls became much like the labor-saving machines that brought them into existence. Girls who played with dolls as they "should" were now forced to keep up with the dolls' inexorable machine pace. To do so required order, discipline, and little imagination. The doll was a machine that performed one specialized function and did so over and over again—at least until it broke. In her autobiography Eda Lord recalled leaving behind "useless things like clockwork toys which had broken down or no longer had a key."[43]

The commercial result was that American male efforts to wrest the doll business from the Germans would not succeed for decades to come. Although the Goldsmith firm supplied Montgomery Ward mail-order customers with five sizes of "Patent Corset Bodies" for 20 to 60 cents, most American manufacturers were unable to capture a significant share of the doll market.[44] Even with his imported machines and German workmen skilled in wax and ceramic manufacture, Goldsmith could not compete with imports, despite the 35 percent import duty levied on foreign goods. The Webber Singing Doll, which came in three sizes and cost between $2.75 and $4 in 1883, was prohibitively expensive for most American families. Even to those who could afford them, American dolls appeared primitive compared with European models. Dollmakers fought a losing battle against doll importers, who flooded the American market with captivating and extravagant dolls, appealing to status-seeking parents of the Gilded Age. Wooden or metal dolls did not reflect the aim of conspicuous luxury. Although American dolls twisted acrobatically, they could not convey the sophisticated beauty that appealed to upwardly mobile American consumers. These dolls stood little chance in either the nursery or the marketplace.

Male inventors remained in the public sphere, insulated from more human and domestic concerns, which they would eventually commercialize to their best advantage. Until they developed sensibilities and skills which enabled them to become fully competitive, these contenders remained in cultural backwaters. Although they largely produced female dolls, their machine-like creations remained as male as those who brought them into being.

CHAPTER THREE

In the Dolls' House:
The Material Maternalism
of Martha Chase,
1889–1914

Although a wax doll in a contemporary children's story boasted that she was "modelled to perfection after the most approved forms of [Victorian feminine] beauty," in contrast, dolls hand-painted with rougher brush strokes at the M. J. Chase Company provided an intentionally realistic texture.[1] Martha Jenks Wheaton Chase (1851– 1925), descendant of early New England settlers, sewed dolls for her own children and those of neighbors and friends in the years before she converted the small cottage behind her home into the M. J. Chase Company. Though locally known as "The Dolls' House" a decade after Henrik Ibsen's *Doll's House* (1879) appeared, it signified neither gender oppression nor domesticity to Martha Chase. Instead, the Dolls' House represented the ways in which Chase drew on the culture of the domestic economy in order to reform dolls and reconstruct gender roles.

What motivated the wife of a prominent physician to go into business to make dolls? The rather limited literature on businesswomen has focused on the enduring influence of the Victorian ideology of domesticity that limited female entrepreneurs to those businesses that catered to women and children. This nineteenth-century trend has been generally interpreted as a capitulation to gender roles and an accommodation to capitalism. The experiences of Martha Chase and other women dollmakers suggest, however, that we need to take a closer look at these feminized areas of the economy for evidence of discontent and reform. If late nineteenth-century dollmakers represented by Chase are any indication, there was widespread resistance to both sex roles and industrial capitalism.[2]

In the last decades of the nineteenth century, Martha Chase and her contemporaries questioned dominant notions about what a doll should look like, what it should represent, and what role it should play in the lives of girls as well as boys. Within a broader cultural climate devoted to "child study" and "scientific mothering," American women voiced their objections to bourgeois childhood and, in particular, to the many heavy, expensive, and dangerous dolls that restricted the range of their daughters' creative play. In their own way, women like Chase set out to reform the doll in an effort to promote doll play among girls and boys.[3] With the dolls she created, Chase was not only redefining what it meant to be a girl but what it meant to be a boy as well.

Women like Chase created dolls whose qualities were rooted in the domestic values and norms of the antebellum households in which they grew up. As girls, they had learned how to nurture family and friends, how to be useful and, at the same time, how to act as cultural guardians in the world besieged by commerce and greed. Thus, Chase's stockinet dolls—as those made by other women—embodied the middle-class conceptions of motherhood and childhood articulated in mother's magazines and books on childrearing. Their dolls combined key features of their creators' antebellum upbringing—sensitivity to the potential of dolls as teaching tools—as well as a social ethos that prized social relationships over material acquisition.

Chase was not only a businesswoman but a social reformer as well. Female dollmakers were inspired by the same social forces that led an army of middle-class women to launch women's clubs and establish settlement houses. Many were "maternalists," a term that describes the ideology of many progressive era reformers whose values and goals were shaped by what they believed to be woman's natural capacity to nurture.[4] Maternalism drew upon Victorian domesticity yet provided women with the moral authority to reform specific areas in the public sector. Businessmen and modern business methods had little influence on the maternalist style of employers like Martha Chase, who blurred the boundary between home life and the marketplace. In the New England "Dolls' House," for example, women dollmakers combined the skills of the antebellum household economy with feminine middle-class Victorian values. In the 1890s, women doll inventors, often in partnership with female kin, established maternalistic labor relations with the women who sewed, stuffed, and painted dolls for them, giving them gifts and birthday parties. Like the male artisans that Herbert Gutman and other "new labor" historians have described, Martha Chase shared stories and laughed with the women who assembled the dolls she designed.

Chase was neither a typical entrepreneur nor an explicit feminist. Still, she was critical of sex-role stereotyping and did bring to her business an ideology comfortably expressed in "things." Unlike the male producers' delight in mechanical objects that served as an outlet for technical innovation, however, her material expressions began, and did not end, with the use to which the dolls would be put. Like other "material feminists," Chase gave feminism tangible form by providing alternative artifacts in the commercial world.[5] She combined business methods with social goals to produce dolls whose mission it was to ameliorate urban conditions and to reconstruct gender roles. Martha Chase's dolls can be read, then, as the material culture manifestation of her maternalist ideology.

"Nine tenths of our well-to-do families rob their children of the right to be happy, by producing 'toy indigestion,'" commented a contributor to *Babyhood* in 1898.[6] What did parents think of talking, walking, creeping, and crawling dolls? In late nineteenth-century America, the effects of the sheer and cloying abundance of dolls worried some adults. They were made anxious by the materialism that dominated the nursery where an overpopulation of dolls were resplendent gentry of their own "mansions" cluttered with their own "possessions." One parent exclaimed, "Too much and too many kinds will confuse the mind!" Others worried that a surfeit of dolls would cause boredom instead.[7]

Mechanical dolls were also compared to monsters, a metaphor widely applied to all machines in America since the publication of *Frankenstein* in 1818. But to mothers and educators, the machine-like mechanical doll, which brought industrialization into the nursery, posed a particular threat to childhood. At the same time, mechanical dolls also appeared as the very personification of artifice to contemporaries who worried that children were also becoming too superficial. These toys became a favorite target among those increasingly dissatisfied with what the expanded consumer market had to offer. Kate Douglas Wiggin, founder of the first American kindergarten and author of *Rebecca of Sunnybrook Farm,* found serious fault with these new mechanical dolls:

> Press a judiciously-located button, and ask [the doll] the test question, which is, if she would like some candy; whereupon with an angelic detached movement smile (located in the left cheek), she is to answer, 'Give brother big piece; give me little piece!' If the thing gets out of order, (and I devoutly hope it will), it will doubtless return to the state of nature, and horrify bystanders by remarking, 'Give me big piece! Give brother little piece!' Think of having a gilded dummy like that given you to amuse yourself with! Think of having to play . . . with a model of propriety, a high-minded monstrosity like that![8]

To Martha Chase and her contemporaries, wasp-waisted, white-skinned dolls and fragile bisque ladies elaborately dressed in the latest cosmopolitan European fashions contrasted sharply with the simpler social order of their childhoods. To them and to other Americans in the process of rejecting European decadence, the overdressed French and German bisque dolls represented a culture of luxury, fashion, and other bêtes noires of the bourgeoisie at odds with domestic values. Chase, born in Massachusetts in 1851, was far more likely to have spent her girlhood making the rag dolls promoted in antebellum advice literature. That dolls were to instruct the young in middle-class values and to prepare girls for their future as domestic managers led one mother to declare: "Long live the old fashioned doll and perish the doll of the 'smart set!' "[9]

As an adult, Chase spent her time watching her daughters at play, as did an increasing number of middle-class mothers in late nineteenth-century America. Adult observation of children's play was in the process of becoming widespread among middle-class parents. Charles Darwin contributed to late nineteenth-century "baby biographies" with the record of his infant son's development. More so than fathers, however, it was middle-class mothers who took copious notes documenting their children's development and also organized nationwide child study groups. Many groups found support and advice from G. Stanley Hall, the American child psychologist who had galvanized the child study movement. From data collected by parents, teachers and students, Hall would publish "A Study of Dolls" in 1896, demonstrating the preferences of girls and boys.[10]

Childrearing dominated the lives of the vast majority of middle-class wives and mothers whose lives were shaped by the precepts of domesticity. As the young wife of a doctor, Martha Chase's life had been scripted by larger cultural forces. The development of a market economy and industrialization in the nineteenth century had carved out separate spatial and social spheres for Victorian women and men. Middle-class husbands in general, as businessmen, professionals, and politicians, provided for their home-bound wives and daughters who sought to emulate the ideal of purity, piety, chastity, submission, and domesticity.[11] Before long, women like Chase would extract their own blend of these honored qualities in their own business products.

The average white American middle-class family was in the midst of a demographic transition. In 1800, the birth rate was about seven children per family; by 1900, it was 3.56. Decreased family size led to increased maternal intimacy, observations, and involvement. Mothers had more time to watch their children because they had fewer of them. Martha

Chase's family of seven children was well above the national average in size although Chase's twins died young. Chase raised her two oldest children in Vienna and Berlin between 1876 and 1878 while her husband completed his medical training in European hospitals. Her European residence led her to observe that German dolls were too heavy for small hands. The weight of the hard-headed china and bisque dolls, for example, was compounded by their equally solid sawdust-stuffed bodies. Mothers worried about the dangers of playing with the new dolls; they often cracked, chipped, melted, or broke. To ensure the safety of child and doll, caretakers restricted doll play to certain times and required adult supervision. Nevertheless, replacing broken doll heads was a routine practice among mothers.

Although elaborately dressed dolls could enchant and mechanical dolls could entertain children (albeit briefly), adult dissatisfaction with them was so widespread that popular women's magazines urged mothers to substitute the "perfect mine of treasures in her kitchen and her sewing basket" to make her own dolls just as "Granny" had done. Articles in popular magazines like *Babyhood* urged mothers to use their artistic skills to make simply-constructed cloth dolls devoid of artifice. Magazine contributors disparaged mechanical dolls and praised cloth ones for their homespun virtue. Urban mothers (separated from kin who perhaps had more experience in dollmaking) received advice and instruction from magazine suggestions and patterns. Women traditionally had created dolls out of household scraps for their children and those of their neighbors, friends, and relatives. When Martha Chase was a child, her mother's friend Izannah Walker of Central Falls, Rhode Island, may have given her one of the dolls which she had designed and produced (fig. 22).[12] As an adult, Martha in turn made dolls for neighborhood children and relatives. Thus, the dolls that women created can be understood within the context of the family, where mothers experienced daily and intimate contact with children.

While today we conceive of dollmaking as a craft or sentimental alternative to mass production, the women who would eventually patent their dolls as inventions with the U.S. Patent Office between 1870 and 1909 demonstrated that this protest eventually became less private and

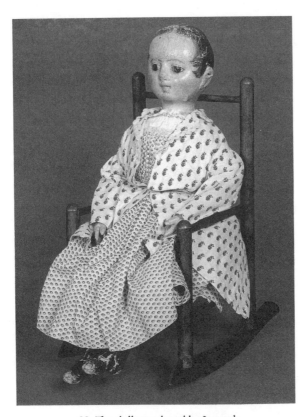

22. The dolls produced by Izannah
Walker were a precursor of those
produced by a generation of women
who also drew upon their familiarity
with textiles to make cloth dolls.
Photo by Mark Sexton, courtesy of
the Wenham Museum, Wenham, Mass.

more public. Although commonly associated with masculine Yankee ingenuity, inventing was also considered an acceptable commercial pursuit
for women; they were even encouraged by womens' guidance books of
the period. Patent lawyers frequently advertised their services in the back
pages of women's fashion magazines like *The Delineator*. Patent records,
however, reveal that the dolls women created provided more than a
"temporary escape into fantasy" as did other aspects of women's fancywork.[13] Drawing upon past skills and present grievances, women, with an
eye toward commercial production, patented dolls embodying a social
agenda with five major areas of concern: softness, portability, durability,
safety, and realism.

With pins and patents, women dollmakers revealed that the first requirement deemed essential for dolls was that they be soft and not brittle
or sharp like those commercially available. Izannah Walker, Martha Chase,
and Ella Smith were typical among dollmakers who were far more likely
to use the textile stockinet because it was lightweight, elastic, washable,
durable, and widely used in everything from therapeutic casts to artists'
mannequins. Julia Beecher (half-sister of Catharine and Harriet), on the
other hand, made her Missionary Ragbabies out of pink or black under-
wear (fig. 23).[14]

As the men used materials well known to them (rawhide, papier-
maché, metal and wood) women used textiles in part because of life-long
domestic familiarity with their properties. Chase spent her days sewing
the children's clothing, sheets, pillow cases, and table linen, as did the
wives of other professionals.[15] Moreover, Chase lived in Pawtucket, Rhode
Island, one of the leading manufacturing centers in the nation in the
nineteenth century. Male inventors, on the other hand, were often disin-
clined to use cloth or rely on sewing skills and often improved upon a
form so as to intentionally obviate the need for sewing.

For middle-class females in Victorian America, however, a background
in the decorative arts was also de rigueur. Art training, considered an
extension of a woman's natural vocation as mother, was a genteel feminine pursuit. Women could also, therefore, draw upon their art training
to design dolls. Ella Smith studied art at La Grange College, and Martha
Chase's daughter Bess Chase (who would become her mother's business

23. Julia Beecher, like her sisters
Catherine and Harriet, was a
reformer who created soft, safe,
durable, lightweight, and childlike
dolls like the one she holds here.
Photo courtesy of Margaret Whitton.

partner) graduated from the Rhode Island School of Design. Ida Gutsell drew from her art education—while still an art student at Syracuse
University she had cast the bust of her mentor George F. Comfort (later
founder of the Metropolitan Museum of Art). Ida A. Squire taught painting and modeling at Norfolk College for Young Ladies in Virginia and
at the New Hampshire Conference Seminary. Doll producer Ella Smith
taught art at Roanoke Normal School in Alabama. In addition to Sunday
school, Martha Chase taught children in the Providence public schools
and in sewing classes at the Church Hill School, and she instructed mill
girls at the Girls' Club of the Lorraine Manufacturing Company.[16]

The second requirement for dolls arising out of women's concerns
was that they be lightweight so that children could handle them more
easily. "A little girl named Pearl," narrated a doll in a contemporary story,
worried that "it might be heavy, and for a moment the recollection of
her little cousin's French doll came across her, for that doll, thought very
slender and genteel, was so heavy that she was moved about on rollers."
Women invented dolls, however, that tended to weigh far less than those
of European origin or those fashioned by American men. Dollmaker
Marietta Adams stated in one of her brochures that each doll weighed
only nine to 24 ounces. Martha Wellington's 24-inch doll weighed two
pounds 14 ounces, as compared to a four-pound bisque-headed, composition German doll of the same size.[17]

The object of her dolls, wrote another dollmaker, was to provide children with "dolls that, first, will be safe and harmless." Thus, cloth dolls
patented and produced by women inventors accommodated the third
concern that naturally arose from observing children's play: safety. Noting
the likelihood of accidents, Izannah Walker claimed that her dolls were
"not apt to injure a young child which may [accidentally] fall upon it."
Cognizant of girls' doll play activities, inventor Olice Agness Flynn constructed a doll capable of enduring rough play. "The fabric casings stuffed
with cotton or other soft yielding material . . . will be flexible and cannot readily be broken by bending or pulling the doll, or by the rough
usage to which such toys are subjected." Because they were safe to play
with, cloth and even soft leather dolls were roundly endorsed by late
nineteenth-century magazines like *The Housewife,* which recommended

the cloth doll because children "can do with it as they like, without fear of injuring the doll or calling down reproof upon themselves." Touching testimonials printed in *Babyhood* magazine included readers' tender anecdotes about infants who played roughly but safely with cloth dolls.[18]

Because cloth dolls had the potential for becoming flimsy, dollmakers strove for durability, the fourth area of concern. In their patents, women inventors touted their inventions for their indestructibility, especially in the hands of a small child. Dollmaker Ella Smith advertised that "we have instances of use [of the Alabama Indestructible Doll] for as long as twenty-two years and thousands of them in constant use five and ten years."[19] After decades of production, other manufacturers' would make the same proud claims.

The stuffing of cloth dolls with soft fibers not only ensured durability but also increased the likelihood that dolls would feel "real," the fifth requirement of doll construction. While female and some male doll inventors aimed for naturalism in dolls, women were more likely to refer in patents to how soft dolls felt to the touch. Displeased with "the rigidity which dolls have now," referring to those stuffed with horse hair and sawdust, inventors used "cotton-batting or other substances which are soft and yielding." Child psychologist G. Stanley Hall reached the same conclusions that children preferred soft dolls.[20]

As alternatives to the European bisque dolls as well as those produced by American businessmen, female dollmakers like Martha Chase created soft and safe dolls that not only felt but also *looked* like children. Often, women used their own children as models, while men—who had a minor role in parenting—did not. Chase used images of real children in order to paint three-dimensional portraits on doll faces with her own recipe of oil paints. The progressive juvenilization in the dolls' appearance already in progress and to which Chase contributed, reversed the appearance of generations of European dolls.[21] In short, dolls started out resembling adult women but, over time, began to look far more like babies.

Because these dollmakers paid close attention to children's proportions, the dolls they created often looked even more lifelike when undressed. To female inventors, the body was something more than just a form on which to hang fashionable clothes. Thus, their naturalism can be distinguished from the functionalism of European and American male inventors. The feet of printed rag dolls pointed in opposite directions until Ida Gutsell created dolls whose feet faced naturally forward.[22] Martha Wellington's dolls had large heads and well-rounded buttocks. Julia Beecher's black and white Missionary Rag Babies had nipples and belly buttons. Martha Chase sculpted her stockinet baby dolls in order to achieve natural-looking cupped hands instead of fingers and wrists in unnaturally genteel poses. Naked toes on broad feet replaced formless stubs and painted stockings with tiny, high-heeled shoes. Even though Chase might have used the bisque doll head of another manufacturer to make at least one of her metal molds, the raised facial features contributed to her dolls' more realistic appearance.

As a result, playing with the dolls women created more closely approximated the sensations and emotions stimulated by handling real babies. "There is a difference," wrote one contemporary observer, "between a real doll baby to be loved and petted [and] an overdressed puppet to be used as an object of vanity." In part, this difference can be explained by the dolls' proportions. According to Konrad Lorenz, both the proportions and the specific features of infants stimulate innate protective, affectionate, and nurturing behavior. More recently, Stephen Jay Gould has argued that, whether a behavior is biologically programmed or learned, "when we see a living creature with babyish features, we feel an automatic surge of disarming tenderness." [23]

Though girls were assumed to constitute the largest consumer market for these dolls, Chase, like other material maternalists, aimed to reform traditional gender roles by producing boy as well as girl dolls. Child psychologist G. Stanley Hall urged that while "the danger . . . of making boy milliners is of course obvious . . . we are convinced that on the whole, more play with girl dolls by boys would tend to make them more sympathetic with girls as children if not more tender with their wives and with women later." [24] Women inventors of designs printed on cloth were even often inclined to design dolls of males rather than of females as did Celia Smith and Ida Gutsell (who had two sons). The Mother's Congress Doll Company produced Baby Stuart, known as the "Children's Favorite," which was a rag doll based on a patent obtained by Madge Lansing

Mead. Ella Smith manufactured boy dolls in addition to girl dolls, and Chase's character dolls of George Washington, Roger Williams, and other male historical figures were intended for her nephews and other boys. Ida Gutsell also patented a doll of "a negro boy" adding to the already large number of black dolls created by middle-class white mothers.[25]

In addition to the impact on girls' socialization, material maternalists aimed to reform those aspects of sex roles that constrained them as middle-class women. Despite the inroads that women had made into the commercially productive and professional sectors of the late nineteenth-century economy, separate spheres persisted. Women's responsibilities were still primarily homemaking, childrearing, and creating a moral and religious homelife. After making dolls for friends and family for nearly five years, Martha Chase received an order from a "quick-witted shop girl" at Boston-based Jordan Marsh, one of the largest urban department stores to emerge in the late nineteenth century.[26] Though evidently delighted with the buyer's persistence, Chase thought that her primary commitment was to her family upon whose consent she felt the venture depended.

Dollmaking businesswomen led conventional lives, and Chase, like the rest, was not likely to disrupt the family—the focus of most nineteenth-century women. Thus, when she converted the small wooden building behind her home into her first workshop, Chase transformed herself from hobbyist to entrepreneur, and from mother to "social housekeeper."[27] Instead of venturing out into the commercial marketplace, Chase, like other women dollmakers, started her business at home, expanding the boundaries of the private sphere women dominated. While dollmakers probably enjoyed sustaining close contact with family, in reality they had no choice but to launch their businesses at home. Women had limited operating capital and little hope of acquiring any from banks.

To Chase and her contemporaries, making dolls for profit probably did not represent the challenge to Victorian gender ideology that female business enterprises actually were. By making dolls for profit in backyard factories, women dollmakers destabilized the boundaries between the private and public spheres. Dollmakers, like other businesswomen, controlled "their places of business, set their own hours and received the net profits."[28] But, for doll entrepreneurs, the home, motherhood, and childcare cloaked their business enterprises. That the artistic skills necessary for doll production were regarded as feminine further served to mitigate apprehensions about business as a masculine endeavor. This mirrored the male dollmakers' protection of their masculine esteem by using "hard" materials and industrial techniques of production. Each wished to stretch, but not break, the separate spheres.

Advice books and other popular literature aimed at an audience of women encouraged them to consider commercializing traditionally feminine household skills like dollmaking. To contemporaries, there was "a certain appropriateness in a woman's entering into the business of doll manufacture." With Martha Chase and others in mind, Laura Starr reported in *The Doll Book* (1908) that "various people in this country have taken the making of rag dolls from the realm of homemade articles into that which might be called home industry."[29] In a letter to *Demorest* magazine, one reader requested:

MADAME DEMOREST: Will you please inform me how I can best employ myself so as to make some money . . . Now, I would like to accomplish something, do something, if it's nothing better nor higher than making rag dolls, for which I hear there is a good market.

ANSWER: But why not start a small manufactory of dolls' . . . clothing where you live, not confining yourself to the common round, but striking out original ideas.[30]

"This shows what enterprising young ladies can do," wrote Mrs. H. R. Bacon about commercial dollmakers Emma and Marietta Adams.[31]

While most did not establish doll "manufactories," of course, women did launch enterprises like food preservation and preparation from the home. In 1890, 16,624 "women proprietors, managers and officials" were counted in the national census, a twofold increase over the 1880 census. In a study of businesswomen in the midwest between 1850 and 1880, one scholar found "an astonishing number of women who ran their own businesses."[32]

Home and family provided women with workers in the form of rela-

tives, in addition to the possibility of using domestic skills for remunerative ends. Many women who produced dolls did so with the assistance of sisters with whom they shared childhood experiences. Three of
Izannah Walker's sisters painted the heads, arms, and legs of the dolls
she invented. In Oswego, New York, Emma Adams and her sister, Marietta, began to make rag dolls for profit in 1891. Emma, who had studied
art and was noted for her crayon portraits, painted the features and hair
on every doll. Marietta kept the ledger and ran the business. "Miss Marietta Adams," reported the *Northern Christian Advocate,* "is as interesting
and refined as she is enterprising and thorough in her business affairs."[33]
Other sisters joined forces in the doll business.

> Elizabeth Chitty made cloth dolls and soon taught her methods to
> her friends Maggie and Bessie Pfohl, who added their own touches.
> Maggie began the dolls in the 1890s, starting with an old German pat-
> tern of her mother's. She painted the heads with house paint, sanded
> them, then applied the features and hair with oil paints and varnished
> them. The dolls had molded features, and carefully stitched fingers
> and toes "and a backbone," she recalled. "You have to have a back-
> bone. If you don't they nod." The sisters made dolls for 40 years, sell-
> ing them and giving some away.[34]

Margaret Ball made the dolls and her sister dressed them between
1885 and 1891 in Brooklyn, New York. Margaret's sister sewed the lace-
trimmed dresses until her hands became so crippled from rheumatism
that Margaret made them instead. "The Hastings sisters of Central New
York made very fine dolls; they are well shaped and proportioned, and
bear little resemblance in this respect to the rag dolls of home manufacture which are usually seen."[35] Although her sisters did not join in her
enterprise, two of Martha Chase's daughters did (fig. 24). After graduation
from the Rhode Island School of Design, Elizabeth (or Bess) painted the
faces on the Chase dolls in the workshop behind the home she shared
with her parents. Her sister, Anna, who married the boy next door, was
separated from the Dolls' House only by the driveway. It was she who
helped manage the business.

Sisters were not the only female kin who designed, invented, and pro-

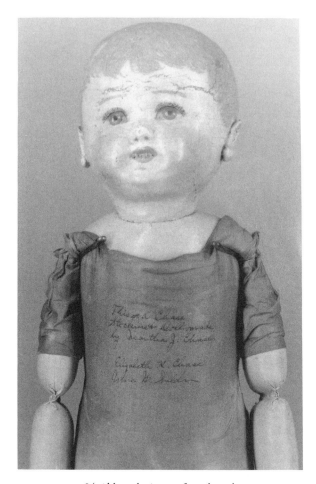

24. Although sisters often shared
dollmaking business partnerships,
Chase produced natural looking girl
and boy dolls with the assistance of
her daughters, whose signatures
appear on the torso of this stockinet
doll. Photo courtesy of the Strong
Museum, Rochester, N.Y. ©1993.

duced dolls together. Roxanna Elizabeth McGee Cole made dolls with her daughter-in-law, Molly Hunt Cole. The handsewn dolls were made of fine muslin, delicately sculpted to shape the chin and dimples of the painted baby faces. Beginning in 1899, Celia Smith made dolls for profit with her sister-in-law, Charity Smith, who also lived in Ithaca, New York. Their partnership combined their best qualities and together they designed, among others, a two-piece calico doll.[36]

In the absence of sisters or female kin, husbands provided their dollmaking wives with financial and emotional support, building factories and confidence. In 1899, doll entrepreneur Ella Smith (no relation to the Ithaca family) took up the needle and the ledger in "a rough, unceilinged, two-storied, building" built by her husband (a local contractor and carpenter) and operated by a dozen women. At the crescent-shaped work bench "Bud" Smith had built to accommodate his wife's rotund form, she designed dolls stamped "Mrs. S. S. Smith," while a parrot perched on her shoulder recited psalms and sang hymns.[37]

Next to the Chase family home was Martha's first workshop, a small cottage that Dr. Julian Chase had had constructed for his wife's fledgling business. In general, backyard cottages were crude and decidedly unmodern. During the winter, only two small coal stoves and occasional sunlight warmed the single-story building. The uninsulated building had no cellar, and the walls were thin and unfinished. To this structure was added another which provided for more space but probably offered even less protection against the cold.[38]

For material maternalists, the middle-class household with a commanding domestic manager became a useful model for doll production. While design, production, and management were separated elsewhere in the business world, in the Dolls' House, Chase supervised the making of the dolls she designed in addition to sewing. Chase spent most of her time stitching up doll parts, putting them together and painting faces, as did her employees (fig. 25). The interdependence between work and family was also exemplified by Mabel (Molly) Jenkinson, who worked for fifty years making dolls. "Molly took care of my father," commented Robert Chase (Martha's grandson) in an interview. She also took care of "all the young girls in the family, then became head gal in the doll factory.

25. Dollmaker Martha Chase, seen
here probably sizing stockinet faces,
recreated the female-centered
nature of the middle-class family in
her backyard workshop. Photo
courtesy of the Chase family.

She was a fixture—practically a member of the family." The rapport between Martha Chase and the women she employed appears to have been familial. "Mrs. Chase was wonderful to us all and most sympathetic," recalled one doll face painter.[39]

For production, design, and business acumen, doll producers relied on a bevy of women. "From a small beginning the [Adams's] business has grown until many women are employed and they cannot keep up with the orders received." In the factory behind her house, 8 to 12 women related by a network of kin assisted Ella Smith (fig. 26). Maybelle and Lorrie Arnett, for example, made dolls in her backyard factory. Production records about the 8,000 Alabama Indestructible Dolls made each year were handwritten in a ledger by Katie Mitchum and Barma Mitchum McCarter, likely relatives of Connie Bonner McCarter and Mrs. E. L.

26. Doll entrepreneur Ella Smith (*top row, third from left*), doll workers, and her daughter Macy (holding the "Alabama Indestructible Doll") in front of the doll factory built by Smith's husband in Roanoke, Ala., c. 1909. Photo courtesy of Gwen Stevenson.

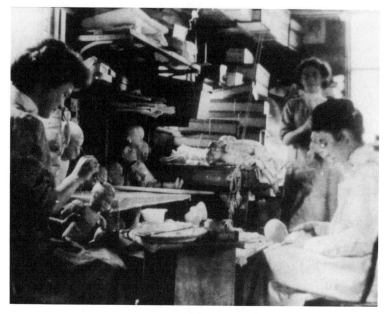

27. Chase doll workers packaged waterproof and cotton-stuffed
dolls around 1915 in the Pawtucket, R.I., "Dolls' House"
workplace, where the ambiance was often more like a parlor than
a factory. Photo courtesy of Marjorie A. Bradshaw.

McCarter. Ella Smith was also known to employ widows and orphans to
make her dolls.

For five dollars a week, a high-school girl worked weekday afternoons
and Saturday mornings, stoking the stove with coal and stuffing envel-
opes with Chase advertisements. She also ran errands such as carrying
Chase mailings to the local post office.[40] Molly Jenkinson sold seconds and
handled repairs; several women painted faces at sunlit elevated tables.
The workroom was also equipped with several sewing machines operated by specially trained workers. In the workshop, dolls were also assembled, painted, boxed, and shipped (fig. 27).

In these backyard cottages, women integrated aspects of feminine,
middle-class gentility with a premodern workers' culture. Doll producers

were concerned with not only the safety of their work force but the congeniality in the workplace as well. At the M. J. Chase Company, employees told stories while they worked and had "the best 'giggle' about things which happened." Martha Chase "had a great sense of humor." The Rhode Island workshop, where birthdays and holidays were celebrated, resembled the family parlor far more than it did the workplace. According to one worker, "when the 13th of the month came on a Friday, it was, in [Martha Chase's] mind, a 'red-letter day' and she gave us a party saying it was our lucky day! At Christmas and at Easter time, and especially on our birthdays, she never forgot us, and all of her helpers had the month of August off." Chase's employees did not relate to their place of employment as most workers might. By coming "to work in what always was called the 'Dolls' House,' never the 'Shop,'" as one worker explained, a sense of factory drudgery was replaced by genteel maternalism. At the Dolls' House, women workers felt close to the dolls they produced. As if taking snapshots for the family album, "when a new member of the doll family appeared, each of us took the one we liked best and had our pictures taken in the yard" (fig. 28).[41]

Like Chase's Rhode Island firm, others also employed women "almost exclusively in the various processes of manufacture." Whether in Brookline, Massachusetts, or Brooklyn, New York, "a large number of girls and women have been enabled to find employment." "Several establishments for the manufacture of these dolls are now being managed by women in different parts of the country," noted the toy industry's trade magazine in 1903. In Brooklyn, two young women opened a dollmaking establishment after the successful reception of their muslin dolls at church affairs. "From so small a beginning, the originators of this rag doll have seen the business grow until the dolls are now found in all parts of the country. Larger orders are received from the West and South, and competing firms have sprung up, which turn out dolls."[42]

By the beginning of the twentieth century, the privatized maternalism practiced in late-nineteenth-century backyard workshops found institutional support from national women's organizations. Mary C. W. Foote had the health of women workers and child consumers in mind when

28. Chase doll workers who did not relate to their place of
employment the same way workers did elsewhere, occasionally
posed for photographs with the dolls they liked best in front of
the Pawtucket backyard workshop. Photo courtesy of
Marjorie A. Bradshaw.

she launched the Fairyland Doll Company in Plainfield, New Jersey. In addition to protecting women workers, Foote shared the goals of other women reformers during the Progressive Era. The bow-shaped labels attached to Fairyland Rag Dolls asserted that "cleanliness [was] guaranteed by the National Consumers' League," an organization formed in 1891 to improve the working conditions of women, to provide protection of child laborers, to eliminate health hazards, and to benefit middle-class consumers.

> Goods bearing this label are made in factories in which: 1. The State Factory Law is obeyed. 2. ALL the goods are made on premises approved by the League. 3. Overtime is not worked. 4. Children under sixteen years of age are not employed. The factory is then occasionally visited by the League agent and the local committee of the League reports to the National Secretary.[43]

Appealing to the concerns of mothers they understood, advertisements in *Ladies' Home Journal* assured consumers that "Fairyland Rag Dolls" were "made in clean, sunny factories" (fig. 29).[44]

Mothers who had been concerned with the cleanliness of dolls welcomed Izannah Walker's claim that her doll was "easily kept clean." Women and other readers of popular magazines had been aware of the danger of microbes years before 1890, when most doctors finally accepted the germ theory of disease. Writers of late nineteenth-century women's magazines frequently warned middle-class readers that dolls made or used by the working class were a possible source of dangerous contagion.[45]

It was not until shortly after the turn of the century, however, that the cleanliness of dolls moved into the forefront of concerns, at the urging of Chase and others. Domestic science and public health advocates, along with other progressives, had concluded that environment rather than personal defects caused poverty and disease. Many of the ills of industrialization, they believed, could be cured by improved sanitation. To this end, women doll manufacturers coated their stockinet dolls with insoluble paint as most cloth-bodied dolls, like the sateen-bodied dolls Chase made early in her career, stood little chance of surviving getting

29. Mrs. Mary C. W. Foote's "Fairyland Rag Dolls," endorsed by the Progressive Era National Consumer's League, appealed to turn-of-the-century mothers alarmed by industrial production, child labor, and the spread of germs. Reproduced from *Playthings,* by permission.

a little wet, much less being washed. Waterproof dolls were not only washable but also more impervious to dirt. In business circulars Chase assured her customers:

> The stuffing of the doll is cotton batting. Neither sawdust, ground cork, nor any of the other common fillers is used. The batting is a good quality, fine textured, white and clean. Since compressed cotton is practically impervious to bacteria and other disease germs, its use renders the Chase dolls to that degree so much the more sanitary . . . The paint used to cover the doll from head to feet has a zinc basis and is the very best grade that can be bought in the open market. Special care has been taken to select a paint that is non-poisonous, and easily cleaned, a paint that is tough, flexible and extremely durable.[46]

Chase also promoted her undressed and dressed 12- to 30-inch dolls among a middle-class clientele of mothers and readers of popular women's magazines like *Mother's Magazine* and *Ladies' Home Journal* in which she advertised. One advertisement explained that Chase dolls "can be washed with warm water, keeping infecting germs from our babies."[47] Chase doll advertisements addressed contemporary maternal concerns with regard to the importance of play and health. Mothers were urged to shop at toy stores such as F. A. O. Schwarz, gift shops, and department stores such as Macy's, Gimbel's, and Wanamaker's—all of which carried the Chase Stockinet dolls. *Children's Magazine* advertised that Chase dolls, "easily washed in lukewarm water, were available at Best & Co. for between $3 and $8.50."[48] By the 1920s, over 100,000 Chase dolls had been sold worldwide despite their high price.

In addition to middle-class mothers, Chase attracted the attention of professional women whose concerns her dolls could also address. Chase developed a 5′4″ prototype of a female figure based on her own height and proportions, clothed her in a dress and hat, then invited friends to tea to meet "Miss Demon Strator." Martha Chase's adult-sized doll was really intended to train nursing students in the proper procedures for handling patients. First tested at Pawtucket's Memorial Hospital, Chase's hospital mannequins were then produced for Hartford Hospital in 1911. In part, Chase had been influenced by a nursing instructor at Hartford

Hospital Training School who had been dissatisfied with the straw-filled dummies available to nursing students at the time. A demonstration of the Chase mannequin at an annual nurses' convention in St. Louis in 1914 would contribute much to its widespread use. As a result, the ubiquitous teaching mannequin became known to nurses and other health professionals in the twentieth century as "Mrs. Chase." [49]

Chase also tapped the needs of other health professionals. She introduced a line of dolls in five sizes, from newborn to four-year-old, according to standard measurements set by the American Medical Association. [50] Dolls, some of which included nasal and otic passages to help demonstrate proper hygiene techniques, were advertised in journals like *The Public Health Nurse* and *American Journal of Nursing*. These dolls were intended to teach working-class mothers how to ensure the normal and healthy development of their children (fig. 30). Chase, affected by changing middle-class ideas about children, family, and "scientific motherhood" and a growing awareness of urban conditions, promoted these washable "sanitary dolls" for use in public demonstrations or proper maternal behavior.

Throughout the nation and abroad, school boards, colleges, mothers' clubs, baby clinics, and welfare workers' schools used Chase "sanitary dolls" to teach and demonstrate the essentials of child care. [51] For material maternalists like Chase, dolls became a vehicle for teaching middle-class values to the poor who lived in communities without sewers, garbage removal, or running water. Chase, like others during the Progressive era, was in the process of elevating motherhood to a profession requiring education as well as practical training. "Teach the facts to the mothers of today and of tomorrow," proclaimed Chase advertisements. Motherhood now required the development of expertise and techniques, not the blossoming of instinct. Scientific mothers aimed to uplift all others. "Not only do healthy babies make strong men and women, but the health and happiness of the household, of the community, and the whole nation is improved by everything done to protect the children." [52]

Chase was committed to purifying, uplifting, and reforming life outside of the middle-class home. Progressive reformers—a loose coalition of middle-class professionals, businessmen, politicians and "maternal-

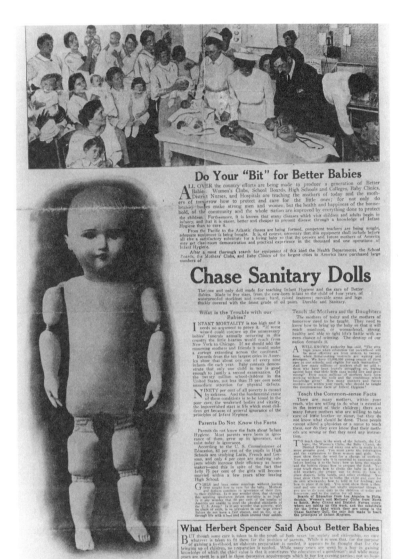

30. Chase's "Hospital Baby" was used widely by reformers in
baby clinics, mother's clubs, in schools and at settlement houses
in order to teach infant hygiene to working-class mothers and
their children. Chase circular, c. 1918. Photo courtesy of
the Chase family.

ists"—found a wide variety of organizations to help families adapt to conditions in modern urban America.[53] Educators and settlement house and social workers sought to educate working-class mothers, and especially immigrants, in the latest principles of "scientific mothering." Teaching foreigners the middle-class values of the home—a feature of progressive social reform—was doomed to fail when newcomers' living conditions made it impossible to meet the new standards of cleanliness.

Most doll collectors have assumed that Martha Chase's husband, Julian, inspired and assisted in the development of the hospital dolls. Martha probably had been influenced by her family—her father, brother, and husband were all doctors. According to contemporary reports, her husband had been one of the first physicians in Rhode Island to use anesthetics, often treating injured textile workers.[54] Her father, James L. Wheaton, had been known for his unconventional homeopathic medicine and political convictions.

Although many have credited the origins of the hospital dolls to the men in Martha Chase's life, however, her mother's influence was especially significant. Anna Maria Jenks Wheaton was eulogized "for the success of various enterprises and organizations [which] gave her a prominence that is allotted to but few women, and endeared her to various persons who were directly concerned in measures tending to improve the public."[55] Martha Chase, like other daughters of the middle-class, was influenced by her mother's charitable activities as well as by the expanded role that other bourgeois matrons carved out for their sex. For twenty years, Anna Wheaton had been engaged in hospital work and had been one of the founders of the Homeopathic Hospital in Providence.

Yet by the turn of the century, the "angels of mercy" of Chase's mother's generation had been replaced by a new generation of "social housekeepers" like Chase who hit their stride during the Progressive Era. During the first decade of the twentieth century, women and children had moved to center stage in a variety of disciplines.[56] John Dewey, G. Stanley Hall, Sigmund Freud, Emmett Holt, and Jane Addams, among others, contributed to a new childhood ideal. These educators, psychologists, philosophers, artists, reformers, radicals, and parents wrote about, photographed, and debated the nature of childhood and the welfare of children. Jacob Riis and Lewis Hine brought into sharp photographic focus the social conditions of children. Maternalist Jane Addams and other middle-class women established settlement houses where they lived for the purpose of educating the poor. Margaret Sanger's birth control clinics aimed to limit the number of unwanted children and thereby raise the standard of living for the urban poor. Charlotte Perkins Gilman argued that professionalized childrearing would benefit children, mothers, and society. And dollmakers like Chase used their talents to teach the urban poor, especially mothers and daughters, practical techniques to care for themselves and their dependents.

Martha Chase and other female dollmakers presented the public with dolls that had been conceived in a separate sphere than the European dolls and American mechanical toys disparaged in the popular press. The women's dolls were safer, more durable, easier to carry, and better suited to the needs of children than dolls invented by men. That Chase dolls were intended to teach personal hygiene, however, could limit girls' doll play to the chores of maternity. Yet maternalistic dollmakers designed dolls not only to foster new attitudes toward children's play but also to alleviate the pressing social problems of turn-of-the-century working-class mothers and children. Unfortunately, the prohibitive cost of Chase dolls insured that they would remain in the hands of middle-class girls.

In their workshops, however, dollmakers provided their female employees with meaningful, safe, and unalienating employment where women workers were not relegated to the least skilled aspects of doll production as was the case in the factories operated by businessmen. The craft nature of women's doll firms unfortunately kept production low and costs high. Still, by stretching the boundaries of the home, doll producers embraced new roles for women. They also contributed to the ultimate breakdown of a culture based on separate spheres that sustained gender stereotypes. Ironically, Chase and others like her provided new possibilities for the next generation of young women to create dolls not in a separate sphere but side-by-side with men. This new collaboration, however, held great promise: to overcome the limitations of both male and female dollmaking cultures.

CHAPTER FOUR

Marketing a
Campbell Kids Culture:
Engendering
New Kid Dolls,
1902–1914

Shortly after the turn of the century, two stocky, well-fed children sporting androgynous haircuts and donning modern, ready-made clothing—the Campbell Kids—strutted across the pages of *Ladies' Home Journal*. The Campbell Kids were part of an extensive advertising campaign designed to promote the new easy-to-prepare and "nutritious" soup by equating its consumption with health and middle-class well-being. The wide-eyed, round-faced, and chubby-cheeked New Kid was another symbol of childhood only recently "discovered" by Progressive Era reformers, philosophers, educators, psychologists—and doll manufacturers as well. The dawning of the new century, Progressive Era optimism, and the influence of middle-class women in the public arena con-

verged in the marketplace. Yet it was not Martha Chase but E. I. Horsman, the late nineteenth-century producer of home amusements, whose
Campbell Kid "character dolls" exuded confidence, demonstrated initiative, and revealed personality, intellect, and wit.[1] The popularity of these
"New Kids" dolls and the culture they spawned led to the construction of
a new commercial childhood ideal.

After years of concentrating on making the bodies, heads, and mechanisms of adult-looking female dolls, American male manufacturers now
produced boy dolls. And the girl dolls they produced were endowed
with attributes more typically identified with masculinity. Although collectors have long credited German doll designers for the influence of
Puppen reform (a doll reform movement initiated by the Germans), the
"character dolls" made by America's first commercially successful doll
manufacturers were, in fact, the result of the industrial experience and
gender ideology of American businessmen at the turn of the century.

In the years before nearly every doll manufacturer promoted their
own "kid," American businessmen produced the stuffed bears made
famous by Theodore Roosevelt. Drawing upon their experience as producers of Teddy Bears, manufacturers endowed the dolls that followed
with a masculine personality and animal features—indeed, these doll
producers were unable to conceive of animals in other than masculine
terms. Billiken—the primogenitor boy doll which launched the modern
American doll industry—had a bearskin body and a Teddy Bear's overall proportions. It took several "generations" for his paws to evolve into
hands and to shed his animal fur. The masculinized Campbell Kid dolls
that resulted would represent an unprecedented moment in the representation of gender.

Although doll collectors trace the origins of the American doll industry to World War I, American producers seem to have been in the process
of carving out their niche in the American market in the prewar years.
In the first crucial decade of the twentieth century, the fledgling domestic doll industry was in the process of defining its identity as America's
first modern doll industry. By drawing upon manufacturing precedents,
a turn-of-the-century businessmen's ethos, the work of the New Women
doll designers, and changes in socialization, producers competed to

create American dolls free of the imported European bourgeois tastes, values, and fashions that had dominated the domestic toy market. Their success can be measured by the fact that in 1910 the industry manufactured and sold more American-made toys than in any previous year. By 1913 *McClure's* magazine would report, "Germany finds itself wholly unable to compete in this branch of the trade."[2]

Despite success, however, the complex evolution of dolls from their origins as masculine stuffed animals into more familiar feminine representations was not accomplished with ease, speed, or foresight. Between 1902 and 1914, American doll producers continued to bumble through production successes and failures as they had during the previous decades. During this period, however, they now sought to define whether dolls should: look like animal or human babies, be masculine or feminine representations, be the lucky charms of adults or the playthings of children. The New Kid dolls that would result fused aspects of late nineteenth-century male and female producers. New Kid dolls were soft, clean, safe, and without springs and pulleys. But, unlike the rag doll, they had ready-made, male personalities.

The ultimate financial success of these producers over their German competition can be attributed to a triumph of marketing of "kid" dolls among women consumers whose concerns they commercialized. After years of advertising their dolls as one would advertise machine parts, turn-of-the-century doll producers marketed newly modern American values along with the dolls. Whether dressed in the latest children's fashions, in Dutch costumes, or as recognizable characters from soup and soap advertisements, New Kid dolls conveyed a sense of health that appealed to progressive-minded middle-class mothers. As consumers in the modern age, New Kids wore jumpers and rompers and thrived in the fresh air. Whether dressed like other middle-class children who donned "rational" clothing or in stars and stripes, they shared a class and national identity forged by American businessmen.

Despite the apparent representation of democratic values, gender and race stereotypes filtered in the doll designs. And at the same time that New Kid dolls were portrayed as representatives of a seemingly universal middle-class, exploited child laborers in urban tenements sewed and stuffed Campbell Kid dolls that their families could not afford to buy. Nevertheless, for the American doll industry, it was the beginning of a marketing strategy that seriously challenged the European doll monopoly.

The origins of the New Kid doll can be traced back to 1902, when Clifford Berryman's cartoon of Theodore Roosevelt sparing a trapped bear cub first appeared in the Washington *Star*. The adorable creature captured the public's sympathy and imagination at a time when "attitudes toward the animal world were being charged with new cultural values and emotional content." Shortly thereafter, toy banks, puzzles, tea sets and paper dolls of Teddy Bears appeared everywhere on sales counters (fig. 31). Even clowns and chorus girls dressed up as bears to entertain audiences of children and adults at circuses and at vaudeville shows. In Brooklyn, Rose Michtom, the wife of a Russian immigrant, sewed her own stuffed bear and placed it, along with the President's endorsement, in the window of the candy store she ran with her husband. Soon dealers including Baker & Bigler, A. S. Ferguson, and E. I. Horsman issued their own version of the Teddy Bear. Dressed as Rough Riders or baseball players, Teddy Bears were widely available at toy stores as well as through mail-order companies like Sears & Roebuck.[3]

Several years later, the E. I. Horsman Company, which had enjoyed success with its Babyland Rag Dolls, searched for a new toy to build on the Teddy Bear's momentum. Horsman, and others, were also eager to capitalize on the changing social, economic, political, and cultural forces that affected children in modernizing America. Unlike Morris Michtom, the co-founder of the Ideal Toy Company who had benefited financially from his wife's creativity, Edward Imeson Horsman was neither an artist nor married to one. Using his financial resources, however, he purchased the rights to the designs of artist Florence Pretz, in whom he found what he had been looking for. While a student at the Craftsman's Guild in Chicago, she had created a figure with a child's body, big ears, a wide grin, and curled-up toes (fig. 32). Hoping to double his company's profits by combining rag dolls and stuffed bears, Horsman modified Pretz's design

31. The Teddy Bear, believed to
have been inspired by a hunting
accident involving President
Theodore Roosevelt, influenced the
production of modern American
New Kid dolls. Photo by Laurie
Minor, courtesy of the National
Museum of American History, Smithsonian Institution, Washington, D.C.

DESIGN.

F. PRETZ.
IMAGE.
APPLICATION FILED JUNE 9, 1908.

39,603.   Patented Oct. 6, 1908.

32. When art student Florence Pretz patented her "Billiken"
design in 1908, she appeared to have been inspired by children,
although her creation's antimodernist philosophy spoke more to
the concerns of anxious adult men. U.S. Patent Office.

and produced Billiken, "the first American-made doll to be really successful."[4]

When Virginia Woolf wrote that human character changed somewhere
around 1909, she was probably unaware that her observation also per-
tained to transformations in human representations as well. When E. I.
Horsman produced Billiken later that year, the figure's childlike body
had been modified to that of a stuffed animal. Moreover, the Billiken doll
now shared far more features with his forebears than with any previous

generation of dolls (fig. 33). To be sure, Billiken shared the same over-all body proportions and shoulder and hip joints with its phylogenetic cousin. It was evident to contemporaries that Billiken enjoyed great popu-larity on Teddy Bear's account, but Billiken was, in fact, a stage between furry stuffed animal and human baby doll. In its own lifetime, Billiken's paws evolved into hands and feet—albeit rather stubby ones—and he

33. E. I. Horsman, Inc., recast
Florence Pretz's design of a Billiken
"child" in the image of a Teddy
Bear, a novelty which by 1909 was
less commercially popular.
Advertisement, *Playthings,* 1909,
reproduced by permission.

shed his rough fur coat for silky-smooth pink skin. Horsman ultimately marketed the doll wearing pajamas.[5]

"The unbreakable doll to-day might be traced directly back to the day when the American Teddy Bear became so popular, an item which was manufactured in large numbers in this factory," reported a spokesman for the Amberg firm years later. It required "many years of experience in making teddy-bears and then animals and doll bodies of all descriptions." An intermediary step in the evolution of dolls from stuffed animals into more familiar representations of children had been dolls of adult men dressed in beastlike garb, like fur-clad Eskimo dolls and mustachioed Arctic explorers. "From the Teddy Bear [also] grew the Teddy Doll, a wonderfully popular novelty which was a distinct outgrowth of the bear, being a Teddy Bear with an imported bisque or celluloid face" (fig. 34). Despite these "mutations," however, preexisting forms, materials, and the skills used to make new toys determined that the pace of change would remain slow. Like Amberg, other American manufacturers who wanted to change toy lines also wrestled with an established continuity. Making dolls look more like human beings and less like beasts, explained Playthings, "requires change after change."[6]

For example, Amberg's New Born Babe doll still had ears reminiscent of his ancestor even though the doll appeared five years after Billiken.[7] Likewise, it would take the entire course of Baby Bump's lifetime to winnow out vestigial features. In 1914 composition hands with articulated fingers replaced paws, yet it would still take several years more for Baby Bumps to learn how to smile and to speak. Although it was Billiken's "fossilized" successor, Baby Bumps, who completed the evolutionary process from furry animal to baby doll at the Horsman firm, the same process occurred at the Amberg factory beginning with the Sunny Jim doll. Advertised as a real, lifelike infant doll, Sunny Jim had a velvet "bearskin" body (one step away from fur), body shape, paw-like hands, and rivet construction that revealed Teddy Bear's enduring influence.

Although Baby Bumps finally shed many of his more obvious animal characteristics, he nevertheless retained the gender identity acquired from male prototypes: Theodore Roosevelt was not only the president but also one of the most important symbols of turn-of-the-century mas-

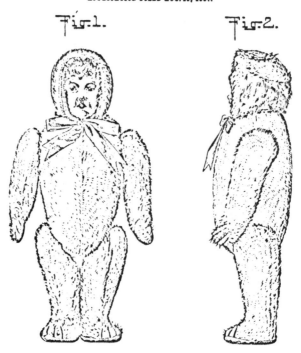

34. Teddy Doll, which combined a doll's face with
a bear's body, represented one stage in the "evolution" from
animal to child, due, in part, to the changing cultural and
industrial production priorities of American businessmen. Photo
courtesy of the Strong Museum, Rochester, N.Y. ©1993.

culinity. At an extreme, Teddy Bear was often portrayed in the new format of the postcard as a hairy athletic man. Like bear dolls, Billikens were also considered male although identified as a "doll" by their label. Although Billiken sometimes sported a pink ribbon (color coding of gender was still in a period of transition), his sex was never in doubt especially after the marketing success of his sibling, Sister Billiken.

Like Teddy Bear, Billiken had originated in the world of men, but Billiken soothed grown men, not children. As "a sure cure" for those suffering from the decline of Protestantism and the effects of overcivilization, Billiken would heal: "The Blues/The Hoodoo Germ/That Solemn Feeling/The Grouch/Hard Luck Melancholia/The Down-and-Out Bacillus." Billiken (like his contemporary, Kill-i-Blues) specialized in helping overburdened men to subdue "the depressing spirit of the blues, which seemed to be pervading . . . the business channels of a great part of the metropolis of the Middle West."[8] A cross between a patent medicine and a primitive talisman, a "dose" of Billken provided men with insurmountable confidence. Billiken was advertised as

a maker of happiness, a chaser of frowns. You must smile back at him. When you smile you are bound to feel in a good humor. When you are in a good humor everything seems brighter; you work with a better vim; you see the hopeful sides of things instead of the worst. He throws a spell over you that has the same effect as mental healing. You feel that you can do anything—and back of all achievement lies confidence.[9]

One of Billiken's competitors, Kill-i-Blues, promised similar results to other adults beleaguered by the modern age.

> Here's some News
> I'm Kill-i-Blues
> That Color Flees
> If at your knees
> I linger still
> So take me in
> Amidst the din
> Of hurried life

I'll show you—Glee!
On land and sea
My all is yours—Depend on me.[10]

It was, in fact, grown men—and not children—whose "worship" of Billiken was, in the words of one contemporary, "spreading all over America." "Billiken, the jolly little god of luck, is being accepted by actors, authors and professors and businessmen in every part of the country as a charm against the grouch, the 'blue devils' and all other human ailments which afflict poor mortals." Retailers reported that men "not only bought the little [Billiken] bruins for their tots, but they bought them for themselves, for decorating their autos" and as protection against "smash ups." A Billiken even perched on the grand piano of L. Frank Baum, author of *The Wizard of Oz* (1900) and a devoted follower of turn-of-the-century "mind cures." [11]

If among men Billiken was little more than an adorable charlatan, among dolls he was a born leader. Billiken led others of his sex—such as Teddy Jr., Little Boy Blue, the Gold Medal Baby, the Uneeda Kid (based on the boy in the advertisements for the cracker company)—from the toy store into the American home. That boy dolls like the Parsons-Jackson Company's "Little Fellows" (fig. 35) were produced at all was a radical departure from the previous century when boy dolls were rarely manufactured by mainstream producers (see chapter 2). In fact, decades before these boys made their appearance, boy dolls represented only about ten percent of all commercially-produced dolls, and the majority were intended for dollhouse play.[12]

Many boy dolls produced between 1909 and 1915 were frequently paired with girl dolls: the Campbell Kids, School Boy and School Girl, and Farmer Boy and Farmer Girl.[13] While the financial benefits are obvious, this duplication had enormous social, cultural, and political consequences for dolls and children who played with them. Instead of boy dolls losing their gender identity as they became less like beasts, it was girl dolls who acquired more masculine characteristics as they became more realistically human. In their new forays into advertising, toy manufacturers now stressed that boy and girl dolls possessed "character."

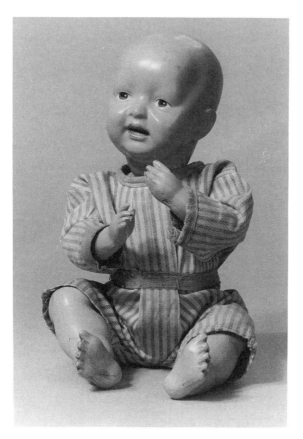

35. In a radical departure from previous generations of female dolls, rock-hard boy dolls like this "Little Fellow" were typical of the New Kid character dolls, manufactured by American businessmen and marketed as having a masculine personality. Photo courtesy of the Wenham Museum, Wenham, Mass.

Among the many manly features that New Kid dolls claimed over generations of vapid-looking female dolls was the possession of intellect. Like proud fathers, manufacturers claimed through their advertisements that their "kid" was smarter than all the rest. While E. I. Horsman bragged that the Campbell Kids were "clever," Louis Amberg asserted that his Bobby Blake and Dolly Drake were *the* "Cleverest Kids in Babyland!"[14] However one measured it, New Kid dolls were smart because of their quick-witted ancestors. Theodore Roosevelt was a Harvard graduate, and Billiken's philosophical speculations into the human condition revealed his intelligence to be well above average. One of Billiken's peers was a doll named "Brighto."

From their male ancestors who had been deep thinkers, New Kids also inherited their "irresistably comical" and "delightfully humorous" temperament. Those like Jolly Joker or a 1915 Charlie Chaplin doll probably learned how to amuse from vaudeville (whose shows were often reviewed in the doll industry's trade journal for businessmen whose work brought them to the nation's doll capital). The wide smiles on the generations of dolls thereafter similarly conveyed happy feelings in stark contrast to past generations of female French fashion dolls whose expressions had revealed neither thought nor emotion. Whereas white dolls were marketed as having a sense of humor, black ones like "little darky doll" or Amberg's 1910 line of "Baby Beautiful" black dolls were made to seem happy-go-lucky. In an advertisement for "a jolly life-like picaninny" which drew upon dominant racist stereotypes, Rastus in Rompers was portrayed as a giddy simpleton. One laughed *at* Cotton Joe (advertised as "one of the most humorous on the market"), whose overalls made him look hickish and old-fashioned.[15]

The representation of happiness was, in many ways, distinctly American. In 1909 Strobel & Wilken Company had advertised an imported all-bisque baby doll whose face revealed a brooding internal state. Perhaps affected by new ideals that afforded children unprecedented opportunities to express their feelings, this baby doll's frown revealed deep pain and suffering. Its raised eyebrows made it look worried and there was no hint of a smile—enigmatic, vapid, or otherwise. This doll import had emerged out of the German *Puppen Reform* (a movement among doll designers) which rejected unrealistic-looking "angel-faced" dolls in favor of dolls that expressed human emotions, especially, it would seem, painful ones. (Depression and unease were two aspects of the European penchant for realism.) The doll looked "lifelike in every detail from the unformed head of the tiny baby boy to the faintly formed double chin, the dimple, the strongly lined bones in the forehead and the round, red, chubby face of the older youngsters."[16]

American producers quickly abandoned the more anxious looking and poorly selling boy dolls for ones with eyes which "are round and full of childlike humor."[17] The large round eyes on these New Kid dolls made them appear far more spunky than sad and more saucey than sweet. New Kids inherited their temperament from their male ancestors (Billiken, Lucky Bill, Sunny Jim, and Jolly Little Joker Doll, among others) who had been "irresistibly comical" and "delightfully humorous" in addition to being thoughtful. Like the Campbell Kids, who were advertised as the "jolliest dolls of all," Bobby Blake and Dolly Drake were considered amusing and lighthearted. Billiken's wit had helped him maintain his even temperament in the face of fin de siècle doom and gloom. With his "lucky grin gloom run out and joy run in." Similarly, dolls like Billiken and Sunny Jim were likely to amuse others because they too resembled vaudeville actors.[18]

Playful teasing turned into suggestive flirting, however, in some girl dolls of the period. Thus "Goo-Goo" eyed-dolls (as they were known in the trade) were intended to arouse more than good feelings.[19] By 1911, Miss Mischief's sideways glancing eyes conveyed an allure of "naughty mischief" that had become an American doll trend. By 1912, many manufacturers had their own appropriately named version of coquette dolls. The New Toy Company produced the Coquette, and Fleischaker & Baum marketed Miss Coquette (previously Naughty Marietta; her name was changed because the Ideal Toy and Novelty Company already had a Naughty Marietta doll). These dolls may have reflected changing sexual mores, although their coy expressions were more likely to have expressed male fantasies rather than female desires. A comparison of images of children with dolls suggests that the large-eyed characters created by women illustrators conveyed innocence, while the dolls produced by businessmen expressed a male sexuality.

While many New Kid girl dolls strutted with confidence and "coquette" dolls exuded provocativeness, others at the time exhibited a bashful innocence. Unlike such dolls as Naughty Marietta, Fairy doll looked innocent and angelic by comparison—a prewar harbinger of the dolls of the twenties. Her eyes were almond shaped, not round and "flirting." "The contour of her face is that of a pensive little fairy of the most lovable sort." Fairy was far more demure than other members of the Campbell Kid family. If the flirting eye dolls seemed lusty, Horsman's Fairy was their antithesis—both ethereal and sublime. Dressed in white and lavender she was also more feminine. "Her underthings are lacey lingerie of the most modern sort." Other manufacturers at the time had competed with their own "fairy" versions. With prewar dolls like these, traditional sex-role stereotypes were in the process of filtering into the material culture of dolls as manufacturers imbued dolls with feminine attributes. These early returns to cliched femininity revealed that, while promoting masculinized New Kid dolls on the one hand, male manufacturers were also in the process of constructing a more feminine girlhood for American girls on the other.

In doll advertisements, both boy and girl dolls projected energy and activity which knew no bounds. Unlike generations of passive female dolls, the Campbell Kid boy and girl sashayed across magazine pages (fig. 36). Likewise, when the Schoenhut Company launched its new era of doll production in 1911, the owner's dancing grandsons appeared on the catalog cover. Schoenhut boy and girl dolls, dressed in "regulation Gymnasium School Suits," represented a new kind of activity for modern American children. Nearly everyone was now convinced that regular physical exercise, especially in the open air, would build a healthier child and a healthier society. (In fact, Theodore Roosevelt, who had dramatically improved his health by a rigorous outdoor regimen, exemplified

Still Another Doll Sensation!

Manufactured by License from Joseph Campbell Company

Heads Reproduced from Plastic Model Copyrighted 1910, by E. I. Horsman Co.

Copyright by Joseph Campbell Company. Protected by International Copyright law.
Above Picture is from Photograph of Dolls Themselves

The Campbell Kids

TRADE MARK

The Jolliest Dolls of All

Familiar Faces Now Transformed into Household Pets,
Beautiful, Artistic, Irresistibly Comical, Washable and Unbreakable

These dolls have heads of the celebrated "Can't Break 'Em" material, the model being the work of an artist of note. The dressing of the dolls has been done with taste and care, with good material and careful finish. They are in short, artistic creations. Each doll packed in a box.

> Campbell Kid Boy, per dozen $8.50
> Campbell Kid Girl, "   "   8.50

A Word to the Wise

Doll Buyers alive to their own interests will buy no
Dolls on Import
until they have seen our new and wonderful doll line for 1911.

E. I. HORSMAN CO.,

DOLL MANUFACTURERS

365-367 BROADWAY, NEW YORK.
Kindly Mention PLAYTHINGS When Writing to Advertisers.

36. The Campbell Kids were an active, strong, intelligent, and witty boy and a masculinized girl; such "character dolls" were often siblings. The commercialization of the Progressive concern over cleanliness was best represented in Dutch doll versions. Advertisement, *Playthings,* 1912, reproduced by permission.

the "strenuous life," a popular movement that advocated physical exercise and moral strength.)[20]

The many representations of athletic activities however, excluded New Kid girls (unless one counts "physical culture" bloomers). Although Amberg marketed a genteel and feminized Little Lord Fauntleroy doll (based on the hero in Frances Hodgson Burnett's 1886 novel), its Swat Mulligan baseball player doll, sold at "cigar stores and similar shops where men congregate," was more typical of the period. American businessmen in the doll industry may have embraced a more rugged masculinity for themselves, yet they appealed to the "masculine domesticity" of turn-of-the-century fathers who spent more time with their sons. The Schoenhut Company produced a uniformed football player doll and another firm advertised Jockey the race horse rider. In addition to boy dolls at play, there were also boys at work such as the entrepreneurial newsboy Mugsey and the assertive messenger boy Buttons.[21]

Although not physically mature enough to engage in a team sport or have a job, baby boy dolls were alleged to possess great physical strength. Hahn & Amberg named their first baby doll Samson and advertised him as "Uncle Sam's Firstborn" (probably a reference to their own idealized beginnings, a growing patriotism, and the Bible). When Samson turned out to be a weak marketplace contender (possibly because of his hard composition body), Hahn & Amberg attached his head to a cloth body. Ironically, the baby boy, given a man's bow tie, was renamed Dolly Strong, and in its new guise was invincible. But competitors made similar inflated claims about physical fitness and invulnerability. One manufacturer marketed the "Kant Krack Kids"—"very STRONG AND TOUGH." (Dolls like Billiken sported a "Can't Break 'Em" head made by the Aetna Doll and Toy Company.) A. Steinhardt & Brothers trademarked its "Never break" character dolls. Fleischaker & Baum claimed that its doll heads were as hard as concrete. Not to be outdone as the producers of the "cleverest dolls in babyland," Amberg once again professed that its was also the "hardest." That manufacturers marketed New Kid dolls on the basis of strength was, in part, the result of technological changes such as steel spring hinges, metal swivel spring joints, and the substance called composition.[22]

Although New Kid dolls embodied the concerns of turn-of-the-century businessmen, they were marketed to "honest, open-hearted," and "child-loving" middle-class mothers. In order to appeal to female shoppers whom manufacturers had targeted as their "most profitable customers," ads for New Kid dolls drew upon American middle-class domestic values.[23] Little brother and sister dolls were likely to live in a middle-class family where fewer siblings permitted greater intimacy and to play in safe playgrounds with neighborhood friends. Like their mothers, New Kids embraced the consumer values of the modern age that were distinctively American and not European. As in other households, the Campbell Kids' "real" human mother probably shopped for the wholesome American food she prepared daily. (Like the Campbell's Soup Kids and the Uneeda Cracker boy, numerous dolls were based on popular images drawn from the recent method of brand name advertising.)

Judging from the innovative stocky appearance of the Campbell Kids, New Kid dolls were not only well fed on American abundance, but they were also consumers of ready-made clothing in up-to-date fashions. Unlike previous generations of dolls and children who wore restricting frilly dresses and button-topped shoes, "children's costumes are [today] replacing the grown-up finery of former times." New Kid dolls arrived from the store with rompers, sun dresses, and overalls—the latest in children's fashions that accommodated liberalizing ideas about childhood in this "Century of the Child." Because modern mothers and other caretakers "were usually too busy to make lots of dainty underclothes, dresses, coats and hats for their doll family," one-piece rompers and play-suits were not only ready-made but also washable.[24]

Doll manufacturers appealed to this cult of cleanliness as they competed for the attention of American women who promoted a knowledge and practice of sanitation, nutrition, and sound health through progressive reform. "[Our dolls'] faces can be washed with soap and water," claimed one doll manufacturer, appealing to middle-class mothers for whom washing with soap was a relatively recent priority. Other manufacturers, like Hahn & Amberg, advertised that their "Original Washable babies" were "Positively Washable." Many dolls like the Bye Bye Kids were advertised as "Strictly Sanitary." In addition to efforts to make the actual dolls washable, New Kid dolls were more often marketed as sanitary by invoking images of cleanliness, particularly Dutch children. Although contemporaries found much about the "new immigrants" from eastern and southern Europe that they did not like, the Dutch represented cleanliness in the minds of many although their real influence on America had been in the previous two centuries. Like the "peaceful, bovine expression" on Amberg's Kids, the "round, red faces" of another manufacturer's Dutch-He and Dutch-She dolls are "the perfect picture of Holland Health."[25]

Doll manufacturers also used soap company advertising images familiar to women who bought cleaning products. Amberg made this association stronger by renaming its Dutch dolls Spic and Span—the "cherubs of cleanliness." Amberg hoped to benefit from a $50,000 advertising campaign conducted in New York for the the new metal and polish cleanser. Horsman's Fairy doll was based on the sprite who sat on the cake of Fairy soap ads for the N. K. Fairbank Company. Under an arrangement between Horsman and Naphtha, a rompered version of Dolly Strong was distributed with Naphtha soap coupons. The acceptability of the Dutch trend overlapped with a Japanese motif that drew upon the popular perception that the Japanese were both childlike as well as untouched by civilization. The Japanese did not emigrate to American cities and could, therefore, remain safely romanticized. The kimonoed Jap Rose Kids were produced under license by the Jas. S. Kirk & Company, a soap manufacturer and a prominent advertiser on the east and west coasts. Horsman's Baby Butterfly doll, who was said to "Exhale the Fragrance of the Blossoms of Japan," also exuded healthfulness.[26]

The domestic values promulgated in the New Kids commercial culture reached beyond the confines of the American household to the rest of the nation. The manufacturer who bracketed his advertisements with "American Dolls for Americans" spoke for the rest. All New Kid dolls had one thing in common: they were advertised as "every inch American."[27] Uncle Sam's patriotic niece and nephew, Hail Columbia and Yankee Doodle, dressed in stars and stripes. As prewar American businessmen switched from importers to manufacturers, they generated a national commercial culture for children that *aimed* to obliterate regional, racial, and class differences.

Although "The Yankee Doll" was claimed to have been "made in Yankeeland," it was not made by Yankees. During the winter of 1912, fourteen-year-old Rose Cattena sat hunched over a wooden kitchen table in the tenement apartment she shared with her family in New York City's Lower East Side. Rose was joined day after day by Tessie who lived downstairs, "deformed" 12-year-old Lena, and a "very deft" 9-year-old, Nettie. At 10 o'clock one night, the little group, which had been sewing for seven long hours, took their last stitches and piled the doll legs into a box bearing the label of a local factory (figs. 37 and 38). With the heavy box cradled in her already exhausted arms, Rose decended the five flights of stairs and walked to the nearby Aetna Doll and Toy Company. From there, the doll parts she and her friends had sewn would become E. I. Horseman's Campbell Kids dolls.[28]

Child laborers like Rose had made it possible for producers like Horsman to market an exalted middle-class New Kids culture to American consumers shortly after the turn of the century. The Campbell Kids, widely advertised since 1905 as happy, energetic, well-fed, healthy, and clean, stood in sharp contrast to the working-class children who sewed Campbell Kids dolls and their dresses at piecework rates. Campbell Kid dolls wore ready-made clothing in up-to-date fashions, not threadbare hand-me-downs as did their young dressmakers. Though the dolls sold for only one dollar, it was more than families like the Cattenas—who lived on about $600 a year—could afford.

While New York City at the turn of the century lured merchants, buyers, and doll importers, the expanding urban economy also attracted many immigrants. Unlike businessmen, however, most immigrants entered the doll industry at the bottom. Seventy-nine percent of all doll homeworkers in New York City around 1910 were immigrants who came from Italian agricultural districts. The recently-arrived settled in overcrowded tenements in Italian neighborhoods in Manhattan, especially the Lower East Side, Greenwich Village, and Brooklyn, areas closest to the commercial doll industry, located south of Houston Street.[29] It was there that immigrant mothers, and sometimes fathers, daughters and sons sewed dolls for doll producers.

37 and 38. Two contrasting photographs intended by
photojournalist Lewis Hine to reveal the class-based nature of
childhood at the turn of the century. Middle class girls (*top*) are
pushing a Campbell Kid doll made by child laborers and their
mother (*bottom*). Photos courtesy of the Library of Congress.

IN FAMILIES DOING NUTS AND DOLLS' CLOTHES

Occupation of Father	Wage per week	Rent per month	Number in family	Number of children	Age of oldest child	Age of youngest child
Baker	$18 00	$14 00	6	4	12	3
Barber	12 00	15 00	3	1	17	......
Bookbinder	12 00	11 50	8	4	15	10
Bottler	12 00	8 00	3	1	......	......
Butcher	18 00	13 00	3	1	14	......
Candy factory	18 00	11 50	8	6	15	5
Cap cutter (in season)	20 00	18 00	6	4	17	4
Carpenter	18 00	12 00	10	8	17	1
Cement	12 00	6 00	4	2	8	3
Chauffeur	12 00	12 00	2	......	......	......
Coal man	12 00	13 00	4	2	16	11 m
Cobbler	18 00	17.50	5	3	7	22 mos.
Cook	9 00	11 00	2	......	......	......
Driver	18 00	11 50	4	2	16	10
Driver	16 00	13 00	5	3	4	2
Driver	13 00	12 50	5	3	13	10
Driver	12 00	14 00	6	4	15	5
Elevator man	9 00	15 00	7	2	7	6
Factory hand	12 00	15 00	7	4	20	9
Furniture cleaner	9 00	17 00	7	5	18	8
Gen. El. Co.	10 00	15 00	6	3	13	9
Hod carrier	15 00	14 00	5	3	11	1½
Insurance agent	10 00	16 00	4	3	13	9
Janitor	10 00	10 00	4	2	9	2
Jewelry mender	12 00	5 00	3	1	......	......
Laborer	15 00	12 00	6	4	17	9
Laborer	9 00	16 00	4	2	14	7
Laborer	9 00	8 00	3	1	6	......
Machinist	12 00	13 00	3	1	1 week	......
Marble cutter	11 00	11 00	2	......	......	......
National biscuit	12 00	11 00	4	2	2	14 mos.
Packer	12 00	13 00	3	2	2	2 mos.
Painter	15 00	12 00	5	3	3	2
Pencil factory	9 00	13 00	3	1	10	......
Plumber	24 00	14 00	5	3	9	5
Policeman	29 00	16 00	8	6	16	4
Polisher (brass work)	12 00	11 00	3	1	14	......
Printer	12 00	7 00	2	......	......	......
Rag man	10 00	13 00	8	6	15	6
Rag shop	10 00	10 00	6	4	18	14
Salesman	15 00	15 00	7	6	19	9
Saloon clerk	9 00	12 00	10	6	16	6
Shipping clerk	10 00	11 00	2	......	......	......
Soap factory	10 00	17 00	6	4	18	11
Stone maker	8 00	12 00	6	......	17	9
Street cleaner	9 00	12 50	5	3	17	9
Switchman	1 050	10 00	7	5	14	7 mos.
Tailor	14 00	16 00	5	3	11	4
Tailor	12 00	13 00	6	4	7	5
Tel. Co.	15 00	13 00	3	1	6	......
Dead	......	12 00	4	2	18	5

39. Nuts and Dolls' Clothes, National
Child Labor Committee for the
Factory Investigating Committee,
1912. Photo courtesy of the
Library of Congress.

Italian men, most with no previous industrial experience, in the best
earning years of their lives, often became day laborers or worked in the
seasonal trades. Few, however, earned enough money to carry their families through the "dull" season or had savings sufficient to weather highly
erratic business cycles (fig. 39). More than one member of a working-
class family had to work in order to make ends meet.

In one family, unemployed Alfonso Ricca cared for his young daughter while his wife sewed rompers for Campbell Kids dolls. Italian immigrant women often turned to industrial homework, a reliable source of income. At home, wives could manage some household tasks, unlike factory workers who had far less control over their time. The doll outfitter company Kahn & Mossbacher reported, "We employ . . . about 300 in their homes, such as housewives and persons who are physically unable to work elsewhere. These people do all our hand crocheting, and though not all of them depend on this for their subsistence, we can safely say that the majority of them do."[30] The company's view was unusual; most doll manufacturers maintained that homework provided mothers with mere pin money. Women, they claimed, were content to earn an extra dollar a week in their spare time.

Overworked and underpaid immigrant women, however, were likely to spend much of their time in an endless routine of household chores assisted by young children, especially daughters, who helped maintain their tenement dwellings. Urban reformers had revised building health and safety codes, yet most families still lived in dark, narrow, cold, and cluttered railroad flats. Although wives and daughters decorated dreary apartments with cheap lithographs, posters, and tradecards, inadequate plumbing and overcrowding made the rising standards of cleanliness advocated by social housekeepers all but unattainable.[31]

Daughters who were old enough often assisted their mothers at piecework as well as housework. Between the ages of 4 and 14, girls often helped to make cloth bodies for dolls, doll clothes, and stuffed animals. These immigrant children, both girls and boys, contributed to the family's livelihood. In the Romana family, "the older boy, about 12 years old, operates the machine when the mother is not using it, and when she operates, he helps the little ones, 5 and 7 year olds, break the thread"[32] (fig. 40).

Although sisters and brothers may have exchanged stories and told jokes while they stitched and snipped, making dolls and their dresses was labor for which few homeworkers were adequately paid. The low wages and lessened status in the dolls' fragmented production could not equal the ambiance of Martha Chase's "Dolls' House." Although children performed various other tasks like turning doll clothing right side out

40. Young girls and boys often helped their mothers, who were
the principal industrial homeworkers, by stuffing limbs, snipping
threads, and turning garments right side out. Older children
occasionally used the sewing machine homeworkers purchased
and maintained at their own expense to make modern rompers
for Campbell Kids dolls. Photo courtesy of the Library of Congress.

or bundling finished pieces into dozened lots, families were paid by the
piece and not according to the labor of each worker. In one typical family
in 1912, "the highest wage was $12.00 a week for operating on dolls'
clothes earned by the combined labors of the father, mother and three
children."[33]

Wages were further lowered because doll workers who sewed in
kitchens and bedrooms absorbed the expense of supplies, machinery,
rent, light, heat, needles, and thread. "All needle workers pay for their
sewing cotton and this one item sometimes amounts to 45 cents a week
for the workers on dolls' clothes." The financial loss from ruined garments was absorbed by homeworkers. Picking up and delivering lots of

garments took time for which homeworkers were not paid. "One woman who lived at a distance from the factory had to go on three successive days. Altogether she earned a dollar, out of this she spent 30 cents for carfare."[34] Occasionally, subcontractors even failed to pay for finished work.

Doll manufacturers had a free hand as state statutes did not prohibit tenement doll production until 1913. One manufacturer of doll goods explained, "We do not investigate the homes . . . I have never gone into any of the places myself, or sent anybody to see under what conditions these dresses are made." Contemporary observers estimated that although some workers who made dolls' clothing in their homes did so in tenements licensed by the Department of Labor, more than twice as many lived in unlicensed tenements.[35]

Reformers who ventured forth into immigrant ghettos were appalled by the suffering and sickness they saw there. In basement apartments they encountered tubercular workers sewing Campbell Kids' pinafores. Reformers feared for the middle-class child whose parents unknowingly purchased an alleged disease-carrying doll produced by infected workers. Popular magazines had exaggerated the spread of contagion since the acceptance of the "Germ Theory" and had provoked unwarranted fears about the working class. A contributor to the trade magazine *Toys & Novelties* thought it likely that "a doll quarantine will be established to prevent the spread of tuberculosis . . . among their flesh and blood foster mothers."[36]

Although the quarantine was never mandated, National Child Labor Committee reformers who investigated tenement house manufacture of dolls employed poetry to evoke sympathy.

> Dolly dear, dolly dear, where have you been?
> "I've been in a world you never have seen."
> Dolly, my dolly dear, what did you see?
> "I saw little children make dresses for me."
> How old were these children, when did they play?
> "They don't play in that world, they work every day."
> Dolly, but dolly, how long does it take?
> "They nodded, we nodded, at night half awake."

Why didn't they feed you and take you to bed?
> "The children who made me were often unfed."

Dolly, oh dolly dear, what were they named?
> "There was Nettie with measles, and Rosalie lamed."

These sick little children, what could they sew?
> "They stitched on my dresses, an arm, then a toe."

Dolly mine, dolly mine, who brought you here?
> "I was squeezed in a box and fainted from fear."

Perhaps it was Santa in one of his Sleighs?
> "Twas a bit of a boy who dodged past the drays."

Happy girls, happy boys joyful and gay,
Think of the children who work all the day,
Making your dolls, your dresses, your food,
With no chance to play, grow strong or be good.[37]

The unhealthy conditions of doll homeworkers despite legislation, contrasted sharply with contemporary childrearing ideals disseminated by home economists and other Progressive Era reformers. Settlement house leaders and others urged immigrant mothers to prepare nutritious food (like Campbell's soup) and keep their homes tidy. Appealing to middle-class consumers, doll manufacturers like E. I. Horsman extolled the virtues commercialized in their advertisements of healthful and cheerful Campbell Kids having fun in playgrounds built by crusading reformers. The components of New Kid dolls may have been in the hands of the child laborers from after school until late in the evening, but the finished dolls remained out of their reach.[38]

The Progressive Era seemed to hold great promise for future generations of dolls and for real boys and girls. Although they charted their own course, American businessmen had arrived at a similar place as had businesswomen who had provided them with a model for social action. Between 1909 and 1914, unprecedented changes had taken place in childhood and dolls. Never before had so many boy dolls been produced *for* boys. The New Kid dolls embodied at least some of Teddy Bear's characteristics, broadened the Gilded Age function of feminine socialization in bourgeois ritual. But unlike Martha Chase's generation's sensitivity to women's concerns, New Kid dollmakers tapped issues of male identity epitomized by Teddy Bear's spiritual father, Theodore Roosevelt, whose strength, vigor, and interest in the natural world was embodied in animals. For girls, New Kid dolls replaced previous generations of fragile fashion plates with strong, sturdy, and independent representations. New Kid girl dolls wore "rational" clothes that no longer restricted behavior but permitted the freedom and range of movement girls themselves preferred. Their intelligence and "character" replaced the genteel, passive mindlessness of previous generations of dolls.

Thus it seemed for a time that the contest between male and female conceptions of boyhood and girlhood waged by way of doll design and marketing was approaching resolution. The anxieties and pride of men at the turn of the century and the concomitant concerns of women were integrated within an American value standard that found a channel in the evolution of dolls. The separation of spheres was mollified by Teddy Bears and Billikens, which, in turn, accommodated the zest Americans believed they possessed.

CHAPTER FIVE

New Women and Talismen: Rose O'Neill and the Kewpies, 1909–1914

Rose O'Neill, an internationally recognized artist, writer, and Greenwich Village bohemian, was best known to contemporaries for her Kewpie characters, which first appeared in popular women's magazines in 1909. Shortly thereafter, the naked Kewpies, with rounded tummies and a sprout of hair, were made out of every substance from china to chocolate.[1] By World War I, the Kewpies were the best-known characters in American popular culture until Mickey Mouse. Most Americans today are more familiar with Kewpies than with their creator. Yet O'Neill was well known at the turn of the century for her creativity and success. To doll collectors since, the legendary O'Neill is considered a child prodigy and Renaissance woman, but historians have overlooked her and the role she played in the history of gender, childhood, and American culture.[2]

New Women like O'Neill shared an outlook on children first articulated during the last decades of the nineteenth century by "material maternalists" like Martha Chase. Although not outspoken child-labor crusaders, these artists pursued an agenda that was nevertheless child centered. Their concern about the nation's children also preempted a more private motherhood. Female artists imbued the "children" they created with features drawn from their own experience, ambition, and ideology. Freed from tradition and convention, they drew representations of children who had experienced a similar emancipation. In the case of the Kewpies, moreover, the creations were exempt from gravity as well. In their imaginations, on drawing boards, or in clay, New Women artists created representations of a life as unfettered for children as they demanded for themselves.

Among her generation, Rose O'Neill was representative of new ideas about gender which influenced the image of the modern children she created in her regularly published Kewpie cartoons. An active woman leading an independent life, O'Neill created images of the self-sufficient New Kid—as vigorous and vibrant as she was herself. Although autonomous, New Women created a peer culture not unlike the Kewpies'. An educated woman with a social conscience, O'Neill designed politically conscious and benevolent Kewpies who, like their creator, carried suffrage placards, debated the opposition, and vigilantly watched over working-class neighborhoods as "social housekeepers." As a cultural feminist and artist who donned rather unconventional but less restricting and more comfortable clothing, she also drew children wearing simple garments—or even nude—instead of in long dresses trimmed with layers of lace. O'Neill, who preferred bobbed hair to chignons, also styled children's hair in more natural top knots. Like the Kewpies she created, O'Neill best represents the thematic continuities manifested in the gender restructuring of her generation of New Women doll designers' lives and the new socialization of children they promulgated in their art.

To Rose O'Neill, the turn-of-the-century American child was not only modern, but androgynous as well. The naked boy Kewpies had no identifiable genitalia (unlike Renaissance cupids), carried books, and donned aprons. They were individuated yet communal. While not powerful on their own, as a group the nimble Kewpies were formidable contenders. The affectionate Kewpies mothered the neglected and adopted the unwanted whereas their masculine namesake—Cupid—made mischief instead.[3]

While O'Neill achieved fame and fortune as a result of her cartoon characters' popularity, the radical nature of her vision was changed with the production of Kewpie dolls. That is, while the Kewpie cartoon characters were androgynous in many respects, they were changed by male doll producers whose conception of gender differed from that of female designers. In the end, Rose O'Neill's radical conception of gender would be subsumed when businessmen often recast her androgynous boy as a bashful girl.

This radical transformation in intention is especially evident in the contrast between androgynous Kewpie dolls and the masculinized New Kid dolls, which were their contemporaries. Whereas community values would dominate the lives of the Kewpies, who lived together as peers, the nuclear family would become a source of identity for most dolls produced after 1910. While the Kewpies had no patriotic allegiance and even boasted an international following, the New Kid dolls produced by American businessmen exhibited specifically American national pride. The Kewpies would be critical of material wealth, convention, and the boredom it bred, but the Campbell Kids celebrated middle-class values.

In 1874, Rose Cecil O'Neill was born in "Emerald Cottage," the O'Neill's elaborately decorated home in Wilkes-Barre, Pennsylvania. Inspired by a recent trip to Italy, her father, William Patrick O'Neill, had commissioned an Italian artist to design Cupid frescoes for the ceiling. William O'Neill, a Civil War veteran and book dealer, journeyed to the Nebraska prairie where he built a sod house instead of an elegant cottage for his growing family. Although the O'Neills were like others who had made the journey westward in the hope of finding greater opportunity, O'Neill, who brought along his "heaps of books," was also driven west by "romantic ideas about country life."[4]

O'Neill, who kept his nails beautifully manicured, moved to the prairie with little intention to farm. Because "he was a romantic with lucid intervals" he established a book business, which encountered little success. That the family was often broke failed to motivate O'Neill to find a more remunerative career. Instead, "in his flowered dressing gown and using his most musical delivery," O'Neill recited Byron to bill collectors. Rose O'Neill's mother, Alice Asenath Cecelia O'Neill, who had been reared in an affluent and genteel Protestant home, was barely better equipped for life in the midwest than her husband. In their sod house, Alice O'Neill covered the earth floors with rugs and draped a single window with a satin curtain. Because "the sort of work [she] had to do was all new to her for she had never cooked, mended, or planted," the family abandoned their homestead and moved to Omaha.[5]

Both husband and wife, it seems, were ill suited to the social roles assigned them by virtue of their sex. William O'Neill "was constitutionally a man of leisure" who was often unable to pay the rent; therefore, the family relocated frequently during the twelve years they spent in Nebraska. Their house was always sparsely furnished, the children shabbily clothed and underfed. Instead of household furnishings it was stacks of books that "occupied most of the room in the moving-vans that took us from house to house." Alice O'Neill, who was more realistic than her dreamy husband, was also more adept at bringing home the bacon than cooking it. Renewing old teaching skills, "Meemie" secured a job in order to support the family. Because Alice O'Neill's school was too far away to return home each night, the occasionally employed William Patrick O'Neill raised Rose and her siblings Mondays through Fridays. But unlike other fathers who might have exercised greater authority, "there were no paternal outbreaks of barbarous behavior, such as keep many children on tenterhooks," recalled Rose O'Neill.[6]

Rose O'Neill's childhood aspirations were shaped by her parents' creative passions. As a teenager O'Neill appeared with a traveling theater company. William O'Neill devoted himself to his daughter's acting career by coaching her in Shakespearean roles for local amateur repertories. "My father had never been an actor," recalled Rose O'Neill, "but he had a passion for rolling forth Shakespearean lines and stabbing pillows." Alice

O'Neill was a cosmopolitan, a cultured, and a "very well-read" young woman who played the violin and organ, taught her daughter to play the piano, and had herself yearned for a stage career. "It was she who taught me to put sense as well as voltage into my dramatic doings," Rose O'Neill wrote. It was William O'Neill, however, who "placed tables of drawing paper in handy spots, accompanied by beautifully sharpened pencils" which he spent hours obsessively sharpening. Rose O'Neill, who consumed "everything and anything in my father's library," especially the classics, could "also sing. I recited. And danced. I made up plays and tormented my brothers and sisters into performing them. I had a little Grocer's book filled with poetry. I had started a novel." At age 13, after winning a children's statewide art competition sponsored by the Omaha *World-Herald,* Rose O'Neill sold her drawings to magazines in Omaha and Chicago. More like her practical mother, Rose O'Neill contributed to the support of her family while still a teenager. Yet it was William O'Neill who determined that his daughters would have careers, declaring that "Theirs is a far different sphere" than the private one.[7]

In 1893, Rose O'Neill, now age 19, moved to New York City in order to gain an education, launch her professional career, and publish her first novel, *Calesta.* In New York, Rose O'Neill exchanged constricting clothing for more comfortably fitting garments. "I was always rebellious against harness and hair-pins, until time and fashion released my viscera—and I cut my hair quite a while before the general cropping."[8] For these New Women, as for others, the move to a big city was motivated, in part, by greater educational opportunities beyond what families and local communities could provide. There were many jobs in the growing urban economy for young women like O'Neill with artistic talent and career ambitions. While the census had reported only 418 female artists and art teachers in 1870, by 1910, there were 15,583 women in art-related fields. O'Neill supported herself and paid for her education by selling her artwork to publishers of popular periodicals and advertisers for modern inventions like the newfangled Jell-O desert introduced in 1904 (fig. 41).

While supporting herself and attending school, Rose O'Neill married a handsome Southern filmmaker, Gray Latham, in 1896 when she was 22. Much like her father, Latham (who often posed for O'Neill's illustrations)

41. Kewpie creator Rose O'Neill
illustrated advertisements for many
products, including Jell-O.
Private collection.

was charming, playful, "very worldly and debonair." He also depended
upon O'Neill to buy his "chic" wardrobe. Too often, O'Neill recalled, he
"would go to offices and collect the money I had earned or was about to
earn . . . and leave me penniless," without carfare.[9] Soon O'Neill began
to feel exploited by Latham, who shared her income with his family and
left none for hers.

In 1901, O'Neill left Latham and New York for the hills of Missouri where her father had meanwhile relocated his penniless family to a 300-acre homestead in the Ozark mountains. "The thought of seeing Meemie and my brothers and sisters . . . was always more than I could bear . . . like one asleep and in a joyful dream." While a satin curtain was draped around one of the log-framed beds, the family was forced to construct chairs, bedboards, and roof supports from William O'Neill's vast book collection. Though the Ozarks "seemed sufficiently wild, being almost inaccessible, and romantic enough" to the rest of the family, William O'Neill preferred the solitude of an Arkansas chasm, and gave up regular family life forever.[10]

One year later, in 1902, Rose O'Neill married Harry Leon Wilson, novelist and former literary editor at *Puck* (where she also worked), but the two were thoroughly mismatched. According to Wilson's biographer, "They were a discordant pair, she ebullient and communicative, and he a dour humorist, given to sardonic silences and frequent hangovers." During the winters at O'Neill's Missouri home, Wilson, who often lapsed in morose silence, was incensed by her animated conversations and other insufferable "characteristics." Feeling himself to be her intellectual superior, he disparagingly nicknamed her "chucklehead."[11]

Instead of being subdued by Wilson's attacks, however, O'Neill proved to be as emotionally resourceful as she was creative. During a summer stay with novelist Booth Tarkington and his wife, O'Neill and Louisa Tarkington invented a Wernicke, "a little creature with [unfolding] gossamer wings and thread-like legs in rubber overshoes, very spry in case of danger, who got out of harm's way by backward flips of witticisms." "The point was that instead of being quelled by our 'Two Bright Men,' we would make escape by way of a backward flip of *espirit*." Despite the support of close friends and imaginary beings, O'Neill's resources were ultimately drained in coping with Wilson. He "had taken away my courage." When she divorced him in 1907, O'Neill declared that she had "withdrawn from marriage."[12]

Both of Rose O'Neill's marriages were childless, a fact that alarmed contemporaries worried about "race suicide" among "the better sort." But, O'Neill "adored" children and especially her younger brother, Eddie. "I used to be enraptured with my baby brother and was always making little drawings of his funny lovely little looks and gestures." Her nephew, Paul, "was beautiful in something the same way as Eddie—a golden baby with golden little curls. They were both fairy-like, meditative and refined babies." But, when two-year-old Eddie died suddenly from a cold and fever when O'Neill was 14, she was devastated.[13]

Although often thousands of miles from her sisters, Lee and Callista, O'Neill remained as close as ever to them and Callista became her life-long companion. One neighbor on Washington Square (where the sisters shared a living space) observed that " 'Rose and Callista are my favor-ite woman.' There was something so satisfactory about the singular-word 'woman,' " recorded Rose O'Neill in her autobiography. The O'Neill sis-ters were good friends, business associates, and also political activists united in the "fight for woman suffrage, marching in parades and wear-ing placards" along with other Village Bohemians (fig. 42). Rose O'Neill, who illustrated suffrage pictures and posters, also addressed crowds to whom she was introduced as the "mother of the Kewpies."[14]

The Kewpies first appeared in the December 1909 issue of *Ladies' Home Journal,* the newly launched magazine that "reassured homemakers of the properness of their traditional roles."[15] Thereafter, *Good House-keeping, Woman's Home Companion,* and *St. Nicholas* all carried Rose O'Neill's Kewpie cartoon series at one time or another. Unlike the Victo-rian cherubic images of children that had dominated magazine pages, the Kewpies looked far more like real toddlers with developmentally accu-rate and distinctive body dimensions. The heads were rounder and made up a larger proportion of the overall height, the eyes were spaced farther apart, and torso and limbs were shorter. The Kewpies' hair grew into a top knot (as had O'Neill's as a child). The Kewpies were so natural in fact, that they wore little, if any, clothing. While most turn-of-the-century women and children were discarding layers of immobilizing garments, unashamed and uninhibited "Plain Kewpies" were already stark naked.

Although the Kewpies lacked identifying physical traits, they had some distinctly male characteristics and were always "he" in cartoon texts. As thoughtful social critics, they analyzed and evaluated the impact of mod-

42. By her own account, Rose O'Neill (*left*) was not much of a
public speaker, even on topics in which she ardently believed like
women's suffrage. She was more likely to contribute posters such
as the one her sister Callista wears. Photo by F. DeMaria & Co.,
New York, courtesy of the O'Neill family.

ern American civilization on the young and old, rich and poor, male and female. In one exploit, three Kewpies parody well-to-do adults overly preoccupied with worldly concerns. Kewpies were free spirits who condemned social conventions and status symbols responsible for such misery. In contrast to the New Kids' embrace of a culture of consumption, Kewpies denounced sour and sarcastic adults for being dreary and dutiful. O'Neill's Kewpies also helped those too "ill with gravity"—as in a story about a wealthy matron and her elderly husband who are bored by the splendor that surrounds them—to find their lost youth.[16]

While unrestricted by clothing and other symbols of the society they criticized, the wise Kewpie boys have been often mistaken for compliant girls because they are represented in ways in which females have been typically represented. Because portrayals of female nudes are far more common than males, one assumes that the naked Kewpies—who are gendered without genitalia—must be female. Moreover, what little clothing the Kewpies wear is easily mistaken for feminine frocks. One dons a Mother-Hubbard-style dress, another wears a sunbonnet, and a third a tiny apron, a common symbol of domesticity in most cultures. The small fluffy wings that Kewpies use for flight make them look more angelic than human and, therefore, more female than male.[17]

Although designated as boys, these androgynous spirits were endowed with stereotypically female qualities. For example, the Kewpies are more likely to cooperate than to compete. When Kewpies find a baby not yet dressed for bed, Wag the "chieftain" observes: "Our education has not led/To putting human babes to bed/Now, here's a chance once seldom finds. A thing like this/We should not miss; It will enlarge our minds."[18] Wag does not command the other Kewpies but instead addresses the problem that the group solves together.

As this example also illustrates, Kewpies are more interested in doing good than in making trouble, unlike Cupid, their namesake. In one episode, the Kewpies transform several miscreants into "respectable lads" by saying nice things to them and giving them a party. By dispensing their "dose of Love," Kewpies similarly transform irascibles like Father Time or a gold hoarder, Samuel Gudge, into sweet and generous men.

In order to teach a little girl how to fly, they imitate a patient mother bird who hovers above her fledglings. Far more like idealized mothers than stereotyped fathers, the Kewpies help distressed children by drying tears, clothing the tattered, adopting the unwanted, and snuggling, caressing, and kissing the lonely.[19]

Motherhood had an explicitly political dimension for the Kewpies, who vigilantly watched over ghetto neighborhoods for those in need of their good works just like the maternalistic "social housekeepers" who were their contemporaries (fig. 43). Unlike the "Yellow Kid" comic strip character, who found humor in the violence of slum poverty since his newspaper appearance in 1896, the Kewpies often helped neglected children of working-class families in city slums, such as Tib McGee, the abandoned daughter of a washerwoman and a rag peddler.[20]

Not all mothers were worthy of the Kewpies' emulation and imitation, however. Working-class mothers, for example, were not necessarily immoral or incompetent; rather, they were burdened by numerous responsibilities and inadequate resources. Little Assunta's mother, for example, works so hard that she has no time even to mend her daughter's torn dress. Kewpies, like other maternalists, often impressed unknowledgeable immigrant working-class mothers with their wisdom and expertise. In one adventure, a desperate Mrs. McShane scrubs her Irish brood at bath time but with too much pressure and too little patience. While a set of twins overwhelm this exhausted mother, they are no match for the energetic Kewpies who "merrily lather them/And into cuddly arms they gather them." The Information Kewp—*the* expert—pronounces, "To wash on Saturday is dutiful, but *daily* bathing makes us beautiful." One mother exclaims: "That's inspirational! No wonder Kewps are reputational!"[21]

Like the social housekeepers they admired, the Kewpies were also feminists who embodied the dominant values of other New Women at the dawn of the century. The more militant Kewpies confronted antisuffragists, raised civil rights questions, and demanded the vote in cartoons and postcards. In 1915, the National Women's Suffrage Association Publishing Company issued postcards by Rose O'Neill showing Kewpies carrying "Votes for Women" placards or marching arm in arm (fig. 44).

43. The androgynous cartoon Kewpie boys, who are often mistaken for girls, were "social housekeepers" devoted to the neglected children of working-class families. From *Good Housekeeping*.

44. Although more of a cultural than political reformer, Rose O'Neill, who often recruited her Kewpies to the cause, illustrated numerous cartoons and postcards in support of women's suffrage. Private collection.

As feminists or as their supporters, the Kewpies were an unusual amalgam of the New Woman and emancipated New Man.[22]

In 1912, the Kewpies captured the attention of some American businessmen looking to develop new products. With the entrance of talented women following Billiken creator Florence Pretz into the work force, manufacturers and importers had found a steady supply of doll designs. In 1912, Fred Kolb, president of George Borgfeldt & Company, approached O'Neill about creating a Kewpie doll prototype. Feeling inexperienced and ambivalent about the project, O'Neill hired an artist who sculpted a more realistic-looking figure from the Kewpie drawings she had made. After a struggle over artistic control, O'Neill fired "Brunnhilde" and reworked the "little darling" to be manufactured out of bisque in German factories.[23]

Her enthusiasm over the Kewpie she had finally sculpted was replaced by horror over the samples sent back to her from the German factories. It was "the most shocking travesty of Kewpish face and form." It had the "shoulders of a pugilist, tummy of a drunken Silenus, the face of an infant fiend—the sidelong eyes and smile, a diabolical leer!" The factory had not cast the Kewpie from her statuette; instead, it had used a copy made by a German doll worker. Fueled by her vision and determination, O'Neill confronted the Borgfeldt management "like a Valkyr, complete with helmet, breastplate and sword" for vulgarizing her carefully-executed model. At her sister's urging, they raced to the doll factories in the Thuringer Wald where O'Neill ordered the firm to destroy the models, molds, and a stock of "ogrelings." She remodeled twelve sizes of Kewpies with the help of another dollmaker more sensitive to her artistic vision.[24] The dolls were then produced in a cottage industry system.

Despite her efforts, Kewpie dolls bore little resemblance to the cartoon characters which preceded them. As dolls and as figurines, Kewpies were lifted out of their thematic context, isolated from their peers, objectified and sentimentalized by those with an eye on the fast-paced novelty market. While O'Neill "wanted a Kewpie that would be soft to the touch," Kewpies were instead made out of hard and cool bisque. Their flight had been graceful as cartoon characters; however, as clay dolls they were grounded by gravity and their larger plumed wings had been replaced with Frankenstein-like electrodes. O'Neill's vision had been further eroded by other German doll mold makers who exercised their own artistic discretion. They modified even Borgfeldt-endorsed prototypes by creating Kewpies in slightly different sizes and in slightly different poses. A wide assortment of accessories or animals were placed in the arms or at the feet of Kewpies for greater variety and obvious commercial appeal.[25]

The ways in which Kewpie dolls now effected change differed from O'Neill's original vision. While social critic Kewpies had caricatured the old order, as dolls they became an antidote to the modern industrial age. As cartoon characters their identity had emerged out of their relationship to others. As static and single figurines, they were deprived of their reformist purpose and the large red hearts on their chests represented love without humanitarianism. Marketed as talismans, Kewpies no longer offered the possibilities they had earlier for women and children.

Advertised (like many New Kid dolls) as "the greatest little gloom, sulk and frown chasers," Kewpies were now marketed to appeal to both unhappy children and anxious adults. Marketed as being "contagiously happy," the Kewpies turned the germ theory upside down while still addressing fin-de-siècle pessimism. The winged Kewpies uplifted the spirits of downcast adults.[26] At a time when Sigmund Freud was developing his most important theories, Kewpies seemed to become psychotherapists who alleviated emotional stress and restored balance. The social criticism, irony, and community context of the Kewpie illustrations became instead a unitary "goodwill" philosophy. Kewpie dolls blended into a euphoric elixir whose source ingredients were nostalgia, romance, affection and religion. The result was a generic antidote to ill feeling, an ideal market item.

For Rose O'Neill, the Kewpies had been a consolidation of a wide variety of cultural, social, and political factors, emotional forces, and psychological fantasies. Although untraditional, unmarried, and childless, O'Neill had been inspired by her brother, Edward, who had "branded me with what became the Kewpie." If the Kewpies were modeled after her baby brother, it was her father who provided O'Neill with the prototype of the androgynous man she had believed in girlhood to be an Irish elf. The cultural influence mingled with other images of pixies, angels, and fairies in American popular culture (products of the sentimentalization of heaven, the feminization of love, the commercialization of romance, and the acceptance of fantasy). Despite this cultural blending, however, the Kewpies resonated with ambiguities for O'Neill. While they embodied what she admired most in her father, they may have also compensated for what she liked least in him and in other men. The Kewpies were reliable, compassionate, caring, and never irresponsible like her father, self-centered like her first husband, nor remote like her second. To O'Neill, Kewpie wings represented neither flight from responsibility nor danger. Unlike her father who "fled" the family, the Kewpies flew *to* those in need of their protection. While O'Neill had lost her "transitory baby" brother, she had created "the immortal elf." [27]

But if the men in her life provided material and form for the Kewpies, the Kewpies were also O'Neill's self-representation. In addition to using the Kewpies to illustrate her thoughts and feelings, O'Neill also used wings to cover mistakes in her correspondence. O'Neill's own signature consisted of stick figures with thread-like legs who occasionally sported a pair of wings. Ultimately, in the Kewpies O'Neill created she represented herself as a New Woman. "Rose O'Neill Wants . . . [Women] Free as Her 'Kewpies'" reported the *New York Times* in 1915.[28]

Although the Kewpies in print had represented new possibilities to their creator, Kewpie dolls were stuck between the older order and more modern notions of dolls. The milky-white appearance of delicate porcelain Kewpie dolls was closer to a pale and sickly Victorian complexion than that of a robust New Woman. Moreover, O'Neill's vision of a free and unfettered childhood differed sharply from the more conventional notion apparently shared by doll producers including the Borgfeldts. The sideways glances of Kewpie dolls, unlike the once wide-eyed, engaged, and exuberant characters in her illustrations, now conveyed stereotypically "girlish" bashfulness and coyness (fig. 45). Despite O'Neill's radical androgynous vision, the Kewpies were reshaped into a new feminine symbol.

45. More stereotypically "feminine"
Kewpie dolls, cultural appropria-
tions of their producers, bore little
resemblance to the androgynous
cartoon characters that preceded
them. Photo courtesy of the
Wenham Museum, Wenham, Mass.

Although the breakdown of separate spheres created the Kewpies, it also led to an assimilation that threatened the integrity of New Women artists and their works of art. With time and the needs of businessmen, the images and the values imbued in dolls were no longer recognizable as the original ones intended by their New Women creators. While the Kewpies had been a personal, political, and philosophical resolution of polarized gender roles for O'Neill, American businessmen like those at the Borgfeldt firm had usurped her more radical vision. These changes would have profound consequences for women professionals, as would the feminization of dolls like Kewpies, for their doll designs.

CHAPTER SIX

Forging the
Modern American Doll Industry,
1914–1929

In 1915, a year after the beginning of World War I, the
Maiden Toy Company was founded in New York City to
produce a "National" doll in the hope of benefiting from
patriotic and xenophobic wartime sentiments stimulated
by other industry leaders. Two years later, the manufacturers renamed the firm the Maiden America Toy
Company to capitalize even more clearly on the international situation. The "National" doll they produced
was, ironically, a copy of a German doll. It did, however,
draw upon prewar American attitudes and aesthetics. The
naked composition doll with a top knot, dot eyebrows,
and upturned hands appeared far more submissive and
suggestive than the popular Kewpies on whom it seemed
to be based. The National doll's naked body was provoca-

tively draped with a red, white, and blue ribbon tied in a large bow above her buttocks.[1]

Like Maiden America, contemporaries draped American wartime manufacturers in the American flag. In historical accounts, American businessmen were either patriotic citizens who liberated children during World War I from the tyranny of the Huns or humanitarians who expressed egalitarian concerns by producing dolls that lower-middle-class girls could afford. According to one writer, the American doll industry "kept moving on progressively, constantly improving, until to-day there are many fine American dolls, the acme of loveliness, that will give way tomorrow to something newer and, perhaps, better. For that is the American way."[2]

In an examination of American businessmen and their relations with doll workers, German producers, and women professionals, a very different picture emerges from the one put forth by collectors. The American doll industry was forged by both industry newcomers and veterans who seized the opportunity to wrest the doll industry away from European competition. They stirred up anti-German sentiments, generated an "us versus them" climate, and utilized their political clout to lobby for protective tariffs. Their advertising campaigns successfully swayed children and their mothers into purchasing toys by using a direct patriotic theme. American businessmen consolidated power by forming trade associations that intimidated doll workers and labor leaders into practices and agreements made on the owners' terms. Finally, businessmen pushed businesswomen and other females involved in dollmaking to the industry's margins.

That they were able to do so was one expression of the postwar shift in cultural attitudes toward women. Early in the 1920s, contemporaries praised male-identified businesswomen for their achievements and success in the marketplace. Utilizing a male model, many women abandoned traditional sewing skills and instead produced dolls molded out of rock-hard composition. Similarly, although nearly all women dollmakers had previously rejected the mechanization of dolls, the first commercially successful American "mama" doll was the brainchild of Georgene Hendren. Though motivated by private gain more than public concern (as the material maternalists had been), businesswomen gave entrepreneurial control of doll firms to husbands due to increasingly conservative values about women's roles. The vast majority of professional women, disillusioned by an economically competitive climate hostile to their interests as women, would, one way or another, suffer defeat by the end of the decade.

"SANTA CLAUS IS A WAR PRISONER," read a 1914 *Newark Evening News* headline describing the ostensible fate of one famous victim of the Great War. In the nation's doll capital, the *New York Times* stated more explicitly, "European War Stops Imports." Although the embargo was lifted to allow four shiploads of Kewpies from Germany to pass through the war zone, thousands of dollars worth of toys, dolls, and doll heads sat idly in warehouses in Rotterdam, hostages of war. In New York, this was bad news for local dealers who depended on "brokers" for dolls and their parts despite prewar American business success. The oldest doll hospital in the city, once successful enough to cater to the carriage trade, suffered from the British war blockades against German ships carrying doll supplies.[3]

Although the newspapers described the war's tragedies, they also found heroes among those American men who used the international crisis to their advantage. In 1914, toy manufacturers stepped up production by running their factories around the clock. In one factory fifty laborers worked day and night in order to produce 7,000 doll heads every 24 hours. Although some prewar firms such as Louis Amberg & Son doubled the firm's capital stock, other industry veterans formed new partnerships in order to take full advantage of unusual business opportunities. In 1914, the *New York Times* enthusiastically reported that "many new firms for toy-making [also] have been organized," some established by displaced suit and cloak makers. By 1920, *Scientific American* estimated that 125 new doll factories had sprung up, expanding the Manhattan toy district from Chambers Street to 42nd Street. According to the *Times,* finally "the American manufacturer had the opportunity he had so long desired."[4]

During the war years, veterans and newcomers alike established specialized businesses to manufacture dolls. The embargoing of ships carrying glass doll eyes led inventors like Samuel Marcus to create machine-insertable "Margon" celluloid-covered metal eyes. At one firm, doll workers operated machines capable of inserting 430 pairs of eyes in assorted sizes in eight hours. *Toys & Novelties* reported that the "lucrative" doll head industry had attracted "several hundred firms." One Canal Street firm produced 1,000 doll heads per week during the fall of 1914.[5]

John Giannone's New York firm, as most others, produced composition heads like those for the prewar New Kid dolls. With wartime expansion, however, "each manufacturer has his own private composition, the components of which are kept carefully secret." Composition was basically of two kinds, either wood pulp or glue and flour, despite the "mystery" surrounding individual recipes. Producers' opinions differed as to the merits of each, although glueless composition heads made of wood pulp would eventually predominate, in part because unsanitary "dolls made from some of the worst disease-breeding compositions in existence, as hide and bone glue and other waste material" were unacceptable to reform-minded consumers.[6]

American manufacturers had been virtually unable to duplicate the bisque production process, even though "for years it has [also] been a dream of the American toy industry to produce an all-American bisque head doll." German doll heads were light, durable and realistically colored, whereas the American products were heavy, coarse, breakable, and far too pink. Anticipating that the war would last for a matter of months and that German doll heads would be shipped to the United States soon, "American capital was shy of making the investment necessary for the production of bisque doll heads." Determined to find an American solution, however, E. I. Horsman Company associates, a chemist, and the Fulper Pottery Company (a producer of high-grade pottery) produced an acceptable American bisque, as did the Fleischaker & Baum firm later. At least some of those who did not actually create bisque did the next best thing—they marketed their composition with buzz words such as "bisquette," "bisque-finish," and "Newbisc," suggesting that despite inroads the Americans had made with consumers, continental doll aesthetics predominated.[7]

American success lay not in the development of bisque, however, but in composition and new ways to make it. Since the 1890s, manufacturers had been using the cold-press method invented by Solomon D. Hoffman. This process consisted of ladling "soup-like" ingredients into individual plaster molds of heads with flange necks, shoulder-and-head forms, and limbs. During the war years, however, innovative manufacturers like Fleischaker & Baum claimed that the cold-press was inferior to the newly developed hot-press method. In an effort to increase efficiency and decrease the need for labor, Louis Amberg & Son modernized its production process further by using brass molds instead of plaster ones.[8]

To run the machines they developed, doll entrepreneurs now electrified their industrial plants as did other manufacturers. Industry trade magazines encouraged the use of electric machines to compensate for the loss of cheap European labor. At Giannone's doll factory, electric air brushes were connected "to a five-horse-power motor, on Edison service" (fig. 46). "The Pullman Doll Company of Chicago, which until recently was producing plaster composition doll heads and sawdust stuffed doll bodies in a small plant, has moved into a larger factory which is electrically operated throughout," reported *Electrical World*. As a result, labor-intensive work was reduced: new electric ovens reduced drying time for doll heads by three days and resulted in fewer cracks.[9]

By 1916, technological advances and opportunity had created "an extraordinary large number of new manufacturers who believed that with Europe at war all one need do to make a fortune was to become a toy manufacturer." The immense number of new businesses launched during the war, however, had glutted the market. The Bleier Brothers, makers of "Bee Bee Brand" character dolls, for example, had not anticipated the frenzied competition, labor militancy, and entrenched consumer behavior and went out of business.[10]

In part because doll producers were so plentiful, raw materials were not. Lumberyard workers served in large numbers in the army, so the scarcity of raw materials like wood (for pulp) and paper (for packaging) led to inevitable price increases. According to *Toys & Novelties,* costs associated with making such a specialized product rose too:

46. During the war years, American manufacturers modernized
their plants by using electric machines designed to make the new
composition dolls. Newcomers with less capital to invest, however,
relied on older methods to paint dolls that were still more
efficient than hand painting. Photo courtesy of the
Library of Congress.

In the manufacture of American dressed character dolls, many chemicals are used in making the unbreakable composition for heads, hands, feet, etc. and the prices of practically all of these have gone up from 15 to 200 percent. Composition heads, which are made by the pouring process, contain a large proportion of glycerine and the cost of this chemical has increased more than 40 cents per pound. When it is known that the largest doll manufacturers frequently use more than 1,000 pounds of glycerine a week during their busy season, the effect of this rise may be better appreciated. The paints used for heads have also experienced a sharp increase in price, particularly red paints, and it would not be at all surprising if the domestic dolls appeared less ruddy this year than in the past.[11]

The cost of percale, the material used for the limbs and bodies, increased, as did the cost of all materials (for example, ribbons, laces) used for making doll dresses. One manufacturer of cloth doll masks that had relied on German imports of cloth had difficulty finding American textile mills able to supply him with the fabrics he needed. Manufacturers who foresaw the shortages bought in bulk, but most could not afford to because "overhead expenses during spring and summer are enough of a risk as it is."[12]

In addition to the inconvenience of the scarcity of raw materials, employers bemoaned the intensive wartime production in other industries that attracted their employees "through high wages." According to the *New York Times,* doll manufacturers found it "next to impossible to secure labor of any kind." Before the war, however, producers had relied on a reserve of doll workers who operated factories at full capacity for about five months out of the year. "During the busy season we employed most of the girls and women in the community. School boys and girls worked during their vacations which was our busy time." During the slack seasons when factories operated at only around fifty percent capacity, "extras" were forced to find alternative employment. Given the "princely salaries in the munitions factories," the absence of a slack season, and an inadequate work force, frustrated doll entrepreneurs were forced to operate at below capacity.[13]

Manufacturers faced union militancy in addition to a labor shortage. In 1916, 1,800 members of the newly organized Stuffed Toy and Doll Makers' Union called a general strike in doll factories in New York City and Brooklyn. After quitting work, the striking workers—half of whom were women —spent the afternoon dancing, an important aspect of their industrial work culture. Doll workers demanded shorter work days, longer lunch hours, a closed shop, recognition of their union, and an increase in pay ranging from 10 to 25 percent. They disagreed with their employers that their grievances arose from "a case of too much prosperity."[14]

Although Joe L. Amberg reported that "only two shops had been unionized," an intercepted strike meeting bulletin reprinted in *Playthings* had the industry worried (fig. 47). "It must be recognized that the labor of this class is restless and that every effort should be made to forestall trouble." In response to the walkout, forty determined doll manufacturers organized against the strikers by forming the Doll and Stuffed Toy Manufacturers Protective Association. From the manufacturers' perspective, "it was a case of radicalism of the worst type pitted against an iron-clad determination on the part of manufacturers to fight for the basic American rights of an employer to regulate his own private enterprise."[15]

Modernization made it possible for manufacturers, who were resolute in facing down labor, to control their workers to a greater extent, but newly introduced automation provided only a limited solution. At the Pullman plant, female workers, who exercised little control over the tasks they performed, painted 8,000 doll heads a day with electric air brushes. Operators who cut through six inches of fabric with a motor-driven knife or who sewed 4,000 stitches per minute on motor-driven sewing machines were forced to give their work their undivided attention. A "small force of boys" operated the new machines that stuffed sawdust into arms and legs for 8,000 dolls each day.[16]

Deciding that the workers' demands would not be met this time or any time, the manufacturers "agreed to work in unison in order to bring about a rational settlement of differences." According to Joe L. Amberg, president of the Manufacturers Protective Association, employers were ready to fight union demands to the end and even considered a lockout. Doll producers used a variety of union-busting methods in 1916 and again in 1920, when the union movement once more swept through the doll industry and doll workers demanded a 35 percent wage increase. Drawing upon previous experience, Amberg & Son hired workers of different nationalities, "because their varied ideas, temperament, racial influences and traditions" would prevent unionizing. Amberg felt confident that his firm had now been "fortified against the possibilities of a strike." The Liberty Doll Company, which manufactured doll heads, was among the firms that hired strikebreakers. Unfortunately, the strikers had little chance against the organized manufacturers, who protected their scabs with the fifty men of the "Amberg Police." This force was organized into

TOY AND DOLL WORKERS
WAKE UP!

GET READY. FOR A ☞ **GENERAL STRIKE**

Come All to Our **MASS MEETING**

on Tuesday Evening, at 8 P. M., at Casino Hall, 85 East 4th Street
on Thursday Eve., at Brownsville Labor Lyceum, 219 Sackman St.

Come All and Bring your Co-Worker. Good Speakers will address

THE EXECUTIVE COMMITTEE

OPERAI SU BAMBOLE DI NEW YORK
ATTENTI TUTTI
LA GENERALE RIUNIONE

AVRA LUOGO QUESTO MARTEDI SERA, Alle Ore 8 p. m., CASINO HALL, 85 E, 4th Street
onde GIOVEDI a la BROWNSVILLE LABOR LYCEUM, 219 Sackman Street
PER DISCUTERE LA QUISTIONE DELLO

SCIOPERO GENERALE

Siete pregati d'intervenire tutti in massa onde prendere parte alla discussione per decidere al riguardo

IL COMITATO

NEW YORKI BABATOMOK ES BABAKESZITOK !
EBREDJETEK !

MOST KEDDEN ESTE 8 ORAKOR, a CASINO HALLBAN, 85 E. 3-ik utca allat
THURSDAY a BROWNSVILLE LABOR LYCEUM, 219 Sackman Street

NAGY NEPGYÜLÈS

LESZ EGY ALTALANOS SZTRAJK MEGBESZELESE VEGET
JOJJETEK EL VALAMENNYIEN ES VEGYETEK RESZT A VITABAN

A VEGREHAJTO BIZOTTSAG

RAISING HADES IN THREE LANGUAGES.
Losing their spring strike the agitators threaten
future trouble.

47. The solidarity of doll workers
of different ethnic backgrounds
threatened doll industry leaders,
who reproduced this 1920 leaflet,
which called for a general strike, in
Playthings, the toy industry trade
journal. Reproduced by permission.

a military "platoon" with lieutenants and captains supervising "squads" of ten men. In addition to the company police, "cooperation among the manufacturers of dolls and stuffed toys brought about a speedy end to strikes started in the factories of the members of the Doll and Stuffed Toy Manufacturers Protective Association." After four weeks of picketing, defeated doll workers tore up their union cards and surrendered to a future of company-sanctioned unions.[17]

The doll workers, who garnered little public attention, were a minor problem for manufacturers compared with German producers, whose wares continued to appeal to American consumers. Unable to attack the producers directly, however, doll industry leaders retaliated instead. They attacked U.S. importers who checked doll industry expansion by importing foreign goods. In October of 1918, the 200 members of the newly formed Toy Manufacturers of the United States of America adopted a resolution: "[We are] shocked at the admittance of German toys into this country at this time, and mindful of the unspeakable outrages upon children perpetrated by the same bloody hands that fashioned these toys." The association, whose us-versus-them slogans pulled American producers closer together, also called upon Congress to enact legislation against the importation of German-made goods during wartime. The manufacturers' association was guided by the patriotic American Defense Committee, which sent telegrams to firms that ordered German cargo, asking them "to demonstrate your 100 percent Americanism and to show Germany that goods made by her bloody-handed baby killers will not be tolerated in America."[18]

Self-preservation, decades of chafing dependence on German doll parts, and a drive for financial success had made American doll manufacturers belligerent. Doll industry leaders aimed to damage the credibility of importers of German goods by demanding public declarations from industry veterans like Louis Wolf & Company and Strobel-Wilken Company. "Yes, I was born in Germany, but I came here when a little boy and I am as good an American as anybody," a certain Mr. Silverman responded defensively to a *New York Times* reporter. "In selling these toys—I am able to buy more Liberty bonds; $100,000 is a lot of money, and I intend to put every cent I take in by selling these German toys into more Liberty bonds." [19]

In order to damage competitors, U.S. doll industry leaders stimulated anti-German sentiments among American consumers by urging shoppers to identify composition dolls as victors in the struggle between American businessmen and their rivals in Germany. Thousands of customers closed their accounts at F. A. O. Schwarz and others ceased to patronize stores known for large inventories of German goods. On Christmas day 1917, the *New York Times* reported that "cargoes of German toys bought before the war, and recently released at Rotterdam, are not wanted here." [20]

Despite these demonstrations of solidarity, however, American producers of dolls were not confident that they had won. They feared that American consumers, given the chance, would once again buy European rather than American dolls. Capitalizing on the war climate, American manufacturers, therefore, advertised their modernized plants with patriotic imagery. They wanted the buying public to believe that the "dirty enemy" made unclean dolls in unclean plants, whereas American superiority lay in the sanitary conditions under which dolls were ostensibly manufactured in the United States. "Tell Mother," read an ad in the *St. Nicholas* children's magazine, "HORSMAN 'ART' Dolls are made in America in a big, airy, sanitary factory." [21] Advertisements of this nature probably were most successful with Americans already sensitized to the importance of cleanliness by material maternalists and other reformers.

While E. I. Horsman capitalized on progressive concerns, firms that had traded on patriotism before the war like Louis Amberg & Son had been among the first to identify themselves boldly as American in an industry long dominated by Germans. But during the war, newly established firms took advantage of this national pride by identifying themselves as American by name: the Made in America Manufacturing Company, American Toy & Doll Manufacturing Company, American Toy Manufacturing Company, and the American Toy & Novelty Company. [22] Competing firms imbued their dolls with patriotic values in order to capitalize on wartime sentiments. The Maiden Toy Company, for example, marketed a doll named "Maiden America," a pun implying that the moral

superiority of American feminine innocence derived from native manufacture.

American superiority in dolls, however, went far beyond the superficial appearance of names and wardrobes. The Ideal Company advertised
that when its composition doll was dropped eight stories, the paint was
barely scratched. Buyers demonstrated durability by jumping on or driv-
ing nails into composition dolls. "Drop [a German doll] on the floor,"
"and the head would usually go flying into a dozen parts, and legs and
arms constantly bled sawdust so profusely as to suggest the carnage of a
European battlefield." [23]

The American doll industry's anti-German sentiment did not abate
with the armistice. *Playthings,* the New-York based trade journal, reprinted newspaper reports about Germany's invisible commercial war.
Inflammatory articles with headlines like "Germany's Plot to Gas the
World Trade" painted pictures of "teutonic cunning and treachery" in the
marketplace. Because the reprinted articles never specifically mentioned
the doll industry, *Playthings* provided ridiculing cartoons of its own to
sharpen the effect (fig. 48).

Producers also fought to keep German dolls out of U.S. homes by
urging parents to buy the new American dolls as opposed to German
dolls of established reputation. Pleased by the growth of their industry
but worried that consumer purchasing would revert to prewar tastes, the
Toy Manufacturers of America mounted several nationwide marketing
campaigns "to prove to the American people [that] there is an American
toy industry." Building on already existing anti-German feeling, the Toy
Manufacturers of the USA, Inc., adopted the slogan, "American toys for
American girls and boys" and conscripted Uncle Sam to their cause. [24]

The "Great National Advertising Campaign" of 1919 was a harbinger
of marketing campaigns that would characterize the twenties. Joe L. Amberg and Bernard Fleischaker were among the doll manufacturers who
devised plans to advertise in "national publications of wide circulation
reaching parents as well as children," use local advertising through window displays, and store cards," and distribute "printed matter which will
be attached to, or packed with, every toy made by members of the association and all contributing non-members." Encouraged by the success

of this campaign, the Association launched yet another "unique selling scheme" in 1920 based on a military model—the "American-Made Toy Brigade." Toy retailers were urged to display "electros" and window cards and distribute free buttons to children in exchange for their pledge "to stick to and ask for American-made toys." In 1920, the Toy Brigade enlisted 197,000 children.[25]

Don't Let 'Em Get Away With It!

48. Cartoon by Clifford Knight, 1919. After World War I, American doll producers continued their anti-German campaign using cartoons in an effort to hold onto the consumer market they had captured during the war. Reproduced from *Playthings,* by permission.

Despite the fanfare and unaware that the German doll industry would soon be devastated, American manufacturers fought to hold the ground they gained during the war. In 1921, the Doll and Stuffed Toy Manufacturers Association appealed to Washington to protect the fledgling industry during this period of readjustment. In hearings before the tariff commission, industry leaders described the need to continue "protection from foreign competition given by war conditions." Another toy-toting delegation representing the 133 members of the Toy Manufacturers Association of the USA, Inc., appeared before the House Ways and Means Committee to argue for a higher duty on imported dolls. After weeks of hearings, the Senate Finance Committee passed the Fordney-McCumber tariff bill, which doubled the previous duty on toys to 70 percent.[26] The manufacturers were pleased, but still anxious.

Using a metaphor of confrontation other than outright war this time, American doll manufacturers took to the streets three weeks before Christmas to "picket" the importation of German-made dolls. The newly organized American Doll Manufacturers Association, which promoted the event, distorted a parental concern they then exploited. E. I. Horsman and other doll industry leaders carried banners inscribed "Avoid Childhood's Tragedy: A Broken Doll" (fig. 49). It seemed that American doll manufacturers wanted parents to believe that dangerous German dolls could leave their daughters both physically and emotionally scarred.[27]

By the early 1920s, American doll manufacturers had succeeded in subduing their work force and eliminating much of their competition, helped especially by the depression of 1921–1922. Yet the immediate postwar period ushered in a new generation of businesswomen inspired by professional opportunities, their new right to vote, a rising standard of living (despite the recent economic setback), and increased leisure. The changes in women's roles served as an impetus to these new industrial entrants. As historian Frank Stricker has pointed out, the census category of "Managers, Officials, and Proprietors" indicated real increases after 1920.[28]

This new generation of women shared features with the female doll producers who preceded them but in other ways were less likely to

49. Members of the American Doll Manufacturers Association
"demonstrated" against German dolls three weeks before
Christmas in 1921 as part of a marketing campaign designed to
alter consumer tastes. *Playthings,* December 1921, reproduced
by permission.

be either artists or do-gooders. For some, the doll industry provided an
alternative to low-paying, low-status jobs. For artist Grace Storey Putnam,
designing dolls was better than teaching, which had offered her low pay
and little else. "I'm mighty glad that I didn't go back to teaching or some
other employment when I was forced to wrest my own living from the
world," agreed dollmaker Mary McAboy. When Georgene Hendren was
diagnosed as an incurable invalid, she declared "that she would never
become financially dependent on others."[29] In order to support herself,
she designed and produced dolls' dresses from her home.

Whether married or single, women who launched businesses attempted to balance career and family responsibilities. Working at first in

the basement of her home, Jenny Graves annexed the garage and base-ment and transformed them into the shipping room, the hub of her Vogue Doll Company. Assisted by "housemaids," Mary McAboy launched her dollmaking business from her father's home. Beatrice Behrman (better known as Madame Alexander) and her three sisters sewed the dolls they sold in their father's doll hospital located in front of their family's dwelling.[30]

Instead of shipping the doll clothes she produced from her Ore-gon home, Georgene Hendren relocated her business to the East Coast, where threatened doll manufacturers refused to do business with her, preferring to hire her on consignment from the other side of the country. Within three years, the determined Hendren, who had recovered from her crippling ailment, owned and supervised the third largest doll firm, according to *Woman's Home Companion*. Similarly, other magazines also carried stories describing the proliferation of "the 'new business woman' and her radically expanding frontiers." Though unusually suc-cessful, Georgene Hendren was in other ways typical of female doll-makers who modeled themselves not after maternalistic businesswomen but after modern businessmen.[31]

In addition to businesswomen who converted households into store-rooms, many more established businesses in industrial plants. Harlem residents Victoria Ross and Evelyn Berry, proprietors of Ross & Berry, Inc., were the first African-American female large-scale manufacturers of black composition dolls. The firm's purpose was the "manufacturing, contract for, sale and purchase of toys, shirts, shirtwaists and other goods." Jessie McCutcheon Raleigh employed hundreds of people in her Chicago fac-tory. In a departure from previous methods of financing their ventures, female entrepreneurs were more likely to incorporate their businesses. Berry & Ross began with a capital stock of $10,000 (2000 shares at $5 each). Estelle Allison incorporated the Allison Novelty Company with a capital stock of $6,000 and working capital of $500 to produce her patented dolls.[32]

Many of these businesswomen were not artists, a factor which may have contributed to their imitation of a male career model. Thus female entrepreneurs were forced to depend on the designs of others, similar to the businessmen who, in the words of Beatrice Behrman, had "no talent." Mrs. Benoliel, for example, was more inspired by money than by a muse: "Both Mr. Benoliel and myself had for two or three years been dabbling around trying to invent some sort of toy that would be a big seller." "One Sunday afternoon while we were reading the comic page to our two babies of one and three years old we suddenly said simultaneously, 'why not make a Skeezix doll?' "[33]

While Mrs. Benoliel based her doll on a contemporary cartoon character, as had businessmen, other women drew upon popular political symbols for their doll designs. Caught up in the male nationalist fervor, many women created patriotic dolls. Jeanne I. Orsini, Grace Drayton, and Jessie McCutcheon Raleigh designed Uncle Sam dolls in a variety of likenesses and an Uncle Sam Jr. doll was also marketed in the "Madame Hendren" line. Designer Estelle V. Allison combined two American symbols when she created "Fan-ie Regiment," dolls whose heads and bodies were made to look like baseballs.[34]

Some women drew upon popular culture figures and others relied upon a bevy of artists for the rights to their inventions, designs, copyrights, and trademarks. In a departure from earlier practices that revealed greater familiarity with commercial production, women inventors nationwide now trademarked their dolls. More also applied for joint patents—few had done so before—in another manifestation of the ways in which women adopted modernized male business practices. Of those who applied for joint patents, roughly twenty percent were sisters and eighty percent were unrelated by birth. To promote their wares, businesswomen often joined a professional organization rather than a reform society. Some even served in an administrative capacity for organizations such as the Pacific Northwest Toy Guild similar to their male associates. "The toy trade has furnished the first woman to address the 'big chiefs' of American business," reported *Toys and Novelties* in 1920. Another trade journal noted, "The significant feature of Mrs. Delavan's appearance at Atlantic City is the victory won for the recognition of women as a vital factor in American business and industry. The invitation to speak before the Chamber of Commerce is probably the highest honor yet bestowed upon an American business woman."[35]

Corena Daugherty, three-term director of the Pacific Coast Toy Fair, was also the "editress" of the West Coast-based *Toy World* trade magazine. New trade magazines provided women with an advertising medium other than the mothers' and children's magazines their predecessors had relied upon. But as an editorial in *Toy World* pointed out, "Most publications, even in so appropriately feminine a field as that of toys and playthings, are edited and managed by men, or at least nominally so, even though a woman or several women may actually carry on much of the work." While the East Coast-based *Playthings* was dominated by a male publishing establishment and carried few articles about women, *Toy World,* under Dougherty's direction, frequently reported on the achievements of women buyers and entrepreneurs.[36]

As the *Toy World* editorial suggests, women entrepreneurs who followed the businessmen's lead were not always welcome. Women professionals in the doll industry gained a lower market share in the 1920s than the numbers suggest. Their impact on the future of the industry would be undermined during this decade by four factors: the ambivalence within the business world about career women who were ordinarily confined to job categories with less mobility, lower status, and smaller remuneration; a loss of control resulting from businesswomen delegating organization to men; marginalization of women entrepreneurs and designers; and erratic business conditions due to rapidly changing public taste to which fledgling businesses were especially vulnerable.[37]

As to the first factor, while initially praised for their success, career women in the twenties faced an increasingly hostile climate which demanded more traditional roles for women. Articles in magazines spelled out the magic formula career women needed to succeed: PERSONALITY, which stood for perseverance, earnestness, reliability, sincerity, optimism, naturalness, ability, loyalty, initiative, tidiness, and yearning. Women's magazines and other publications heralded the businesswoman but mostly those who commercialized maternal skills. To the extent that they posed a threat to the social construction of gender in the twenties, they were portrayed as undermining the stability of family life. Moreover, a bill making Mother's Day a holiday had elevated motherhood to the status of a sanctified national symbol. In the context of a newly resurgent domesticity, businesswomen, like feminists in the twenties, were viewed as both selfish and strange. One contemporary recalled that businessmen perceived businesswomen as "undainty." Some women in the doll industry adopted the professional appellation "Madame" to combat stereotypes of mannish businesswomen. The courtesy title cloaked business with continental sophistication and Victorian gentility and focused attention on "madame's" feminine role as wife and mother. Female dollmakers would present themselves to their public in advertisements as nurturing mothers amid a bevy of dolls (fig. 50).[38]

Despite the projection of maternity, the actual accommodation to a male business style often worked against businesswomen, many of whom abandoned traditional skills as they attempted to mass-produce dolls. Mary McAboy renounced the skill of apple carving learned at her mother's knee when her Skookum Indian dolls became popular.

> It was easy enough to make the dolls on a small scale, a few apples at a time. But when I started making them by the thousands, then my trouble began. Instead of drying, hundreds of dollars worth of apples rotted after they had been carved, because of the moisture in them. I tried to dry them on an oil stove. They got all smoked up and for a day my girls and I carried apples into the front yard and blew the soot from them.[39]

Because the Skookum dolls could not be made on a large scale with a pen knife, McAboy "had a die made to cut them out." McAboy also "went to the state university and to the state chemist to learn how to keep them [apples] from rotting." For some, modernizing meant using composition, by now the businessmen's most favored material. Skookum dolls made out of composition ultimately replaced early apple versions. Jessie Raleigh obtained the services of research departments at several large universities in order to make satisfactory composition. This development boded ill as businesswomen now hired men to work on aspects of doll-making with which the women were unfamiliar. In order to produce the doughy composition doll, which was heavy, businesswomen were similarly forced to rely on a largely male work force.[40]

For seasoned material maternalists like Ella Smith, modernization,

First Aid to Santa Claus

Jessie McCutcheon Raleigh, who modeled the "Good Fairy" statuette, has now turned her artistic imagination to building up the American toy industry, and is making dolls that are real personalities

50. In the 1920s, a return to more traditional gender roles led to the portrayal of Jessie McCutcheon Raleigh and other businesswomen in the doll industry as nurturing mothers. Photo courtesy of the Strong Museum, Rochester, N.Y. ©1993.

combined with a tragedy, brought failure instead of fortune. A local businessman encouraged Smith to modernize her business by moving from the wooden shop her husband had built to a plant across town, purchase modern equipment, and increase production of her Alabama Indestructible Dolls. The businessman and his partner, a local druggist who had invested in Smith's business, headed to New York City to solicit orders. According to the Roanoke *Leader,* however, the two were killed when their passenger train derailed and plunged off a trestle. Losing a law suit filed by the widows, Smith was forced to compensate them for their husbands' investments. Broke and disillusioned, she moved her molds and paints back into the old structure.[41] Unable or unwilling to produce a doll alien to her aesthetics and in so doing abandon the culture that had nurtured her business endeavor, Ella Smith closed her factory in 1925.

Dependent on businessmen for more modern skills and experience in production, some women began to reevaluate their attitudes and aspirations in the face of increasingly pervasive notions of feminine helplessness. Mary McAboy renounced her role as entrepreneur for a less stressful position as an employee at H. H. Tammen Co. "I knew so little about business that I was awfully frightened . . . My business had grown so that I was buried in details, and could not keep up with the supervision of the making of the dolls. . . I was glad to shift part of the responsibility on stronger shoulders." Overwhelmed by the success of her firm, the Live Long Toy Company, Eileen Benoliel explained that the business "had grown too large for me to handle alone."[42]

Instead of increasing their power base, many like Benoliel would narrow it. After an establishment's success had become apparent, husbands often assumed its control. When Benoliel's "business had assumed such large proportions . . . Mr. Benoliel was obliged to resign from his [insurance] position." Benoliel's husband, who drew from his experience gained while working for Sears, Roebuck, Butler Brothers, and Marshall Field, took full control of his wife's rapidly growing business. In New York City, Beatrice Behrman's husband, Philip, quit his job with a hat firm to run his wife's doll business. When Paul Averill, a "keen" New York toy buyer with his own company and connections (he was also the nephew of Averill Harriman), married Georgene Hendren, he assumed the presidency of Mme. Georgene, Inc.[43]

While businesswomen provided spouses with new routes for upward mobility, they also closed off some of their own. In the past, sisters might have divided business acumen and artistic skills between them, but in the 1920s husbands and wives ran business according to more traditional gender roles. A typical example is Philip Behrman, who took over the business end of his wife's Alexander Doll Company while she continued to design dolls. According to *Toy World,* with Mrs. Morrill's business a success, "the mother takes a much needed rest, knowing the father, now resigned from a former position to take over the business end of the firm, will handle the army of workers who are now employed in the business of the Morrill Mfr. Co." Just as in the confessions of "ex-feminists" published in magazines like *Harper's* and *Scribner's,* businesswomen in the doll industry also "turned their backs on the work place to find fulfillment at home."[44]

Whether *Toy World* described Mrs. Morrill's actual motivations and feelings or reflected the domestic ideal of the postwar period, it seems likely that businesswomen faced numerous conflicts as they attempted to combine work roles with family life. Although "to significant numbers of women, marriage and work no longer seemed like mutually exclusive alternatives," combining them remained difficult. One of Jessie McCutcheon Raleigh's sons recalled "being taken to the annual Toy Fair in New York as a small boy where mother displayed her wares along with the nation's other key toy manufacturers." Eileen Benoliel explained, "I had intended to make these dolls in my spare time at home while still taking care of my babies." The growth of her business, however, had made her plan unfeasible. Grace Storey Putnam confided, "I am a woman who wanted motherhood and art too." But juggling work and family was a difficult task for this generation of women faced with increasing household and family responsibilities.[45]

The alternative of designing dolls, while it reduced the burdens of entrepreneurship, had its own problems. The professionalization of designing provided security and status for Mary McAboy, but it left some women with no authority over their creations—as had been the case with

Rose O'Neill and her Kewpies. With little control over production, designers depended on others to transform their models into dolls. Problems emerged when women designers and the businessmen who employed them found themselves at odds over what a doll should look like and what values it should represent. New standards for dolls formulated by businessmen in the industry further undermined the artistic independence of female designers.

Borgfeldt, Fleischaker & Baum, and many others promoted infant dolls which were uniformly symmetrical, proportional, cute, and content. Although relatives of the German "character dolls," they lacked the realistic rolls of fat, uneven features, and sulky, unhappy expressions. In the context of these new doll versions, women designers found that they did not share the aesthetics of businessmen nor draw from the same parenting experiences. "Men did not seem to like it at all," wrote Grace Storey Putnam about her Bye-Lo doll (fig. 51). "They shook their heads over it," rejecting it for its "unattractive realism." It "was too like their own babies," suggested Putnam. "They do not care for their own new babies until they are old enough to smile at them." They complained that "the eyes [were] not large enough." They "failed to understand that the eyes were half closed." She preferred the doll to be "a little wobbly—as real babies are," but the manufacturers did not. She wanted the doll made out of rubber, but they preferred bisque.[46]

In the course of the decade, designers like Putnam would have difficulty holding on to what little was left of a female aesthetic, especially when Georgene Hendren would market the first modern American mama doll with little opposition from mothers. Putnam's Bye-Lo, however, was about neither the joys of marriage nor the importance of domesticity in the lives of girls. Instead, Putnam's work flowed from her experience with matrimonial failures. The Bye-Lo doll had been modeled by the recently divorced Putnam after the infant of an unmarried woman at a Salvation Army nursing hospital. "I was creating a baby" not a doll, wrote Putnam candidly.[47]

Putnam was clearly not alone, as children continued to inspire women designers as they had for generations. The *New York Times* would report that other "women sculptors design new life-like faces," and *Toys*

51. In the 1920s, Grace Storey
Putnam, creator of the Bye-Lo doll,
was the first designer to produce a
commercially successful infant doll.
Its many commercial versions,
however, would bear little
resemblance to this original
prototype shown with her.

and Novelties agreed, "It is a long, long reach from the stiff, kid-bodied, bisque-headed dolls of a few years ago to the life-like infant . . . that is one of the results accomplished by Mrs. Helen Speer, of New York." Jessie McCutcheon Raleigh modeled her bent-limb dolls after "little American children," and Jenny Graves and Beatrice Behrman's earliest dolls were modeled after their daughters.[48]

When given the chance, women customers and department store buyers offset the conservatism of businessmen, even though the control of many buyers had eroded since wartime. Businessmen declared that they "would not dream of putting such a doll on the counter" yet "it was only women who saw the real value of the baby [doll]." Women "raved over the Bye-Lo" because it affected them in personal ways. According to one female owner of a doll hospital, the Bye-Lo was "so soft and warm and lifelike in texture and coloring, that you would think that you were holding a living, breathing infant." Eager women consumers lined up outside toy stores just before Christmas 1922 in order to purchase the "Million Dollar Baby."[49]

Despite the Bye-Lo's success with women customers, all its commercial versions disappointed and disillusioned its creator. The artistic independence of designers like Putnam had been undermined as new standards for doll designs were formulated, marketed, and advertised by the male-monopolized industry, as we shall see in the next chapter. The Bye-Lo had been stripped of its "unattractively realistic" features in the doll sold by George Borgfeldt & Company. In the end, wrote Putnam, "the model had been 'softened.' Clay had been smoothed over the creases that I had so carefully molded." The construction of the neck had also been changed so that "the baby head could roll a bit . . . it was simpler for the manufacturer—and less expensive."[50]

Legal suits were yet another manifestation of increasing conflict between designers and manufacturers. Unlike Putnam, other designers became entangled in legal battles to protect their doll creations. Estelle Allison lost her case against Borgfeldt on the grounds that she had failed to submit copies of the alleged copyright infringement.

In addition to court battles, business mergers threatened the autonomy of small businesses. The Pollyanna Company took over the Rees

Davis's Doll Company, established by an actress turned entrepreneur. The Tillicum Manufacturing Company that Harriet M. Robinson established to make educational wooden dolls merged with Craigcraft in 1928. "Although Mother's big customers promised they would not desert her . . . they did," recalled Jessie McCutcheon Raleigh's son. When the firm closed its doors in 1924, it had succumbed to the pressures of a volatile market subject to powerful cultural and economic forces.[51]

Consolidating trends that had emerged between 1910 and 1920, the doll industry in the 1920s had become dominated by male manufacturers, jobbers, importers, and wholesalers. Businessmen from other industries and artisans in other trades had taken advantage of opportunities created by the defeat of the Germans, which vanquished its doll industry as surely as its armies. American men developed new materials as well as more efficient methods for making dolls which they had marketed as patriotic American products superior to those of German manufacture. Newly formed trade associations aggressively stimulated anti-German sentiments for marketing purposes. Trade associations worked closely with trade journals, retailers, and wholesalers to expand the toy industry within its own model and extend its influence.

Between 1919 and 1929 women doll designers faced accommodating this firmly entrenched male industry at the cost of their fundamental beliefs. Although some integrated traditional female patterns along with more assertive male behavior, others rejected the outdated separate spheres model and mimicked businessmen instead. They hoped that these patterns would lead to success, but such was often not the case. Despite the fact that women followed male businessmen's leads by producing composition dolls, establishing networks with colleagues of the same sex, modernizing their plants, relying on the expertise of spouses, and capitalizing and incorporating their businesses, by the end of the 1920s many women dollmakers were disillusioned. The emergence of a new domestic ideology placed working women in the doll industry in despair. A decade later, a reporter for the *Independent Woman,* a magazine published by the National Federation of Business and Professional Women's Clubs, would note that "men chiefly are in charge of this vast industry."[52]

CHAPTER SEVEN

Children's Day:
Constructing a Consumer
Culture for Girls,
1900–1930

In 1913 an estimated 5,000 girls jammed the roof garden "decorated like a fairy park" to attend a dolls' tea party at a California department store. One year earlier on the other side of the country, another department store had invited 2,500 girls between the ages of four and twelve to a dolls' tea. "In the tearoom there are groups of dolls everywhere and the little ones come out all excited about the kind they want Santa to bring them." After the party, the children, who wore numbered tags, were picked up by their parents who held the duplicate ticket. With pre-war marketing spectacles like these—which commodi-fied both parties and players—businessmen rehearsed the consumer culture they would generate in the post-war years.[1] Commercial holidays like Children's Day of the late twenties would attempt to extend the reach of American business-men into the purse of every American mother and into the heart of every American daughter.

How had girls raised between 1900 and 1920 responded to elabo-rate marketing events, tantalizing shop windows, and illustrated trade catalogues that advertised active New Kid dolls along with others? How had doll play changed since the previous century and what meaning did it have for girls? Although many waited for repaired or newly dressed Christmas dolls, others plied the commercial market for the best doll deals they could find. Yet, not all girls' lives revolved around playing with dolls or shopping for them. Memoirs, autobiographies, contempo-rary studies, reformers' reports, magazine exposés, and oral histories reveal the many changes despite obvious continuities with past genera-tions. Most important, by the early twentieth century, dolls would cease to be the objects of resentment and resistance manifested in previous generations. Those doll players who accommodated themselves to the new domestic ideal were more likely to be nurturing than nasty.

Why? Unlike Victorian girls, the majority of girls from coast to coast were less restricted in their play and enjoyed broadened social re-strictions. Bicycles and movies transported the energetic daughters of farmers, commuters, and laborers beyond the safety of the dollhouse hearth. During the first two decades of the century, the changes in gen-der socialization explored by some adult New Women permeated the younger generation of girls, who were, in fact, the New Kids that the in-dustry portrayed as dolls. Ironically, real New Kids were not so interested in playing with New Kid dolls.

That many girls preferred other activities to "playing house" posed a threat to the doll industry's market and profits. Thus, the industry reacted vigorously to these developments, marketing an idealized femininity through dolls that were more sweet than sassy. Condescending pam-phlets printed by one doll manufacturer, for example, instructed mothers in how to use dolls to teach etiquette to their young daughters. During this "age of play," manufacturers—in cooperation with retailers who re-sponded to financial incentives—strove to widen the consumer market through Children's Day, the commercial holiday they created. Although doll manufacturers expanded the consumer market, they also redefined play more narrowly for this generation of girls. By selling impossibly "perfect" baby dolls that idealized motherhood and homemaking and flirtatious dolls that modeled husband-getting, businessmen hoped to re-store traditional gender roles for American girls.

"I remember I got a note from Santa Claus that they were going to take Bubbles," recalled one girl about the doll her aunts had given her shortly after 1900. "I must have carried Bubbles by the feet; I was short and her head was badly damaged. Santa Claus was going to fix her. They took her. I had a little playroom off the dining room and I can remember being very lonely without Bubbles." Often at Christmas, old and damaged dolls like this girl's were repaired and poorly attired ones newly outfitted. The dolls' absence meant a new wardrobe for some girls: "Every Christmas [my dolls] vanished because Santa Claus took them and made new out-fits for them." Another doll got new eyes and a new wig every Christmas until it finally broke. "I had a funeral for her in the back yard with a cold cream jar for a headstone. And it broke my heart."[2]

This doll was undoubtedly replaced by a new one the following Christmas. Dolls with china heads and cloth bodies were often found on the morning of December 25 sticking out of the tops of stockings, tokens of affection from parents, grandmothers, aunts, or uncles. One girl's uncle gave her a doll when she was one year old. A great-uncle who won a doll at an office raffle saved it for his niece instead of exchanging it for some-thing for himself.[3]

Unlike those before them, however, many girls born in the prewar years were not obliged to wait until Christmas to have their wishes granted. Instead of having to endear themselves to adults, many used their own money to buy dolls of their own choosing. "The money came from windfalls from visiting relatives," one woman recalled, "or through the proceeds from that budding new feminine profession, baby-sitting and baby-walking. Fresh air was a new vogue for infants and little girls pushed carriages for busy mothers who had no other child to saddle with the job. The pay wasn't good but it was steady work a good many months of the year."[4]

According to Catherine Brody, who tended children after school along with other girls on her Manhattan block, "the babies came in baby carriages. We parked the carriages, generally at the edge of the sidewalk and placed kitchen chairs or footstools together." In addition to baby-sitting, girls also earned money by running errands for mothers and neighborhood wives. Nearly one-fifth of the middle-class girls in California earned money in this manner, according to one 1897 study. Little girls ran most errands "because little boys just were not around when they were needed." Fortunately for girls, while running errands they could survey stores' current doll stock and select dolls "for which they were saving."[5]

Although the wages earned from running errands, baby-sitting, or other jobs were usually small, they must have seemed substantial to the young workers. "Francie had a nickel. Francie had power," noted Betty Smith about the eleven-year old heroine in her autobiographical novel *A Tree Grows in Brooklyn*. "The first year we were turned loose at the bazaar to do our own shopping. . . I went fiercely alone, my small wash-leather change purse clenched in my hand," recalled Ethel Spencer of her Pittsburgh childhood. Although some girls were undoubtedly spendthrifts, others who shopped sought the best bargains. One girl matched wits with local shopkeepers: "It was never considered good purchasing strategy to let the storekeeper know how much money you could or would spend because your hands were then kept off the 19-cent or 29-cent dolls if you only had a dime."[6]

Husbands and wives ran some toy stores, yet especially in small towns women proprietors made up a healthy proportion of toy dealers. A great many wholesale and retail toy and novelty establishments employed women and girls because the toy industry considered the required effort:

light enough for women whose physiques would not be strong enough to stand the strain of conducting a store of some other kind. In fact, the work in the store is mild and the articles for sale are not heavy or of great bulk. Women have a knack of keeping toys and novelties in order-and holding the trade of women and children especially . . . There is that mysterious something about a toy and novelty shop which makes women employees seem in the right place as are girls behind the ribbon counters.[7]

Despite the expectations of the industry, however, penny candy stores, the new five-and-dimes, and other shops operated by widows, spinsters, or unmarried heads of households had little patience for "small buyers." One girl recalled that "these were usually the last ports of call." Moreover, they would "go on strike against a store with no compunction whatever" if a girl from a neighboring town appeared with a doll purchased for less than the price on the local market.[8]

These marketwise shoppers utilized discriminating consumer strategies. "The first time I saw the brown-eyed girl doll," one woman recalled, "she stood on a display stand with dozens of other dolls. I circled the table several times examining all the dolls." Sometimes choosing the right doll required the help of experts, but rather than shopkeepers, sales clerks, or mothers, trustworthy friends assisted young shoppers. "The purchaser usually brought along a couple of her friends or a visiting child to make sure she did not get a doll with crossed eyes, a thin wig, or, heaven forbid, a smaller size than could be found in another store or in another town." The recent widespread availability of bicycles enabled girls to save time and have fun while they canvassed nearby stores. When the girls descended on dry goods or hardware stores, "the entire contents of the box or boxes [of dolls] had to be examined." After her new doll purchase, one girl who carefully budgeted her funds spent the remaining 15 cents on a bag of peanuts for a Saturday afternoon movie. "We tucked the brown paper bag which contained our prize [the doll] under the rubber of a bloomer leg so that our hands were free to crack peanuts or clap."[9]

Thus not all little girls spent "all their time with dolls, embroidery, and the applied arts." In South Carolina in 1900, playing with dolls narrowly edged out jumping rope as girls' favorite activity (28.7 to 21.6 percent). Girls enjoyed a variety of outdoor games, recalling that friends "walked fences, flew kites, [and] belly bumpered down hills on our own sleds." One girl raised in Rochester, New York, caught fireflies with her cousins, and other girls wandered through woods, romped through fields, and waded through streams instead of playing with dolls.[10]

Although G. Stanley Hall's 1896 study of girls revealed how widespread doll play had been, it decreased in the two decades thereafter. Studies conducted between 1898 and the mid-1920s showed that the domain of girls had grown considerably larger. One 1918 survey of girls reported that dolls had, in fact, dropped to eighth place. Calling for a balanced adult view of what constituted appropriate play for girls, purported experts were not at all opposed to girls' outdoor recreation, which they believed to provide a salutary influence in adulthood. Popular magazines and professional journals regularly featured articles describing the benefits as well as warning of the dangers of recreation to girls and to society.[11]

Middle-class girls usually played with sisters, neighbors, and school friends—often boys—whom they raced on bicycles or on ice skates. "My sister that raised me had five boys and then a girl at the end [so] I didn't have girls to play with," recalled R. Brown, who became a "tomboy" instead. "A girl should be a tomboy during the tomboy age and the more of a tomboy she is the better," wrote playground advocate Joseph Lee. Janet Gillespie recounted throwing cherry tomatoes at her brother Aldie in their aunt's garden one Sunday afternoon before tea: "We were happy, intoxicated by the obvious havoc we were causing. I knew perfectly well we were being naughty but I also knew with calm certainty that we were naughty only in grownup terms. Since all the really interesting and original things we did were labeled 'naughty' by the adult world, I didn't mind being naughty at all. I liked it and so did Aldie. We were not interested in goodness; it was too boring."[12] Tomboyism was tolerated as long as feminine decorum was not sacrificed in the end. "To the coyness of a kitten, let a girl add the friskiness of a colt," urged a Mrs. Roessing writing in the *Pittsburgh Playground Journal.*[13]

Most girls still wore dresses that restricted them in one way or another, but new clothing fashions enabled many to pursue action and adventure with fewer recriminations about soiling or tearing their garments. "Healthy girls like healthy boys are rough on clothes," read an advertisement for overalls designed to be worn over dresses. Girls whose bloomers matched their dresses could even borrow boy's bikes without worrying about being immodest. Although many girls hated the new bloomer style, they were also aware that it contributed to a "new liberty."[14]

"Millions of us lived in small towns where we . . . had complete freedom of movement on foot, roller skates, [and] bicycles," recalled one woman about her girlhood. Susanna Dakin remembered spending her afternoons riding bicycles with her friends, which seems to have been typical at the time, for at least one contemporary survey reported that dolls could hardly compete with bicycles' popularity. One girl born shortly after the turn of the century recalled going to a toy store where there were "dolls in starched organdy dresses standing in cardboard boxes" in addition to the fire engines and shiny tricycles she rode down the cluttered store aisles. Another girl liked her baby doll but loved her tricycle more. In the absence of wagons, doll carriages were put to other uses. One girl born in 1905 enjoyed pushing her sister in her doll's carriage despite her mother's repeated warnings not to ride too fast.[15]

To some extent girls raised in the first two decades of the new century played with dolls less often than in previous decades because of the wider variety of toys available to them. The worries of contemporaries were justified when many girls preferred their stuffed animals to more gender-appropriate toys. In 1908 one author lamented, "The dear little girls who have always cried for dolls at Christmas, are this year crying for Teddy Bears, and dolls are left on the shelves to cry the paint off their pretty cheeks because of the neglect." Instead of taking her dolls for a stroll in the park, one girl took her menagerie of stuffed animals to the movies. Girls "loved" their teddy bears.[16]

At the turn of the century, girls whose families were not of the middle class also played in less gender-appropriate ways, but this was not necessarily because they had *more* toys. Nearly half of the recently arrived immigrants from eastern and southern Europe were too poor even to maintain minimum standards of health, let alone spend money for toys. One woman recalled never having received "a lot of presents because we . . . didn't have the money." In New York City, the average working-class family in the early twentieth century earned between $600 and $700 a year. "I can't remember any toys in those days," recalled Ester Cohn. "Practically none of the kids at that time . . . had dolls." Kate Simon, the

52. Immigrant working-class children around the turn of the
century were unlikely purchasers of dolls whether displayed in
enticing department store windows or in illustrated mail-order
catalogues. Photo courtesy of the Library of Congress.

daughter of poor Polish-Jewish immigrants, could only window-shop for
the dolls she saw along Third Avenue (fig. 52). One girl who grew up
in an immigrant neighborhood in Brooklyn recalled that in her family,
"there was just one person earning and it had to go a long way when
you had seven children." "Did you have any dolls?" an interviewer asked
Ethel Merchey, an immigrant from Russia. "Never," she replied.[17]

Working-class girls in the early years of the twentieth century were
less likely to "play" house than to run it. "I had to do a lot of chores 'cause
I was the oldest," recalled Ethel Merchey. "I would do the washing, iron-
ing, cooking, baking." Immigrant men who boarded with other families
often added to the burden of young girls who assisted their mothers with
routine shopping, cooking, and cleaning. As in many immigrant families, one girl recalled that "my mother never worked" outside the home,
being far too busy cooking and cleaning. In Anzia Yezierska's autobio-

graphical novel about immigrant family life on the Lower East Side, ten-year-old Sara peddled herring in order to help make ends meet. Other girls snipped threads on the Campbell Kid doll clothes that they helped their mothers sew.[18]

Although urban reformers like photojournalist Lewis Hine, who presented Campbell Kid child laborers as thoroughly deprived of all sanguine opportunities, even girls who regularly contributed to the family economy spent much time outdoors. "Little Mothers" who cared for younger siblings may have spent more time sitting on stoops than bending over stoves. Because small tenement dwellings were crowded and cramped, girls often "played outside with all the rest of the children." Even in New York City, Elizabeth Stern and Kate Simon recalled taking babies outside for "fresh air." "Sometimes I go to play a little while at night with the other children," reported an eleven-year-old girl, "but I must mind [my brother] Danny there."[19]

Fortunately, girls entrusted with responsibility for younger siblings usually joined other children with similar charges. Girls from families with fewer or older siblings, or those with greater resources, however, could spend more of their time playing with the neighborhood girls. The working-class daughter of an Italian family recalled being "always out," and because her older sister helped out at home, she was able to go skating and play jacks and other games with her friends. Similarly, Ester Cohn was able to play with her friends and attend the school, library, and exhibitions of the Educational Alliance in New York City.[20]

In cities, girls also went to inexpensive neighborhood theaters to see movies with "forbidden subjects" which were popular with the working-class. While vice commissions and the Society for the Prevention of Cruelty to Children feared that girls' innocence would be compromised by sexually aggressive boys in the "house of dreams," girls nevertheless frequented turn-of-the-century nickelodeons in record numbers. At the age of three or four, one girl who lived in a downtown neighborhood often went to the local movie theater. "I'd watch the old pictures and when it was all finished, I turned around and go home which was right next door." Most girls had less spare change than their brothers who worked the "street trades" as "newsies," although according to a member of the National Child Labor Committee, "It is so easy for a girl, when sent to the corner grocery for 15 cents worth of coal oil, to get a dime's worth and save a nickel for the show."[21]

By the 1920s, American businessmen who had promoted an active girlhood in the New Kid dolls they marketed felt uneasy about the future of their own industry. If "tomboyism" had been quietly tolerated by parents of preadolescent girls, to businessmen it represented a loss of profits.[22] Thus, whether through mail-order catalogues or in toy departments, doll retailers, wholesalers, and manufacturers would spend the decade devising new ways to convince mothers and daughters to buy dolls, at higher prices, in greater quantities, and more than once a year. Like other entrepreneurs after the war, doll producers were eager to exploit the new American predilection for play and to direct it to their product line.

If American mothers and their daughters thought that they were making independent decisions about which doll to buy at what price, for whom, and when, they were wrong. Relying on studies of consumer spending, retailers found that women purchased "dolls which cost $5 for their children, while for neighbor's children they spent between $1 and $2.50." Displaying the expensive dolls together with the lower priced doll will in case after case "influence customers to purchase higher priced dolls than they had originally intended to purchase."[23]

Although most retailers appealed to mothers, some department stores tried to attract fathers through aggressive merchandising. A father, unlikely to browse in the toy department, was more likely to purchase a doll strategically placed in the men's department to catch his eye. Retailers were still less interested in making fathers steady purchasers of dolls, as they knew that most dolls were bought by women. One store buyer told a *New York Times* reporter in 1920 that "his wife may not be a customer of the store, but if father's toy is approved, she may start to investigate other purchasing opportunities which the establishment offers."[24]

Retailers relied on a well-trained sales force to attract and advise customers. Male and female salespeople were taught to play to their gender strengths. Salesmen were instructed to cultivate and exhibit "masculine" qualities and to impress their female customers with their expertise. "Being men we think like men, act like men, buy like men and try to sell [to] women as though we were trying to sell men," explained one toy buyer. Salesmen were encouraged to visit doll factories where they could pick up "illuminative explanations, supplemented by pertinent phrases." Nonetheless, in general, doll departments were a female world of saleswomen selling female dolls to mothers and daughters. Saleswomen were hired to use their maternal qualities to sell dolls, according to a survey of saleswomen at leading department stores in Brooklyn and Manhattan. In addition to cultivating their nurturing qualities, saleswomen were encouraged to develop other "feminine" attributes like patience, attentiveness, and sensitivity. At Best & Company, older female assistant buyers or an older, more experienced saleswoman helped new and younger saleswomen get acquainted with doll stock. Katherine Fleischman was not only the assistant toy buyer but the "doll expert" at Gimbel Brothers.[25]

Retailers depended upon adults to provide consumers with direction, yet *Playthings,* the trade journal of the toy industry, encouraged hiring children as "child promoters" as well. Girls were offered one or two percent of the total sales made to customers sent to the store by them. To girls in need of ways to earn money, this opportunity had obvious appeal. Child sales promoters were probably expected to badger family, friends, relatives, and neighbors into making purchases and provide efficient word-of-mouth advertising to audiences missed by traditional means.[26]

In addition to the retailers, American manufacturers appealed directly to consumers using new methods, images, and advertising copy. Tailoring publicity was essential: "Effanbee Campaign Gets Sales by Helping Parents Buy Toys," reported *Printers Inc.* "While the language appeals definitely to parents, for whom, of course, it is written primarily, it has the simpler appeal to the child which arouses its interest." Publications like *Advertising to Women* (1928) suggested that because women made the vast majority of purchases, advertising should be written in a language they could understand. Utilizing the burgeoning advertising industry of the 1920s, leading American manufacturers like Fleischaker & Baum advertised dolls in popular women's magazines like *Children, Ladies' Home*

Journal, Child Life, and *Good Housekeeping,* as well as in children's publications like *John Martin's Book* and *St. Nicholas.* In its ads for Vanta Baby, Amberg hoped to reach 17,000 women by advertising through "national mediums." In addition to the middle-class urban market, because fifty percent of all dolls were sold in towns of 2,500 or fewer inhabitants, American doll manufacturers appealed to girls whose families lived in rural communities through advertisements in magazines like *Farm Life.* [27]

Movies also played a role in this strategy, and dolls even made cameo appearances in *Jane Goes A-Wooing* and Cecil B. de Mille's *We Can't Have Everything.* "These pictures are seen by millions of youngsters who are sure to want the kind of toys the Little Folks in the movies have, and by millions of mothers who resolve to buy the toys they see on the screen. That should be a sufficient hint to manufacturers of toys to see to it that the motion picture producers are kept fully supplied with the latest novelties." Kate Simon recalled seeing movies in which "mothers in crisp dresses stroked their children's heads tenderly as they presented them with the big ringletted doll." [28]

Wholesalers similarly stepped up their marketing efforts by producing richly illustrated mail-order catalogues with expanded "Doll Departments." Butler Brothers, for example, steadily increased the number of catalogue pages devoted to dolls from just under two in 1889 to twelve by 1928. Advertisements in the Sears, Roebuck catalogue appealed directly to young female customers: "Girls: Did you ever imagine such lovely dolls for such small prices?" The entire process was bewildering to at least one girl, who thought that "Mr. Searsanroebuck lived in Chicago in a big red brick house (the picture was in the catalogue) full of dolls, gingham, hats, corsets, shoes, horse collars, and kitchen cabinets." [29]

The throngs of children who crowded toy department aisles by the mid-1920s were a testament to the success of those who had earnestly believed that they had only to "bring the children into the store and the parents will follow." Although they flocked to toy counters, children and their mothers too often steered clear of cash registers. Studies of parents' buying habits suggested that "parents are usually lookers instead of buyers when they have little Mary or Little John in tow." While one store found that it paid "to keep children out of toy section," something had to be done to encourage mothers to open their purses.[30]

To this end, the Better Play for Childhood League was formed late in 1926, the brainchild of one doll industry leader who gathered together buyers, manufacturers, and leading New York department store owners. To "advertise" the new organization, notices of the league's formation had been sent to the *New York Times* and 900 other newspapers across the country. Although the league's philanthropic impulse was emphasized by the presence of prominent social service leaders on the board of directors, the venture was neither conceived nor initiated by social reformers. The ostensible purpose of the league was "to stimulate normal play" and emphasize the "right kind of play for all children." These aims were to be achieved through the promotion of Children's Day, a national holiday to be celebrated on the third Saturday of June, after children had been dismissed from school and "turned more or less on their own resources for two or three months." The month of June, the manufacturers argued, was a propitious time of the year for parents to display their affection and reward their children's school achievements with gifts. Although a cautious representative of Marshall Field reminded the industry, "we must be careful that the public does not view the day as only a commercial expedient to sell toys," Children's Day fell exactly halfway between the Christmas shopping seasons and during the slow summer months.[31]

Although store merchants often created holidays "to justify their right to exist and to command large markets," the idea of a special day for children was not a new one, and had been promoted since the Progressive Era with varying degrees of enthusiasm by Protestant church leaders concerned about Sunday School attendance. In the early twenties a coalition of social reformers, labor unions, and manufacturers' trade associations had labored in behalf of America's 35 million children. Although President Calvin Coolidge endorsed Child Health Day, as did twenty organizations from the General Federation of Women's Clubs to the Milk Producers' Association, it was not proclaimed a national holiday until the early twenties.[32]

Whereas Child Health Day focused on health, hygiene, and education,

Children's Day centered on play. Promoters called special attention to the dangers children faced at play on city streets, after school, and during summer recess. Children's Day borrowed a theme from the more focused "No Accident Day" declared in New York City the year before honoring "the memory of 7,000 boys and girls killed in traffic accidents." Children's Day promoters' appreciation of the streets' dangers, which they shared with social reformers, was to be one variable of the toy industry's formula for its own health. "Most child accidents took place between 4 and 5 p.m. (5 p.m. was the deadliest hour), on nonschool days, and during summer months, when children played on the streets with minimum adult supervision." Children in New York and other major cities had shown an overwhelming preference for city streets over playgrounds despite adults' partiality to enclosed play spaces. Only four percent of all city children used even the few playgrounds that were available as opposed to 96 percent who played in the streets.[33]

Fast-moving automobiles were seen as the "menace," according to James V. Mulholland, supervisor of public recreation for New York City and an active Children's Day supporter who had been converted by toy industry leaders.[34] Approaching horse-cars had given ample warning to pedestrians and playing children, but automobiles and trolley cars did not. Furthermore, old streets were in the process of renovation and new ones were being built to connect city and state roads with a national highway bearing denser traffic. Over the next ten years alone, the number of registered drivers would soar from 8 million to 23 million.

Children's Day supporters and many others believed that irresponsible mothers had failed to provide adequately for their children. The Childhood League took on the task of teaching parents how to raise their children by providing them with advice in order to counteract the negative effects of family erosion, parental indifference, and specifically maternal negligence. "The matter of directing the play instincts of their children rests upon the shoulders of parents," wrote Dr. Selina Caldor, psychologist at the Childhood League. Although praised for the "two washes in the morning," American women were also criticized for the "bridge party at night," and for flirting with the latest recreational fads and fancies. But the responsibility for insuring that their children did not "gang around with the wrong companions" rested ultimately with mothers. They were chastised to forego golf and bridge and to limit public service club meetings. Mothers, who were seen as the single most important person in a child's life, were exhorted by experts to get involved with child study groups, school activities, and playground supervision and to transport their children to and from extracurricular lessons in the family car. Many took up the challenge, as did mothers in the typical American community of Muncie, Indiana. Yet experts argued that maternal neglect was pervasive across the country and its consequences profound. In 1922, the *Woman's Home Companion* entitled an article "Are You a 100% Mother?" Ida Cash, a New York City probation officer and *Playthings* contributor, also reproached inattentive middle-class mothers for their negligence. In their pursuit of selfish recreations, mothers had failed to provide their children with both a proper play environment as well as the "right tools" for childhood.[35]

> Join in the game and shout "Hurray"
> The play's the thing for Children's Day.
> Your little girl needs you, your home, your care
> Your tenderness and that great treasure rare
> Your understanding heart. And when you feel
> That you have given her a splendid deal
> In house and ground and comforts that you find
> With dollar bills, turn over in your mind
> Her dolly's tea-party. Did you attend?
> Were you too busy to play "Let's pretend?"[36]

The solution to maternal guilt the industry induced was safe, wholesome play—with dolls, naturally. But Children's Day merrymaking was not to obscure the fact that this holiday had "deep significance," as did Mother's Day and Father's Day.[37]

The success of Children's Day depended on its promotional committee, which included some of the doll industry's leaders and was funded by toy merchants and manufacturers. In its trade literature, the American Doll Manufacturers Association's advertising committee unabashedly claimed credit for "the entire campaign" they also financed. The committee, which sent articles to hundreds of newspapers nationwide, was chaired by B. F. Fleischaker and included I. E. Bernhard (both principals in Effanbee) and R. A. Hopf of Averill. Newspaper editors, school superintendents, playground supervisors, and other officials in more than 1,500 cities throughout the country received information about Children's Day from the committee. In 1927, more than 500 advertisements were placed in newspapers from coast to coast by cooperating stores that pooled resources and split the costs. Forty-four newspapers published Children's Day sections, and Marshall Field was among the department stores that printed Children's Day inserts in summer catalogues.[38]

A *Playthings* poster symbolized the importance of appropriate toys and environment for children (fig. 53). The poster depicted a pre-industrial, one-room school house perched on a grass-covered hill— the pernicious influences of modern cities were noticeably absent. "Too many parents fail to realize that character is built outside the school house when the child is free from the restraint of the classroom," wrote Dorothy Lewis, president of the Childhood League.[39] At the base of the slope in the poster, two groups of children, one with toys and one without, foreshadow possible scenarios for youngsters during summer recess. Rather than cooperating or competing, children without playthings are mischievous and belligerent, pulling hair and punching one another. Another group of children, clearly influenced by the bed of flowers and gender-appropriate toys, are delighted to play and were intended to be delightful to watch. Babies and baby dolls provide girls with maternal contentment and baseball bats give boys confidence.

The poster was made available to local merchants by the doll manufacturers association, and mayors were urged to recognize officially the sample Children's Day proclamations sent to them. In 1928, 71 mayors declared war on the "jazzization" of American society, according to *Playthings*. New York governor Al Smith became an enthusiastic supporter of Children's Day. Reflecting upon his immigrant background, Smith wrote in a letter to the children of the city of New York that, "when I was a child parks were a long way from my home and we could only go on rare occasions . . . I hope that during this vacation . . . every child will make a new friend, read a good book, attend the neighborhood playground, and

53. This Children's Day poster
depicted the importance of gender-
appropriate toys. Reproduced from
Playthings, by permission.

take a long walk." Unfortunately for the holiday's promoters, he made no mention of buying a new toy.[40]

Children's Day consisted of contests and competitions to demonstrate traditional gender roles. In 1928, all Manhattan playgrounds held Children's Day contests, as did 1,000 playgrounds in 167 cities. For boys, boat races and other events brought them as close to nature as was possible in an urban environment. The Toy Manufacturers Association provided toy prizes for playground competitions and the Doll Manufacturers Association awarded trophies.[41]

Special activities for girls consisted of doll carriage contests, doll competitions, and doll parades (fig. 54). Although doll parades were not a Children's Day innovation, they were nonetheless a relatively recent phenomenon. A 1922 contest in New Bedford, Massachusetts, drew 500 young contestants. One hundred and fifty girls pushing doll carriages were given the right of way over street traffic in one doll parade. While boys received trophies, girl winners were awarded points toward a regional playground banner. For girls in Louisiana, the main event of Children's Day was a doll contest and doll carriage competition for the "pretti-

54. Although doll contests were more typical, girls dressed like dolls also competed for prize cups awarded by the American Doll Manufacturers' Association on Children's Day. This doll buggy parade took place in Evanston, Ill., in 1927. Reproduced from *Playthings,* by permission.

est, funniest, oldest and newest doll." Naturally, "the last feature meant a run on doll[s] . . . prior to the parade."[42]

Merchants were encouraged to make use of an Association publication, *American Dolls—How to Show and Sell Them,* which emphasized "general" and thematic window displays. Retailers and dealers all over the country participated in the contest, following the rules of the window dressing competitions established by the American Doll Manufacturing Association to motivate retailers. Editors from trade magazines specializing in display techniques judged the results. In keeping with the excess of the times, winners received cash awards in gold.[43]

Award-winning Children's Day windows cloaked urban reality with pastoral beauty and reinforced traditional views of femininity and family. Merchants' displays with rural imagery stood in stark contrast to the experience of most American children. One department store won a Children's Day prize for its window display of dolls sitting in a grassy field beneath an arched hedge. In addition to closeness to nature, displays also evoked girls' traditional future roles as wives and mothers. Bride dolls with bouquets were displayed in outdoor wedding party scenes, sprinkled with apple blossoms strewn by dolls dressed as flower girls. Bridesmaid dolls wore large flowered hats. In case the point was lost on mothers who were preoccupied by their bridge clubs, such scenes often included conspicuous reminders: "BUY HER A DOLL."[44]

American doll manufacturers presented themselves to mothers as members of the growing number of "experts" on child care and female socialization. By sending in a coupon from Fleischaker & Baum ads in *Ladies' Home Journal,* mothers could receive a 16-page instructional booklet entitled *How to Select the Proper Doll to Suit your Child's Age* that showed how dolls might assist the necessary task of teaching good manners and eliminating bad habits. Mothers were informed through pamphlets that dolls could impart lasting lessons in hygiene and feminine etiquette to young daughters. Doll companies in the 1920s further aimed to make sophisticated ladies out of unsocialized girls. While many adolescents and adult women donned shift dresses, bobbed their hair, and assumed a more boyish appearance, girls were instructed in the essentials of more traditional femininity. These dolls taught skills useful to the duties of modern motherhood and to the conduct of an American middle-class life. Fleischaker & Baum enclosed with each doll purchased a pamphlet entitled *How to Play with a Doll* that provided "scientific" advice to the little girl. The booklet instructed the younger player "to name her doll, teach her to dance, wash her face, put her to sleep, make her hats and dresses and give her parties."[45]

In addition to learning etiquette and child care from playing with dolls, girls were taught that they served important emotional functions in the modern home. Effanbee dolls, manufactured by Children's Day promoters Fleischaker & Baum, taught girls to love their dolls "with the golden hearts." Whereas New Kid dolls had conveyed intelligence and insight, Effanbee dolls elicited love and affection. For six cents and a coupon, a little girl could purchase a heart pendant to match the one her doll wore. Infant dolls were marketed to inspire affection as well as a specifically "maternal instinct" (fig. 55). The Ideal Toy Company advertised "Hush-a-Bye Baby . . . on the lips and in the hearts of America's little mothers." A psychologist suggested that doll play would nurture the maternal instinct in young girls and prevent companionate marriages and "one-child mothers."[46]

Long- and slender-legged girl dolls with typical American names such as Sally or Patsy were advertised with stereotyped feminine identities, as was Vanity Flossy. The head of temperamental Soozie Smiles, for example, could swivel to reveal a pouting face. When the anxious prewar Baby Grumpy dolls were reissued in the late twenties as pouting Grumpykins, only the female versions dressed in frills and furbelows were manufactured. This doll, proclaimed an Effanbee advertisement, was "especially appropriate for Children's Day." While a majority of dolls encouraged girls to imagine themselves to be mothers, other dolls, like Flossie Flirt, taught girls how to make themselves attractive to boys. The ArranBee Doll Company advertised its doll as a coquette: "She flirts! Her head moves from side to side when she walks."[47] While New Kid dolls had been marketed as siblings, Skippy was introduced as Patsy's boyfriend, Jimmy as Dimmy's boyfriend.

Dolls in the twenties made girls into little mothers and they now made boys into real men. While boys were now hardly targeted as a consumer

55. In a departure from the turn-of-the-century New Kid dolls,
nearly all manufacturers in the 1920s marketed their infant and
Ma-Ma dolls to emphasize domesticity, maternity, and femininity,
as in this Sears, Roebuck catalogue page from 1924.

market, they could impress their imaginary playmates with their masculine prowess by bossing their dolls around if they so chose. In the twenties, bad boys—not merely the insouciant New Kid—had become fashionable once again. For example, it was Skippy (Patsy's boyfriend) who was described as "mischievous" in advertisements (fig. 56).

Rather than Skippy, however, it was Peter Pan who came to symbolize the values that Children's Day promoted. When the Childhood League designated Peter Pan the "patron saint" of Children's Day, they could not have made a better choice; Peter Pan represented the spirit of play, valued by children and adults alike, like the Kewpies. He immortalized childhood as "the boy who would never grow up." "I'm youth, I'm joy," said Peter when asked who and what he was. This "Playfellow of Children's Day" remained suspended in time, never outgrowing his need for play. To toy entrepreneurs, this perpetual child was the industry's dream. The 1924 Paramount movie *Peter Pan,* based on J. M. Barrie's story, was shown throughout the country on Children's Day. One firm in Des Moines, Iowa, rented the local movie theater for more than 100 children to see it. At the Boston Store in Chicago, a saleswoman dressed as Peter Pan entertained young children. In Sioux City, Iowa, the movie was shown free to 2,000 children. Movie stills decorated the pages of *Playthings* intended to "show toymen what Peter Pan should wear."[48]

Peter Pan was also a critic of contemporary self-absorbed mothers whom he regarded as "overrated persons." The charming, though "cocky" Peter Pan and his band of motherless "lost boys," represented a romanticized and sanitized version of the prewar street urchin or postwar juvenile delinquent who concerned social reformers and urban professionals. Despite the indictment of mothers, "the spirit of Peter Pan crowds out the demons of worry and trouble in us, and we become again, children with our children," wrote a psychologist for the Childhood League.[49]

Peter Pan's appeal was virtually universal among various subcultures, each of whom found meaning in his multivalent messages. The androgynous Peter Pan appealed to boys and girls—he was a young boy acted by a young woman. "Any store could arrange to have one of the sales girls or a bright boy dressed in the costume of Peter Pan." Several stores planned to hold contests for Children's Day in 1928 to crown "Peter as King and

And Now "Patsy" Has a Boy Friend

The Famous Mischievous

SKIPPY !

Millions of children and parents follow with delight the antics and adventures of Skippy in the leading newspapers and magazines of the country. This perfect doll reproduction of Skippy will make an instant appeal to them. He will equal Patsy's popularity.

We have secured the exclusive rights for doll reproduction of Skippy from his creator, Percy Crosby.

FLEISCHAKER & BAUM

Originators of Doll Hits and Makers of Quality Dolls

Office and Factory: 45 Greene Street, New York

Salesrooms: 45 East 17th Street, New York

"OF COURSE, IT'S AN EFFANBEE DOLL"

56. Boyfriend and girlfriend doll couples replaced sibling dolls of the Progressive Era. Whereas female dolls transformed girls into cultivated young ladies, mischievous dolls like Skippy made it clear that trouble-making was now reserved for boys. Advertisement, 1929, reproduced from *Playthings,* by permission.

the winning girl as 'Pan,' Queen of Children's Day." [50] Wendy, on the other hand, made a more symbolic appearance representing motherhood and domesticity to the "lost boys." Peter Pan, essentially a New Kid, was selling idealized infant dolls to girls who needed to be taught how to be the "good" mothers their own mothers were not.

Although many girls provided the doll industry with a ready market for their wares between 1900 and 1920, others had demonstrated their preference for other toys and activities. Cutting across geographic, ethnic, and class lines, bicycles, jacks, and movies had won favor with modern American girls who faced far fewer social restrictions than previous generations. After spending nine years with her grandparents, another girl born in the twenties returned home along with her dolls. Because the children who came over to play were too rambunctious, "I put my dollies away and we went out and played rough games" instead.[51]

To counter American girls' indifference to their products and promotions, American businessmen had generated a culture of consumption for little girls through the mass marketing of a new generation of dolls that represented abundance, domesticity, and maternal self-fulfillment. The doll industry could claim at least a partial victory, in that girls raised in the 1920s played with dolls in harmony with the more domestic role they were expected to play. Rather than scolding or smacking their dolls, girls' largely nurturing doll play consisted of dressing and undressing, feeding, bathing, and putting their dolls to bed. When one girl saw the baby doll she had longed for on Christmas morning, "I don't remember being able to speak at all. I simply clutched my baby to me in ecstasy . . . It was very like birth. I was a mother, no doubt about it." [52]

Agents or Agency—
Dolls in Modern America
Since 1930

By the end of the 1920s, dolls manifesting a mentality articulated by late nineteenth-century women producers had been largely excluded from the market. The breakdown of separate spheres (which had led to co-optation, not collaboration), the rise of a consumer culture, and the collapse of the postwar German economy had led to the rise of a male-dominated industry. Not all the priorities of women producers had been lost, however. Manufacturers in the twentieth century had yielded to the concerns of middle-class women for lifelike materials, safety, and cleanliness. This search for a softer surface material (combined with the men's greater fascination with durability) continued into the thirties when manufacturers revived the nineteenth-century producers' experiments with rubber dolls. Rubber was used sporadically over the next several decades until the development of more satisfactory synthetics, either soft latex (referred to as "magic skin") or hard plastic. By the 1950s, American dolls were made out of plastic and vinyl.

Dolls that felt more "human" were one of the legacies left by women producers. But the relentless quest for the imitation of human behavior (offered in lieu of doll qualities that nurtured human relationships) did not cease with Edison's attempt to apply phonographic technology. Since then, manufacturers have used tape recorders and computer chips to make dolls seem more "human." In 1937, Fleischaker & Baum advertised its Dy-Dee Baby doll as "almost human."[1] More recently marketed dolls have "hearts" that "beat."

In their attempts to make dolls more "realistic," however, modern manufacturers have relied on numerous demeaning stereotypes about females despite "gender-bending" attempts. The scatter-brained Chatty Cathy doll of the 1960s talked too much and Barbie hates math. More recently marketed dolls serve a single aspect of self adornment: applying makeup, wearing jewelry, or combing, curling or crimping hair. Many dolls like lacy-lingeried Barbie, the Goo-Goo-eyed doll of the early 1900s, and Little Miss Mermaid of the 1990s are also eroticized, providing masculine messages about female sexuality. Susie Cupcakes (on toy shelves in the 1980s and 1990s) seems to look like a prom-night girl doll in a floor-length dress. But the instructions implore girls to lift Susie's dress over her head to turn her into a scented cupcake.

In addition to static stereotypes, dolls have been affected by a variety of contemporary social, cultural, economic, and political forces. Barbie made a comeback in the extravagant 1980s as the ultimate consumer, especially among the daughters of postwar baby boomers, themselves former Barbie owners. Barbie has more recently acquired a computer (pink, of course). Changing demographics as a result of new immigrants and the commercialization of the "cultural pluralism" debate has led to a dramatic increase in the number of Hispanic, Asian, and African-American dolls (with their modern origins in the civil rights era.) Dolls representing premature babies and pregnant women appear to have been shaped by the "family values" agenda, abortion, and feminism.

Yet images made popular in the commercial culture like the Campbell Kids in the 1910s have continued to provide manufacturers with the greatest marketing opportunities. Doll producers drew upon new sources as movies surpassed comic strips and advertising for reaching children. By 1935, for example, Sears catalogues advertised a doll of child film star Shirley Temple. Even during the Depression, one woman recalled, "everybody had a Shirley Temple [doll]."[2] Movie characters were joined by a host of toys inspired by television programs (especially cartoons) beginning in the 1960s. While glittering versions of cartoon-based She-ra dolls were marketed for girls in the 1980s, more masculine "action figures" like G.I. Joe, Rambo, and He-man are dolls whose roots unmistakably lie in the New Kid dolls of the early 1900s.[3] The progeny of New Kid dolls were as active as their forebears, even more superhumanly "heroic" as the times required. Although some "action figures" can also fly, they share few gender similarities with the androgynous Kewpies who preceded them. Working-class neighborhoods are no match for far-away galaxies, and righteous violence is at the heart of many television cartoon scenarios.

While the Kewpies' social reform mission has vanished, the point of their popularity and commercial success was not lost. American toy firms have continued to launch new marketing campaigns—like the one establishing the Cabbage Patch Kids, which arrived with "adoption" papers—by drawing upon well-tested strategies from the past. In 1931, masters of marketing Fleischaker & Baum produced *My Doll's Magazine,* a miniature publication with realistic articles, notices, and advertisements. Ostensibly written by "Aunt Patsy," Effanbee pamphlets included *What Every Young Doll Mother Should Know* (1937). Ownership entitled girls to become members of a larger "community" of Patsy Doll Club "fans" who read the same marketing "literature." [4]

Although the conservative climate of the doll industry in the 1920s made it more difficult for women to transform dollmaking hobbies into lucrative businesses, some women continued to try. In the case of an enterprising farmer's wife, "A Peter Rabbit Doll *Made* Her Fortune," reported *Forbes* magazine. Despite female dollmakers' tenacity, however, by 1940 "there [were] more women buyers and clerks than entrepreneurs." Jenny Grave's company, Vogue Inc., survived the conservative climate of the twenties, the economic depression of the thirties, and the wartime scarcity of the forties and went on to major success with the Ginny doll in the domestic 1950s: a testimony to her overall assimilation. By carving out a marketing niche as a manufacturer of a doll "elite," Beatrice Behrman was able to sustain the Madame Alexander firm from World War I to the present. That local newspapers today still feature articles about women entrepreneurs who launch doll companies from their kitchens, illustrates that, while the dominant doll culture is not yet theirs, there is a flicker of cultural resistance. The recent appearance of a far more realistically proportioned "Happy to Be Me" doll by a woman designer-turned-entrepreneur provides further evidence that this might be the case. Despite the success of this pioneer, however, professional-ization has continued to be as double edged for many designers today as it was for Rose O'Neill nearly a hundred years ago.[5]

Consumers who shop for dolls today—mostly women—also find themselves in a difficult bind created by the collision of personal values, childrearing ideals, and a consumer culture. How many adults have sub-mitted helplessly to a daughter or young friend's longing for a doll (in-variably spawned by a TV commercial), even though it costs a small for-tune, is poorly constructed, and promotes a discomforting ideology? When a much begged-for doll affords little more than a quarter hour's pleasure to the recipient, the giver's initial ambivalence often yields to anger over having been somehow defrauded. Although some girls are every bit as submissive to the doll manufacturers' intentions as they are portrayed to be in commercials, many others, as always, simply spurn doll play for activities they feel are more exciting. The never-ending phe-nomenon of dolls being desired, bought, and then ignored suggests that the struggle for the control of dolls and of girlhood continues.

NOTES

ABBREVIATIONS

DD	*Doll's Dressmaker*
DR	*Doll Reader*
GH	*Good Housekeeping*
HB	*Harper's Bazaar*
LHJ	*Ladies' Home Journal*
NYT	*New York Times*
PT	*Playthings*
SA	*Scientific American*
TN	*Toys & Novelties*
TW	*Toy World*
WHC	*Woman's Home Companion*

INTRODUCTION

1. See, for example, Dorothy S. Coleman, Elizabeth A. Coleman, and Evelyn J. Coleman, *The Collector's Encyclopedia of Dolls,* 2 vols. (New York: Crown Publishers, 1968, 1986); Jurgen Cieslik and Marianne Cieslik, *German Doll Encyclopedia, 1800-1939* (Cumberland, Md.: Hobby House Press, 1985). Both are highly valuable for the thumbnail sketches they provide.

2. Kathy Peiss, *Cheap Amusements: Working Women and Leisure in New York City, 1880-1920* (Philadelphia: Temple University Press, 1985); Janice Radway, *Reading the Romance: Women, Patriarchy, and Popular Literature* (Chapel Hill: University of North Carolina Press, 1984); Lawrence Levine, *Highbrow/Lowbrow* (Cambridge: Harvard University Press, 1988); T. J. Jackson Lears, "The Concept of Cultural Hegemony: Problems and Possibilities," *American Historical Review* 85 (1985): 567-593.

3. Donald W. Ball, "Toward a Sociology of Toys: Inanimate Objects, Socialization, and the Demography of the Doll World," *Sociological Quarterly* 8 (1967): 447-458; Selma Greenberg, *Right from the Start: A Guide to Nonsexist Child Rearing* (Boston: Houghton Mifflin, 1978), 187-193.

4. This quote and the one above draw upon Laura Starr, "The Educational Value of Dolls," *Pedagogical Seminary* 16, no. 4 (Dec. 1909): 567.

5. T. J. Schlereth, *Material Culture Studies in America* (Nashville: American Association of State and Local History, 1982); Mary Douglas and Baron

Isherwood, *The World of Goods* (New York: Basic Books, 1979); Daniel Miller, *Material Culture and Mass Consumption* (Oxford: Basil Blackwell, 1987), 83-130.

CHAPTER ONE
The Politics of Dollhood in Nineteenth-Century America

1. "The Natural Instincts of Boys and Girls," *Babyhood,* April 1905, 143.
2. Mary Lawrence, "Dolls: Logically Considered," *Babyhood,* Oct, 1895, 330–331. On conspicuous consumption, see Thorstein Veblen, *Theory of the Leisure Class: An Economic Study in the Evolution of Institutions* (New York: Macmillan, 1899).
3. Catherine E. Beecher and Harriet Beecher Stowe, *American Woman's Home* (1869; rpt. Watkins Glen, N.Y.: Library of Victorian Culture, 1879), 298. On children and the American family see John Demos, *A Little Commonwealth: The Family in a Plymouth Colony* (New York: Oxford University Press, 1970); Bernard Wishy, *The Child and the Republic: The Dawn of Modern American Child Nurture* (Philadelphia: University of Pennsylvania Press, 1968); Joseph Kett, *The Rites of Passage: Adolescence in America, 1790 to the Present* (New York: Basic Books, 1977); Philip Greven, *The Protestant Temperament, Patterns of Child-Rearing, Religious Experience and the Self in Early America* (New York: New American Library, 1977); Michael Gordon, ed., *The American Family in Social-Historical Perspective* (New York: St. Martin's Press, 1983); N. Ray Hiner and Joseph M. Hawes, eds., *Growing up in America: Children in Historical Perspective* (Chicago: University of Illinois Press, 1985); Steven Mintz and Susan Kellogg, *Domestic Revolutions: A Social History of Family Life* (New York: The Free Press, 1988); Mary Lynn Stevens Heininger, "Children, Childhood, and Change in America, 1820–1920," in Mary Lynn Stevens Heininger et al., *A Century of Childhood, 1820–1920* (Rochester, N.Y.: Margaret Woodbury Strong Museum, 1984), 6. Childrearing literature included Theodore Dwight, *The Father's Book* (1834), Dr. John Abbott, *The Mother's Book* (1844), and Catherine Beecher, *Treatise on Domestic Economy* (1847); see Mary P. Ryan, "The Empire of the Mother: American Writing about Domesticity, 1830–1860," *Women and History,* no. 2–3 (Summer-Fall 1982).
4. Beecher and Stowe, *American Woman's Home,* 299. Eliza Leslie, *The American Girl's Book or Occupations for Play Hours* (New York: C. S. Francis, 1831), intro. This book appeared one year after the very popular *American Boy's Book* and went through 14 editions, the last published in 1849. Mary Sewell quoted in Linda Pollock, *A Lasting Relationship: Parents and Children over Three Centuries* (Hanover, N.H.: University Press of New England, 1987), 103–104.
5. Lydia Maria Child, *Girl's Own Book* (New York: Clark Austin, 1833), iii, iv.
6. Mary Ryan, *Cradle of the Middle Class: The Family in Oneida County, New York, 1790–1865* (Cambridge: Cambridge University Press, 1981), 161; *Mother's*

Monthly Journal, July 1837, 127; Richard Meckel, "Educating a Ministry of Mothers: Evangelical Maternal Associations, 1815–1860," *Journal of the Early Republic* 2, no. 4 (Winter 1982): 402–423. Nancy F. Cott, *Bonds of Womanhood: Woman's Sphere in New England, 1780–1835* (New Haven: Yale University Press, 1977), 43. Paula Petrik, "The Paraphernalia of Childhood: New Toys for Old and Selchow & Righter Co., 1830–1870," typescript, 5. "Pincushion," Work Department. *Godey's Lady's Book* 74, Aug. 1867; "Doll Pin-cushion," *Peterson's* 48, Sept. 1965, 209; "The Little Companion," *Peterson's* 47, Jan. 1865. "Fancy Pen Wiper," *Godey's Lady's Book* 60, July 1884, 66, cited in Beverly Gordon, "Victorian Fancywork in the American Home: Fantasy and Accommodation, in Marilyn Ferris Motz and Pat Browne, eds., *Making the American Home: Middle-Class Women and Domestic Material Culture, 1840–1940* (Bowling Green, Ohio: Bowling Green State University Popular Press, 1988), 63.

7. Cott, *Bonds of Womanhood,* 43; Susan Strasser, *Never Done: A History of American Housework* (New York: Pantheon, 1982); Ruth Schwartz Cowan, *More Work for Mother: The Ironies of Household Technology from the Open Hearth to the Microwave* (New York: Basic Books, 1983), 63, 66, 201. Beecher and Stowe, *American Woman's Home,* 298.

8. Lucy Larcom, *A New England Girlhood* (Boston: Northeastern University Press, 1986), 29. Jean M. Thompson, "The Story of Rosamond," *HB,* May 1906, 474. S. Anne Frost, *The Ladies' Guide to Needlework, Embroidery, Etc.* (New York: Adams & Bishop, 1877), 132–138; Child, *Girl's Own Book,* iii, iv.

9. Paintings in the National Gallery of Art, Smithsonian Institution, Washington, D.C.; Inez McClintock, *Toys in America* (Washington, D.C.: Public Affairs Press, 1961), 68.

10. "Two Sisters," reprinted in *Children's Stories of the 1850s* (Americana Review). Emily Wilson, *The Forgotten Girl* (New York: Alphabet Press, 1937), 7.

11. Wilson, *The Forgotten Girl,* 14–15; Harriet Robinson, *The Loom and the Spindle: or, Life Among the Early Mill Girls* (1898; reprint, Kailua, Hawaii: Press Pacifica, 1976), 23.

12. Suzanne Lebsock, *The Free Women of Petersburg: Status and Culture in a Southern Town, 1794–1860* (New York: W. W. Norton, 1984), 64. Larcom, *New England Girlhood,* 29; Leslie, *American Girls' Book,* 287–288; see also Maria Edgeworth and Richard Lowell Edgeworth, *Practical Education* (New York: Harper, 1835), 16–17.

13. Larcom, *New England Girlhood,* ch. 1; Kathryn Kish Sklar, *Catherine Beecher: A Study of American Domesticity* (New York: W. W. Norton, 1973), 9; Wilson, *Forgotten Girl,* 14–15. In fact, mothers were also advised to permit their middle-class daughters, most of whom still lived in rural areas, to participate in outdoor games. In *The Mother's Assistant and Young Lady's Friend,* Sarah S. Ellis advo-

cated "exercise in open air" as an antidote to "artificial habits" causing a "host of numerous maladies" in genteel daughters. Karin Lee Fishbeck Calvert, *Children in the House: The Material Culture of Early Childhood, 1600–1900* (Boston: Northeastern University Press, 1992); Bernard Mergen, *Play and Playthings: A Reference Guide* (Westport, Conn.: Greenwood, 1982), 25; Robinson, *Loom and the Spindle,* 23–24; Anne Scott MacLeod, "The Caddie Woodlawn Syndrome: American Girlhood in the Nineteenth Century," in Heininger et al., *A Century of Childhood,* 97–120.

14. *Ridleys' Fashion Magazine,* cited in Foulke, "Dolls of the 1880s," *DR,* Nov. 1988, 98. "A Doll's Story," *DD,* May 1893, 103.

15. *Ridleys' Fashion Magazine,* cited in Foulke, "Dolls of the 1880s," *DR,* Nov. 1988, 103.

16. J. E. Jeuck, *Catalogues and Counters: A History of Sears, Roebuck & Co.* (Chicago: University of Chicago Press, 1950); Joseph J. Schroeder, Jr., ed., *The Wonderful World of Toys, Games, and Dolls* (Northfield, Ill.: DBI Books, 1971), intro.

17. Susan Porter Benson, *Counter Cultures* (Urbana and Chicago: University of Illinois Press, 1988), 14. Macy's "was one of the first, if not the first, to sell toys in a department store"; see *PT,* Oct. 1903, 6. Philip G. Hubert, Jr., "Some Notes as to Christmas Toys," *Babyhood,* Dec. 1893, 15–16.

18. William Leach, "Transformations in a Culture of Consumption: Women and Department Stores, 1890–1925," *Journal of American History* 71 (Sept. 1984): 319–342; Elaine S. Abelson, *When Ladies Go A-Thieving: Middle-Class Shoplifters in the Victorian Department Store* (New York: Oxford University Press, 1989). *Harper's Bazaar* (1881) cited in Jan Foulke, "Dolls of the 1880s," 94. "A Doll's Story, Told By Herself," *DD,* Jan. 1891, 5. *DD,* May 1893, 101–102. For other shopping recollections see Una Atherton Hunt, *Una Mary: The Inner Life of a Child* (New York: Scribner's, 1914), and Meta Lilienthal, *Dear Remembered World: Childhood Memories of an Old New Yorker* (New York: R. R. Smith, 1947).

19. Elizabeth Seelye, "Suggestions Concerning Toys and Amusements," *Babyhood,* Dec. 1890, 17; "Toys for Children," *DD,* Nov. 1892, 283. Mary Hunt's uncle gave her a French bisque doll (Hunt, *Una Mary,* 161). Lilienthal, *Dear Remembered World,* 43.

20. H. Coyle, "Papa's Weary Head," *DD,* May, 1891, 98. Wishy, *Child and the Republic,* 16; Heininger, "Children, Childhood," in *A Century of Childhood,* 19–20. *DD,* May, 1891, 100; *Babyhood,* Jan., 1891, 5. Louisa May Alcott, *A Doll's Journey* (Boston: Little, Brown, 1873), 5.

21. One author of a study of Polish children found that doll play ceased at age 10— earlier than among American children (Madam Anna Grudzinska, "A Study of Dolls Among Polish Children," *Pedagogical Seminary* 14, no. 6 [Sept. 1907]: 385–390). L. Emmett Holt, "Infant Feeding," part of an address given before the

Cleveland Medical Society, Oct. 26, 1900, 10, and *The Diseases of Infancy and Childhood* (New York, 1897), 158, cited in Kathleen W. Jones, "Sentiment and Science: The Late Nineteenth-Century Pediatrician as Mother's Advisor," *Journal of Social History* (Fall 1983): 86; Janet Golden, "Trouble in the Nursery: Physicians, Families and Wet Nurses at the End of the Nineteenth Century, in Carol Groneman and Mary Beth Norton, eds., *"To Toil the Livelong Day," America's Women at Work, 1790–1980* (Ithaca, N.Y.: Cornell University Press, 1987), 126.

22. *Youth's Companion* was founded in 1827, *St. Nicholas* in 1873, *Children's Magazine* in 1879. Other children's magazines include *Harper's Young People* and *Frank Leslie's Chatterbox*. Mintz and Kellogg, *Domestic Revolutions,* xix; Daniel Scott Smith, "Family Limitation, Sexual Control and Domestic Feminism in Victorian America, *Feminist Studies* 1 (Winter-Spring, 1973): 40–57. *A Tribute to Margaret Woodbury Strong* (Rochester, N.Y.: Margaret Woodbury Strong Museum, 1986), 7.

23. "A Doll's Story, Told By Herself," 5. During the Gilded Age, Americans became participants and spectators of baseball and football as specific forms of leisure and amusement.

24. J. M. Barrie, *Peter Pan* (1911; reprint, Toronto: Bantam, 1985). The Division of Domestic Life of the National Museum of American History (Smithsonian Institution, Washington, D.C.) has an extensive collection of Victorian juvenile furniture.

25. My thanks to John Gillis for bringing out this point.

26. *Pretty Pursuits for Children* (London and New York: Butterick, 1897), 61; *The Doll's Tea Party* (Boston: Lothrop, 1895); "Dressing Dolls," *DR,* June 1892, 145.

27. "Dressing Dolls," *DR,* June 1892, 144; Evelyn Jane Coleman, *Carte de Visite; Album de la Poupée,* 1978 reproduction; *Pretty Pursuits,* 78; "Styles for Dolls," *Delineator,* Nov. 1897, 558; Mrs. H. W. Beecher, *Monthly Talks with Young Homemakers* (New York: J. B. Ford, 1873), 293.

28. *Victorian America: Transformations in Everyday Life, 1876–1915* (New York: Harper Collins, 1991), 290–293; Harvey Green, *The Light of the Home* (New York: Pantheon, 1983), 165; Karen Halttunen, *Confidence Men and Painted Ladies: A Study of Middle-Class Culture in America, 1830–1870* (New Haven: Yale University Press, 1982) ch. 5; Ann Douglas, *The Feminization of American Culture* (New York: Avon, 1978), ch. 5. McClintock, *Toys in America,* 78; Barbara Pickering, "In Loving Memory—Dolls and Death," *DR,* Nov. 1988, 132.

29. C. Kurt Dewhurst, Betty MacDowell and Martha MacDowell, *Artists in Aprons* (New York: E. P. Dutton and the Museum of American Folk Art, 1979), 60–62; 66–70; Rozika Parker, *The Subversive Stitch: Embroidery and the Making of the Feminine* (New York: Routledge, 1989). Kate Douglas Wiggin, *Rebecca of Sunnybrook Farm* (1903; rev. ed., Middlesex, U.K.: Puffin, 1985), 63. Mary Alves Long,

High Time to Tell It (Durham, N.C.: Duke University Press, 1950), 23. Slave children staged funerals as well, according to David K. Wiggins, "The Play of Slave Children in the Plantation Communities of the Old South, 1820–1860," in Hiner and Hawes, eds., *Growing up in America,* 178.

30. Mrs. (Richard Henry Horne) Fairstair, *Memoirs of a London Doll, Written by Herself* (London: 1846; reprint, New York, 1967). R. Gordon Kelly, ed., *Children's Periodicals of the United States* (Westport, Conn.: Greenwood Press, 1984); R. Gordon Kelly, *Mother was a Lady; Self and Society in Selected American Children's Periodicals* (Westport, Conn.: Greenwood, 1974). *The Doll's Own Book* (Ohio, n.p., 1882); many also had large print, such as, *Twilight Stories* (New York, London, Manchester, Glasgow: n.d.). See issues of *Doll's Dressmaker* for other installments by the same author. Mrs. Jane M. Besset, *Memoirs of a Doll: by Itself* (Philadelphia and New York: American Sunday School Union, 2nd. ed., 1856).

31. Reynale Smith Pickering, "Christmas in Song and Story," and "The New Christmas Doll Complains," (poems) *LHJ,* Dec. 1908, 126. See also the poem by Laura Starr, *The Doll Book* (New York: Outing Co., 1908), 199.

32. S. K. Simons, "The Happy Doll," *DD,* April 1893, 90.

33. This notion of love also laid the basis for inevitable frustration when girls got older. Among middle-class Americans and the British, love had been "feminized"—caring and loving had become the work of women while support and protection that of men. Gillis, "Ritualization," 15; Fancesca Cancian, *Love in America: Gender and Self Development* (Cambridge: Cambridge University Press, 1987). "Dolls: Logically Considered," *Babyhood,* Oct. 1895, 330–331.

34. In stereographs and illustrations, boys often played the role of doctor as well. Thompson, "Rosamond," 474; Heininger, "Children, Childhood," *in Century of Childhood,* 26–27; see also: Anita Schorsch, *Images of Childhood: An Illustrated Social History* (Pittstown, N.J.: Main Street Press, 1985), ch. 6; "The Tragical-Comical Tale of Mrs. Kennedy and Punch," *Frank Leslie's Chatterbox,* 1885–1886, 10.

35. For an example of a taunting monkey, see: "Naughty Jacko," in *Dolly in Town.* In "The Little Doll," a poem by Charles Kingsley in *The Water Babies,* a wooden doll's arms are "troddened off by cows," See "Kate Douglas Wiggin's Poetry for Children," *LHJ,* Oct. 1907, 50. Aunt Laura (pseud.), *The Dolls' Surprise Party* (Buffalo, N.Y.: Butler, 1863).

36. Beatrix Potter, *The Tale of Two Bad Mice* (New York: F. Warne, 1904), 46, 59.

37. Louisa May Alcott, *Little Women* (1868; reprint, New York: Penguin, 1989), 39. Schlereth, *Victorian America,* 197.

38. Hubert, "Some Notes as to Christmas Toys," *Babyhood,* Dec. 1893, 14. Emily Kimbrough, *How Dear to My Heart* (New York: Dodd, Mead, 1944), 76–77; Lilienthal, *Dear Remembered World,* 20–21;

39. "The Doll of the Colored Children," *Babyhood*, Oct. 1894, 351. Hunt, *Una Mary,* 20. A. C. Ellis and G. Stanley Hall, "Study of Dolls," *Pedagogical Seminary* 1, no. 2 (Dec. 1896):134. "Home-Made Rag," *Babyhood*, Sept. 1908, 417. David Katzman, *Seven Days a Week* (Urbana: University of Illinois, 1981). Ellis and Hall, "Study of Dolls," 141.

40. M. H. Jones, "Dolls for Boys," *Babyhood*, June 1896, 216. "Of average city school children below 6 years, 82% of boys . . . played with dolls; between 6 and 12 yrs., 76% of boys" (Ellis and Hall, "Study of Dolls," 155); For more examples see Calvert, "To Be a Child," 156; *Maiden America & Friends: Parade of Playthings,* Nov. 1984, 51; Dorothy Washburn, "Report: Preliminary Results, Doll Oral History Project," 2, Margaret Woodbury Strong Museum, Rochester, N.Y., doll 79.9962.

41. Ellis and Hall, "Study of Dolls," 145.

42. According to one ten-year-old boy, "My doll used to get angry and I would grab her by the hair and threw her down stairs but afterward give her a nice piece of mud cake wit raspberries on it." Ellis and Hall, "Study of Dolls," 145, 147, 149, 150–151; Jones, "Dolls for Boys," 216.

43. T. R. Croswell, "Amusements," 347. Eleanor Abbott, *Being Little in Cambridge When Everyone Else was Big,* cited in Bernard Mergen, *Play and Playthings: A Reference Guide* (Westport, Conn.: Greenwood, 1982), 186–187. Croswell, "Amusements," 5; Brian Sutton-Smith, "The Play of Girls," in Clare B. Knapp and Martha Kirkpatrick, eds., *Becoming Female* (New York: Plenum, 1979) 229–230. "The Natural Instincts of Boys and Girls," *Babyhood*, April 1905, 143.

44. Ellis and Hall, "Study of Dolls," 146–147; "Young Mrs. Wink-et Scolds her Dolly," *Babyhood* 2, 1 (Boston: Lathrop, 1878), 10. Death and burial were the subjects of late nineteenth-century schoolgirls' ring games; see Brian Sutton-Smith, "Play of Girls," in Knapp and Kirkpatrick, eds., *Becoming Female,* 232; Schlereth, *Victorian America,* 292; "Burying Baby Dolls," *DD,* Nov. 1891, 240; Ethel Spencer, *The Spencers of Amberson Avenue: A Turn of the Century Memoir,* ed. Michael P. Weber and Peter N. Stearns (Pittsburgh: University of Pittsburgh Press, 1983), 65; Alice Kent Trimpey, *Becky My First Love* (Baraboo, Wis.: Remington House, 1946), 1–2; According to one nine-year-old, "doll broken, funeral just for fun" (Ellis and Hall, "Study of Dolls," 146).

45. Calvert, "To Be a Child," 153. Lawrence, "Dolls: Logically Considered," 330–331. "The Natural Instincts of Boys and Girls," *Babyhood*, April 1905, 143. Ellis and Hall, "Study of Dolls," 140, 141.

46. James Sully, *Children's Ways* (New York: Appleton, 1897), 492.

47. Hunt, *Una Mary,* 14. Zona Gale, *When I Was a Little Girl* (New York: Macmillan, 1913), 196.

48. Hunt, *Una Mary,* 163–165.

49. Aunt Laura (pseud.), *The Dolls' Surprise Party*. Victoria Bissell Brown, "Female

Socialization among the Middle Class of Los Angeles," in Elliott West and Paula Petrik, eds., *Small Worlds: Children and Adolescents in America, 1850–1950* (Lawrence: University of Kansas Press, 1992), 246. Hunt, *Una Mary,* 20.

CHAPTER TWO
Masculinity, Technology, and the Doll Economy, 1860–1908

1. Dorothy S. Coleman and Evelyn J. Coleman, "'All Steel' Dolls Made in Pleasantville, NJ," *DR,* Oct. 1987, 113–115.
2. See Louise C. Amati, "Schoenhut Dolls: The Beginning of Commercial Dollmaking in America," *Hobbies,* Oct. 1984, 42. Marcell Kahle was only 15 when he left his home in Lauchbeim, Wurttemberg, and his brother would follow close behind. "Death Claims Marcell Kahle," *TN,* Jan. 1910, 11.
3. John G. Cawelti, *Apostles of the Self-Made Man: Changing Concepts of Success in America* (Chicago: University of Chicago Press, 1965), 3.
4. As Oscar Handlin observed, "Generally, the only opportunity for aliens to figure in commerce or finance grew out of the patronage of their own communities" (Oscar Handlin, *Boston's Immigrants: A Study in Acculturation* [Cambridge, Mass.: Belknap Press of Harvard University, 1979], 67). Such was the case for Edmund Ulrich Steiner, who came to America from Sonneberg as a young man; he would work at nearly all the major doll distributing firms, including Strobel & Wilken and Louis Wolf & Co. After an unsuccessful entrepreneurial venture as a principal in Curman & Steiner, importers and jobbers, he returned to manage Strobel & Wilken's doll department. Dorothy S. Coleman, Elizabeth A. Coleman, and Evelyn J. Coleman, eds., *The Collector's Encyclopedia of Dolls,* 2 vols. (New York: Crown Publishers, 1968, 1986), 1:593 and 2:1115–1116. In 1865, Strassburger's in New York City hired George Borgfeldt, an immigrant from Meldorf (Schleswig-Holstein) who would work his way up to be managing partner. The proliferation of businesses like Strassburger's, which imported and distributed toys and dolls in the postwar years, gave young German men solid opportunities for employment in surroundings that were probably less impersonal than at other businesses. A. S. Ferguson, George Riemann, and others all found jobs at Althof, Bergmann & Co. According to Louise Amati ("Schoenhut Dolls," 4), Schoenhut was first employed by Wanamaker's department store repairing toy pianos. On Schwarz, see "F. A. O. Schwarz: The Toyshop," *Fortune,* Dec. 1940, 85–86.
5. In 1882, Geo. Borgfeldt & Co., soon to become one of the largest wholesale firms in the United States, moved to the intersection of 4th and Wooster Streets in New York City. Mueller & Westfall, an importer and distributor of dolls, settled nearby on lower Broadway. Out-of-state importing firms established branch

offices or relocated entirely. The Cincinnati doll-importing firm of Strobel & Wilken opened a branch office in New York which soon became the main office. Amberg, Brill & Co., one of the largest toy jobbers and doll importers in the midwest, moved to New York in order to expand its import and whole-sale business nationally. *Collector's Encyclopedia*, 2:544; Margerie W. Davies, *Woman's Place Is at the Typewriter: Office Work and Office Workers, 1870–1930* (Philadelphia: Temple University Press, 1982).

6. In Cincinnati at the age of 21, Goldsmith established a 25-cent store with his brother Henry. Goldsmith's brother Alex sold his share in the business to the father of Philip's wife, Sophia Heller. Louis and Frederick Althof established one of the largest importing firms of the period, Althof, Bergmann & Co., with Charles and Hermann Bergmann and, later on, Augustus Bergmann. George Borgfeldt joined with the Kahle brothers, also employed at Strasburger's, to establish Geo. Borgfeldt & Co. in order to display samples of European dolls that customers could order.

7. Peter Stearns, *Be a Man! Males in Modern Society* (New York: Holmes & Meier, 1979).

8. Barbara Welter, "The Cult of True Womanhood, 1820–1860," *American Quarterly* 18 (Summer 1966): 161–174; Carroll Smith-Rosenberg, *Disorderly Conduct* (New York: Oxford University Press, 1985), 197–216.

9. Cawelti, *Apostles,* 5. Henry Ward Beecher, *Lectures to Young Men* (Boston: J. P. Jewett; New York: M. H. Newman, 1849), 41, 152, 120–127; Karen Halttunen, *Confidence Men and Painted Ladies* (New Haven: Yale University Press, 1982), 25–26, 47–48. Henry Seidel Canby quoted in Lewis A. Erenberg, *Steppin' Out: New York Nightlife and the Transformation of American Culture, 1890–1930* (Chicago: University of Chicago Press, 1981), 6.

10. At the top of the doll industry pyramid were paternalistic businessmen, *verlegers,* who "produced" dolls. That is, they designed, modeled, financed, organized, col-lected, and distributed dolls. Although manufactured by others, the dolls bore the assemblers' trademark. Most often, the major doll producers, without facto-ries of their own, arranged for manufacturing firms to make the dolls. Each of these factory owners, in turn, depended on cottage workers—pressers, carvers, turners, voice and body makers—who worked at home assisted by wives and children, and often under squalid conditions. Delivering completed doll parts to factories was the task of child homeworkers or delivery women who transported huge wicker baskets on their backs. As many as 25 factories could contribute to the production of one doll. Either factory owners or the verlegers assembled the dolls and arranged for their distribution and export, exchanging inventory notices with German immigrants in American importing businesses.

Trow's New York City Directory for 1864, vol. 77. Hawkins' business was at 381 Canal Street.

By 1866 Ellis's sales amounted to more than $100,000, according to Eleanor St. George, *Dolls of Yesterday* (New York and London: Charles Scribner's Sons, 1948), 13. Due to the flood that carried away Ellis's $40,000 plant, in 1869 the toys were manufactured at the Vermont Novelty Works, also in Springfield.

11. Inventors filed only 36,000 patents with the U. S. Patent Office between 1790, when the the patent system was created under the Constitution to "promote the Progress of Science and Arts," and 1860. Between 1860 and 1920, however, 1.5 million patents were granted.

12. Blair Whitton, "Joel Ellis," *DR,* Aug.–Sept. 1988, 117; Ellis also patented a "splint farm basket." Inez and Marshall McClintock, *Toys in America* (Washington, D.C.: Public Affairs Press, 1961), 208.

13. A. W. Nicholson, U.S. patent 88,197, March 23, 1869; Charles Pfanne, U.S. patent 237,897, Feb. 15, 1881; William. H. Hart, Jr., U.S. patent 157,394, Dec. 1, 1874. Madeline O. Merrill and Richard Merrill, "Dolls Made in America Prior to 1925, Part II," *DR,* April–May 1982, 135. In the second year of production the manufacturers made improvements by providing the Webber Singing Doll with a limber body (of American origin) though the heads continued to be imported. In 1882, the doll cost between $2.75 and $5; the following year, the chemise cost 25 cents extra; see *Collector's Encyclopedia,* 1:645.

Mary Beth Norton et al., *A People and a Nation: A History of the United States,* 2 vols. (Boston: Houghton Mifflin, 1982), 2:481. "Edison's Phonograph Dolls," *SA,* April 26, 1890, 263.

14. Daniel T. Rodgers, *The Work Ethic in Industrial America, 1850–1920,* rev. ed. (Chicago: University of Chicago Press, 1978), 68; Blair Whitton, *American Clockwork Toys, 1862–1900* (Exton, Pa.: Schifter, 1981), 3; Robert J. Clay invented a mechanical animal and William F. Goodwin invented a walking horse before they patented their mechanical dolls. *Collector's Encyclopedia,* 1:454; Morrison was granted two patents, in 1862 and in 1869; see clocks division, National Museum of American History, Smithsonian Institution, Washington, D.C. Permitting children to crawl on all fours had been a relatively recent change in childrearing practices, replacing more rigorous requirements to stand and walk as soon as possible. Karin Calvert, "Cradle to Crib: The Revolution in Nineteenth-Century Children's Furniture," in Mary Lynn Stevens Heininger et al., *A Century of Childhood, 1820–1920* (Rochester, N.Y.: Margaret Woodbury Strong Museum, 1984), 44. In 1871, Robert J. Clay invented a "Creeping Doll" with two large gears protruding from its baby body. When the doll was wound up, the arms and legs moved in "a life-like crawling and creeping action." The following year,

George P. Clarke, employed by Clay, patented his invention as an "Improved Creeping Doll." A year later Clarke's original creeping baby was altered so that it cried as well.

15. Dominico Checkeni, U.S. patent 52,782, Feb. 20, 1866. Fritz Bartenstein, U.S. patent 243,752, July 5, 1881. This invention had been filed in Germany on Oct. 28, 1880 with no model. See illustration for doll head in *Collector's Encyclopedia,* 1:49. One of Bartenstein's doll heads is in the Chester County Historical Society in Pennsylvania. Rudolph M. Hunter, U.S. patent 634,143, Oct. 3, 1899. Heinrich Graeser, U.S. patent 440,706, Nov. 18, 1890; Numerous other patents were filed for "Constructing Doll Heads," "Manufacturing Doll Heads," "Apparatus for Moulding Doll Heads," and "Coloring Doll Heads." "More patents have been obtained for the movement of eyes than for any other item" (quoted in Pidd Miller, "The Eyes of Schoenhut Wigged Child Dolls," *DR,* Aug.–Sept. 1986, 127).

16. Lacmann, U.S. patent 113,532.

17. Montgomery Ward catalogue for 1889 in Joseph J. Schroeder, ed., *Wonderful World of Toys, Games and Dolls* (Northfield, Ill.: DBI Books, 1971), 36. Charles T. Dotter, U.S. patent 235,218, Dec. 7, 1880. See patents for Charles Louis Parent, Joel Ellis, Wesley Miller, and Kimball Atwood; see *Collector's Encyclopedia,* 1:327. Mason and Taylor, U.S. patent 242,210, May 31, 1881.

18. *Collector's Encyclopedia,* 1:326. Jacques had patented a phonographic doll which he had assigned to the Edison Phonograph Toy Mfg. Co. In 1890, Thomas Edison obtained a patent for a "Phonograph for Dolls or Other Toys." Whitton, *American Clockwork Toys,* 37.

19. Business directory from 1863 cited in McClintock, *Toys in America,* 212–213. Victor S. Clark, *History of Manufacturers in the United States, 1860–1893* (New York: McGraw-Hill, 1929); Madeline O. Merrill and Richard Merrill, "Dolls Made in America Prior to 1925, Part I," *DR,* Feb.–Mar. 1982, 3. Jurgen Cieslik and Marianne Cieslik, *German Doll Encyclopedia, 1800–1939,* 1st ed. (Cumberland, Md.: Hobby House Press, 1985), s.v. "Edison," and p. 285; *Harper's Young People* (1889) quoted in *Collector's Encyclopedia,* s.v. "Edison"; Each of five monthly shipments of dolls cost $6,000 according to a letter from the treasurer of the Edison Phonograph Toy Mfg. Co. (Jan. 29, 1890), cited in Simonelli, "Edison Talking Doll—An Idea that Failed," *DR,* June–July 1988, 82.

20. *Collector's Encyclopedia,* 1:18 and 2:423. Goodyear Rubber Co., trade journal (1881), 22–24. One of the "chief merits" of Emil Verpillier's doll joints were their construction. One of Frank Darrow's and Deon Peck's goals was to make a "more durable article" than any other. Though children could not easily break the hard and stiff rawhide dolls he produced, rats could eat through them and did. Sybill McFadden, "Mr. Edison's Astonishing Doll," *Hobbies,* Aug. 1983, 42.

21. Kimball C. Atwood, U.S. patent 186,919, Feb. 6, 1877.

22. McClintock, *Toys in America,* 215. F. W. Darrow, U.S. patent 52,142, Jan. 23, 1866. Darrow and Peck, U.S. patent 52,142, Jan. 23, 1866.

23. Wives helped with sewing especially among Jewish Germans, such as the Goldsmiths. Sophia Goldsmith, *In Remembrance,* typescript, 53; in addition to Goldsmith, immigrant dollmakers' wives like Mary Arnoldt made dolls' clothing for the domestic and imported dolls handled by her husband at Arnoldt's Doll Manufactory; see *TN,* June 1911, 75. Goldsmith, *In Remembrance,* 23. One contemporary study suggests that a similar division of labor existed in the German doll industry as well; dolls' outfits were made by working-class wives and widows (see Cieslik and Cieslik, *German Doll,* 201).

    Doll dealers also relied on a pool of women workers to clothe dolls; according to Charles Dickens, "The maker gives out the calico and the stuffing; and women and girls are paid so much per dozen . . . for sewing the former and putting in the latter" (*Household Words* [11 June 1853], 353). The sewing of dolls' dresses was mostly a home industry where all costs (thread, sewing machine, spoilage, and the like) were absorbed by women workers who were paid by the piece. Firms like F. A. O. Schwarz in New York and Heyer Bros. in Boston employed additional "girls" to sew dolls' dresses during the sixteen weeks before Christmas. For German, American, and Irish women in Boston, home sewing had been a reliable source of income since before the Civil War. The great fire of 1872, which scorched 65 acres of Boston including parts of the business district, probably shut down the Heyer firm. As a result, two hundred dolls' dressmakers were left unemployed.

24. "The labor of stitching and sewing [is] avoided altogether," wrote one inventor. Charles F. Blakslee, U.S. patent 45,691, Jan. 3, 1865. Bruckner obituary reprinted in *Collector's Encyclopedia,* 2:193.

23. Horsman Dolls, "Babyland Rag Dolls," catalogue c. 1912; Donald M. Lowe, *History of Bourgeois Perception* (Chicago: University of Chicago Press, 1982). John Berger, *Ways of Seeing* (Middlesex, England: Penguin Books, 1979), 46.

26. "For years and years these soft dollies with their pretty painted faces were turned out by the thousand, and then there suddenly came a great change, a new sort of rag doll appeared, something totally different from the original variety," explained a writer in *PT,* Nov. 1907, 48.
    Philip Goldsmith, U.S. patent, Dec. 15, 1885.

27. Wolf Flechter, U.S. patent 371,751, Oct. 18, 1887.

28. I have borrowed the term "iron hands" from Adrienne Rich, who uses it to describe forceps in *Of Woman Born* (New York: Bantam, 1977), 132. "Edison's Phonographic Dolls," 263.

Harper's Young People reprinted in *Collector's Encyclopedia,* 1:208.
It has been suggested that the inventor of the doll pressing machines demanded
"excessive royalties" beyond the firm's budget (1:310). St. George, *Dolls of
Yesterday,* 11–12; McClintock, *Toys in America,* 206–208.
St. George, *Dolls of Yesterday,* 15. Instead of designing his own machinery, Philip
Goldsmith transported from Nuremberg a machine for making kid leather doll
bodies, as well as workers skilled in the dollmaking technique. When proprietor
D. M. Mason hired Luke Taylor to build machinery capable of making a wooden
doll in 1879, the firm, established at midcentury, altered its course of business.
Mason, who traveled frequently, was probably inspired by the doll ventures of
others in Vermont. Beginning in 1879, the dolls (later patented by Mason and
Taylor) were produced "in the old clothespin shop" owned by Smith, Mason &
Co.
Herbert Ellis, *The Ellis Jointed Dolls* (published privately, Oct., 1942), 3.
McClintock, *Toys in America,* 342–343.

29. Stearns, *Be a Man!,* 41.
30. "Manufacture of French Toys," *TN,* Oct. 1909, 8.
31. For Edison, financial dependence on the modern corporation formed for the
    mass-production of his dolls stymied, in part, his future as a doll producer. On
    Oct. 6, 1890, Edison requested that his stockholders form a new board of direc-
    tors in order to adopt new methods of production. But the angry stockholders
    turned him down. He informed them later in that month that "manufacture
    is entirely suspended owing to lack of funds." Simonelli, "Edison's Talking
    Doll," 83.
    Ellis, *The Ellis Jointed Doll,* 3. "Mary had a little lamb" were the first words
    Edison recorded on the phonograph he invented in 1877. See Thomas J.
    Schlereth, *Victorian America: Transformations in Everyday Life, 1876–1915*
    (New York: Harper Collins, 1991), 191.
    St. George, *Dolls of Yesterday,* 9.
32. See photograph in Dorothy Coleman, "Philip Goldsmith," 3. "Edison's Phono-
    graphic Dolls," 263.
33. While the patent was pending, Ellis established the Co-Operative Manufacturing
    Co. in Springfield and signed over the rights to the patent in exchange for capital
    stock in the doll-producing firm.
    St. George, *Dolls of Yesterday,* 15, 32; Smith-Rosenberg, *Disorderly Conduct,* 90–
    108; Mary P. Ryan, *Cradle of the Middle Class: The Family in Oneida County, New
    York, 1790–1865* (Cambridge: Cambridge University Press, 1981).
    "Great American Toy Industries," *PT,* May 1908, 90; see Davies, *Woman's Place Is
    at the Typewriter.*

34. *Collector's Encyclopedia,* 1:526, 259. Louis Amberg's son, Joshua, joined his father in business after graduating from college, Joshua L. Amberg, obituary, *NYT,* 25 Sept. 1949, 92. "E. J. Horsman, Jr., Dead," *NYT,* 29 July 1918, 11; "F. A. O. Schwarz," 86.

35. Coleman, "Philip Goldsmith," 5; *PT,* Dec. 1908, 119.

36. "Mrs. E. J. Horsman Dead," *TN,* June 1909, 39; on Goldsmith: "From the River," *The Cincinnati Commercial-Gazette,* 12 July 1894, n.p., in Levenson family papers, Cincinnati, Ohio.

37. When the Goldsmiths moved above their own dry goods store in Chicago, "how happy I was," wrote Sophia Goldsmith, "to be nearer to my dear Philip and could assist him." In Cincinnati, "after being through with my work I assisted in the store when the children were asleep." After a while, she recalled, "We kept a little girl [to help] as I was continually in the store." Like others, Sophia Goldsmith had her own work experiences to draw from. Prior to her marriage, she had assisted her brother in the store he had owned in Chicago. Sophia Goldsmith, *In Remembrance.*

38. Stearns, *Be a Man!,* ch 5.; E. Anthony Rotundo, "Boy Culture: Middle-class Boyhood in Nineteenth-Century America," in Mark C. Carnes and Clyde Griffen, eds., *Meanings of Manhood: Constructions of Masculinity in Victorian America* (Chicago: University of Chicago Press, 1990), 15–37.

39. George H. Howard, U.S. patent 268,020, Nov. 28, 1882.; Wesley Miller, U.S. patent 164,582, June 15, 1875. *Harper's Young People,* 27 Jan. 1891, reprinted in *Collector's Encyclopedia,* 1:208.

40. McFadden, "Mr. Edison's Astonishing Doll," 44.
    Letter to Edison Phonograph Toy Mfg. Co. from Horace Partridge, April 15, 1890, cited in Simonelli, "Edison Talking Doll," 82.
    Letter from C. H. Kimball to Edison Phonograph Toy Mfg. Co., April 24, 1890, cited in Simonelli, "Edison Talking Doll," 82.

41. Catalogue page reprinted in Whitton, *American Clockwork Toys,* 33. The dolls were set to run in a circle, "thus obviating the necessity of frequently reversing them, an objection so frequently raised against the original Walking Doll." Although Althof, Bergmann & Co. imported 95 percent of its stock, it domestically manufactured mechanical dolls like those advertised in Goodwin's 1874 catalogue. Perhaps this was due to the influence of Louis Althof, who, along with another inventor, obtained a patent for a mechanical doll with a bell and hoop. Althof, Bergmann & Co.'s display at the 1876 Philadelphia Centennial Exhibition consisted chiefly of mechanical dolls; see *Collector's Encyclopedia,* 1:14–15. Mary Schweitzer Lallik, "The Webber Singing Doll," *DR,* Feb.–Mar. 1990, 70.

42. A. Caswell Ellis and G. Stanley Hall, "A Study of Dolls," *Pedagogical Seminary* 1,

no. 2 (Dec. 1896), 142. Polish children did not like dolls that walked, talked, or boxed, according to Madam Anna Grudzinska, "A Study of Dolls Among Polish Children," *Pedagogical Seminary* 13, no. 6 (Sept. 1907), 388.

43. Robert Harold Bretherton, *The Child's Mind* (London: John Lance, 1903), 14–15.

44. Rodgers, *Work Ethic,* 68. I have applied Rodgers' insights about the impact of mechanization on workers and doll players.
Eda Lord, *Childsplay,* cited in Bernard Mergen, *Play and Playthings: A Reference Guide* (Westport, Conn.: Greenwood, 1982), 189.

44. Montgomery Ward catalogue, 1889, in Schroeder, *Wonderful World,* 36.

CHAPTER THREE
In the Dolls' House

1. Brenda (Mrs. Castle) Smith, "Victoria-Bess: The Ups and Downs of a Doll's Life," in *Victorian Doll Stories* (1879; reprint, New York: Schocken, 1969), 15; *Dolls of Rhode Island,* author unknown, Chase family papers (Bronxville, N.Y.) 4.

2. Marilyn Ferris Motz and Pat Browne, *Making the American Home: Middle-Class Women and Domestic Material Culture, 1840–1940* (Bowling Green, Ohio: Bowling Green State University Popular Press, 1988), 7; Rozsika Parker, *The Subversive Stitch: Embroidery and the Making of the Feminine* (New York: Routledge, 1989).

3. The vast majority of American-born women doll producers, inventors, and designers lived in New England and New York State. Lucinda Wishard, who lived in Indiana, and Ella Smith, in Alabama, were more typical of women who obtained patents after 1900; see chapter 5.

4. Jill Conway, "Women Reformers and American Culture," *Journal of Social History* 5 (Winter 1971–72): 164–177; Robyn Muncy, *Creating a Female Dominion in American Reform, 1890–1935* (New York: Oxford University Press, 1991).

5. Dolores Hayden, *The Grand Domestic Revolution* (Cambridge, Mass.: MIT Press, 1981), 1.

6. "Occupations and Pastimes, Use & Abuse of Toys," *Babyhood,* Feb. 1898, 61.

7. Julia E. Peck, "Misdirected Selections," *Babyhood,* Aug. 1893, 280.

8. Kate Douglas Wiggin, *Children's Rights: A Book of Nursery Logic* (Boston and New York: Houghton Mifflin, 1892), 60–61.

9. Susan H. Hinkley, "The Doll of the 'Smart Set,'" *Babyhood,* Mar. 1896, 119.

10. Martha Chase, personal journal, Oct. 1876-July 1878, typescript, Archives of the Margaret Woodbury Strong Museum, Rochester, New York. Elizabeth M. R. Lomax, Jerome Kagan, and Barbara C. Rosencrantz, *Science and Patterns of Child Care* (San Francisco: W. H. Freeman, 1978), 31–36. A. C. Ellis and G. Stanley Hall, "Study of Dolls," *Pedagogical Seminary* 1, no. 2 (Dec. 1896), 129–174.

11. Nancy Woloch, *Women and the American Experience* (New York: Alfred A. Knopf, 1984), ch. 8; Gerda Lerner, "The Lady and the Mill Girl: Changes in the Status of Women in the Age of Jackson, 1800–1840," *Midcontinent American Studies Journal* 10 (Spring 1969), 5–14; Margerie W. Davies, *Woman's Place is At the Typewriter: Office Work and Office Workers, 1870–1930* (Philadelphia: Temple University Press, 1982); Carl Degler, *At Odds: Women and the Family in America from the Revolution to the Present* (New York: Oxford University Press, 1978); Nancy F. Cott, *Bonds of Womanhood* (New Haven: Yale University Press, 1977); Carroll Smith-Rosenberg, "The Female World of Love and Ritual: Relations Between Women in Nineteenth-Century America," *Signs* 1 (Autumn 1975).

12. Mary Hunt Hood, "Nursery Helps and Novelties," *Babyhood,* Feb. 1895, 87–88; "Making a Rag Doll," *Babyhood,* Jan. 1907, 507; M. E. Acker, "Home Made Dolls, *Harper's Bazaar,* Jan. 1902, 72; "Mothers Corner," Elisabeth Robinson Scovil, ed., *LHJ,* Dec. 1890, 16; Butterick issued its first pattern for making a cloth doll in 1882, and *The Delineator* and other women's magazines provided step-by-step instructions as well. See "Pattern for a Jointless Rag Doll," *Delineator,* Nov. 1894, 612. Advertisement, "A Child's Love for a Doll," subscription premium to "Comforts," in *Delineator,* Mar. 1893. Articles like "Making a Rag Doll" regularly appeared in *Babyhood,* which provided instructions for making rag dolls stuffed with cotton batting, their features painted with oil paints, India ink, or indelible ink "These rag dolls are so easy to make, and so superior to any bought ones," commented one mother in "Making a Rag Doll," 507. Dr. James L. Wheaton, Sr., *Recollections* (Pawtucket, R.I.: E. L. Freeman, 1913), 10.

13. *Women Inventors to Whom Patents Have Been Granted by the United States Government,* 1790 to July 1, 1888 (Washington, D.C.: Government Printing Office, 1888); Appendix 1 (July 1, 1888 to Oct. 1, 1892), 1892; Appendix 2 (Oct. 1, 1892 to March 1 1895), 1895.
   [Mrs.] M. L. Rayne, *What Can a Woman Do: or, Her Positions in the Business and Literary World* (Petersburgh, N.Y.: Eagle Publishing, 1893), 115–118. Advertisement, *Delineator,* Mar. 1893, n.p. See another advertisement for patent attorney Franklin H. Hough in same issue. Suzanne Lebsock, *The Free Women of Petersburg: Status and Culture in a Southern Town, 1784–1860* (New York: W. W. Norton, 1984).

14. See artists' mannequin in the National Museum of American History, Smithsonian Institution, Washington, D. C. Martha Wellington stayed away from inelastic woven fabrics because they were not "well adapted to my purpose" (U.S. patent 285,448, Sept. 25, 1883). Margaret Ball and her sister made dolls out of "stout corset jean stuffed with cotton and dressed in simple wash calico" (Marilyn Harris, letter in Coleman private collection, Washington, D.C.).

15. Susan Strasser, *Never Done: A History of American Housework* (New York: Pantheon, 1982).

16. Considered here are all United States patents granted between 1790 and 1910. Mary Lou Ratcliff, "Those Ithaca Ladies and their Commercial Toys and Dolls: Ida A. Gutsell," *DR*, Feb.–Mar. 1987, 84; Ann Cipperly, " 'Indestructible Dolls' Still Glowing After Decades," *Opelika-Auburn News*, Oct. 12, 1980, n.p. "Notice" of the Pawtucket Industrial School, in Chase family papers. Marjorie A. Bradshaw, *The Doll House: The Story of the Chase Doll,* privately printed, 1986, 30.

17. Adams brochure eprinted in *Maiden America: Parade of Playthings,* (Massachusetts: Yankee Doodle Doll Club, Nov. 1984), 49. for Wellington patent see note 14. *DD,* Jan. 1891, 5.

18. Rebecca Johnson, U.S. patent 336,730, July 19, 1887. Gussie Decker asserted that with her leather doll, "the children cannot themselves be injured by biting them or otherwise placing them in the mouth" (Gussie Decker, U.S. patent 724,822, April 7, 1903). Izannah Walker, U.S. patent 144,373, Nov. 4, 1873. O. A. Flynn, U.S. patent 958,387, May 17, 1910. Quoted in Constance Eileen King, *The Collector's History of Dolls* (New York: Bonanza, 1977), 445.

19. "Homemade Rag Doll," *Babyhood,* Sept. 1903, 417. "The object of my said invention," wrote one inventor, "is to produce a cheap and at the same time practically indestructible doll." Lucinda B. J. Wishard, U.S. patent 280,986, July 10, 1883. Rebecca Johnson declared that her patented dolls "are far more durable than more expensive dolls, especially for the use of younger children" (Johnson patent, see note 18).

20. *Atlanta Women's Club Cookbook* (1921) cited in Judith Whorton, "The Alabama Indestructible Babies—Fable and Fact," *DR,* Feb.–Mar. 1988, 70; Advertisement in the cookbook reprinted in *Doll News,* May 1971, 19. Wellington 1883 patent (see note 14).

21. Ellis and Hall, "A Study of Dolls," 129–174.

22. Stephen Jay Gould, *The Panda's Thumb* (New York: W. W. Norton, 1980), 97–107; Ratcliff, "Those Ithaca Ladies," 85.

23. Ratcliff, "Those Ithaca Ladies," 85; Elizabeth Eggleston Seelye, "Suggestions Concerning Toys and Amusements," *Babyhood,* Dec. 1890, 17; Konrad Lorenz, *Studies in Animal and Human Behavior,* cited in Gould, *Panda's Thumb,* 101.

24. Gould, *Panda's Thumb,* 101.

25. Ellis and Hall, "Study of Dolls," 161. Ida A. Gutsell, U.S. patent 503,316, Aug. 15, 1893. Celia M. Smith, U.S. patent 22,178, Jan. 31, 1893; on clothing fashions for example, see *Delineator,* Nov. 1892, 480. Madge Lansing Mead, U.S. patent 661,185, Nov. 6, 1900. On Baby Stuart, see Genevieve Angione, "Philadelphia's Own Rag Dolls," in Albert Christian Revi, ed., *Spinning Wheels' Complete Book of Dolls* (New York: Galahad Books, 1975), 28. See photo in Whorton, "Alabama Inde-

structible," 73; Robert Chase and Olga Chase, interview with author, Bronxville, N.Y., summer 1986.

26. Ida A. Gutsell, U.S. patent 22,946, Dec. 5, 1893. "The Chase Stockinet Doll, A Tradition in American Families," (M. J. Chase Company brochure, c. 1935). Others have attributed the order to a "buyer" of undetermined sex; see Bird-Ellen G. O'Keefe, "American Women's Role in the Development of the Nineteenth-Century Doll Industry," *DR*, Dec. 1982-Jan. 1983, 56.

27. Olga Chase, "Twenty-Four Park Place," (typescript, Dec. 1980), 8; Robert Chase and Olga Chase, interview with author, Bronxville, N.Y., summer, 1986. Collectors have written numerous articles about Martha Chase: see Mrs. Jessie M. Ramsbottom, "The Chase Stockinet Doll," *Hobbies,* Apr. 1938, 22; Betty Wilson, "Martha Chase's Famous Dolls," *The Antiques Journal,* May 1972, 45–46; Vyrlin Bruce, "The Chase Doll: An American Classic," *DR,* Aug.–Sept. 1981, 18–20; Margaret Whitton, "Martha Jenks Chase: Turn of the Century American Doll Manufacturer," *DR,* Oct. 1984, 94–99; Dorothy M. Dixon and Winnie Langley, "The Stockinet Dolls of Martha Chase," *Collectors' Showcase,* June 1987, 30–34; Florence Theriault, "Cloth Dolls in Turn of the Century America," *New England Antiques Journal,* Aug. 1987, 24, 70; Margaret Hartshorn, "George Washington, a doll by Martha Chase," *Doll News,* Summer 1988, 46–47, 50.

28. Lucy Eldersveld Murphy, "Her Own Boss: Businesswomen and Separate Spheres in the Midwest, 1850–1880," *Illinois History Journal* (Autumn 1987): 158.

29. Laura Starr, *The Doll Book* (New York: The Outing Co.), 200.

30. *Demorest,* Jan. 1874, 33.

31. Mrs. H. R. Bacon, quoted in "Columbian Dolls," in *Maiden America,* 47.

32. Janet Hooks, *Women's Occupations Through Seven Decades* (Women's Bureau Bulletin no. 218) (Washington, D.C., 1947), 183; Murphy, "Her Own Boss," 157.

33. The Adams sisters were assisted by both their mother and their father. Featured at the World's Columbian Exposition in Chicago in 1892, they received a diploma of merit and their doll was honored with the name, "The Columbian Doll." Just how financially successful the sisters were is impossible to determine, yet Marshall Field & Co. of Chicago catalogues that carried their dolls reveal that they reached a wide market of mail-order customers. Though Emma Adams died unmarried in 1900, her sister, Marietta, who married six years later, carried on the dollmaking business for at least a decade more. Mary Lou Ratcliff, interview with author, summer, 1987. See also Ratcliff, "Those Ithaca Ladies," 84–87; Dorothy S. Coleman and Evelyn J. Coleman, *The Collector's Encyclopedia,* 2 vols. (New York: Crown Publishers, 1968 and 1986), 1:5–6; O'Keefe, "American Women's Role" 56–58; "A Unique Enterprise," *Northern Christian Advocate,* reprinted in *Maiden America,* 48.

34. Mary Louise Morris, "Dolls of Old Salem," *Hobbies* (July 1971), 46–50, quoted from Wendy Lavitt, *American Folk Dolls* (New York: Knopf, 1982), 12–13.

35. On the Balls: *Dallas Daily Times Herald,* 9 June 1880, according to Dorothy and Evelyn Coleman; Margaret Ball was listed as a "Toy Dealer" doing business at 464 Bergen Street in *Lain's Business Directory* of Brooklyn, in 1886, 248. For 1886–1887, however, she was listed as a doll manufacturer, Ibid., 39. Jennie Fenn was listed as a manufacturer of dolls' hats, caps and dresses at 2129 Bergen Street in Brooklyn, according to *The Trow Business Directory of the Borroughs of Brooklyn and Queens for 1899* but not after 1900. See also letter in Coleman private collection. On the Hastings sisters: Starr, *Doll Book,* 201.

36. On the Coles see "A Famous Dollmaker," (Boston) *Advertiser,* 1898. Molly Cole continued to make dolls after her mother-in-law died. On Celia and Charity Smith: *Collector's Encyclopedia,* 2:83, 298.

37. With dolls in the back of his Ford automobile, Bud Smith traveled to several states selling and delivering the dolls his wife manufactured ("History of Randolph County," Alabama, 1957). A special thanks to Gwen Stevenson for sharing her collection of Ella Smith sources with me.

38. Bradshaw, *Doll House,* 14–15.

39. On Jenkinson: letter to Margaret Whitton from Mrs. William G. Bradshaw (niece of Mabel Jenkinson), Jan. 9, 1985, Chase file, the Margaret Woodbury Strong Museum, 2–3; see also Henry H. Smith and Harry A. Scheer, "Hospital Dolls," *Providence Sunday Journal,* June 3, 1945.

40. Interview with Robert Chase and Olga Chase; quotation cited in Clara H. Fawcett, "Chase Stockinet Dolls," *Hobbies,* Oct. 1903, 39.

41. "A Unique Enterprise," *Northern Christian Advocate,* reprinted in *Maiden America,* 48. A workbook was kept by both Barma and Katie Mitchum, 1911–1912. Private collection. Martha Ann Calvert, "The Indestructible Dolls of Roanoke, Alabama," *DR,* Aug.–Sept. 1983, 128–130. According to Calvert, while the production records kept by Katie and Barma reveal that they painted, sewed, and repaired dolls, other sources suggest that there might have been a greater trend toward specialization. Minnie Martin (Mrs. Jack Martin) painted the dolls' hair, eyes, and lips. Nancy Brown helped mold the heads and traded her rough black coat with Ella Smith who used the coat for hair on the black dolls. Gertrude Waller painted the dolls. Outside the shop, "boys made pocket money by cutting small sticks and delivering them to the doll factory."

42. Fawcett, "Chase Stockinet Dolls," 39. Chase hid the "secret" of the stockinet dolls even from the women she employed. It has been suggested recently that she probably used German bisque doll heads as models, although it is not known how she achieved the childlike countenances of her dolls from such models.

According to Marjorie A. Bradshaw, at Christmas each doll worker could choose a favorite doll (*Doll House,* 16). "How Rag Dolls Are Made," *PT* (Sept. 1903), 24–25.

43. "Manufacturers Authorized to Use the Label," National Consumer's League, Nov. 1906, Manuscripts Division, Library of Congress, Washington, D.C.

44. Advertisement, *LHJ,* Nov. 1907, 88.

45. Walker, U.S. patent; JoAnne Brown, *Next to Godliness: The Pursuit of Cleanliness in America* (Cambridge, Mass.: Harvard University Press, forthcoming). See, for example, "In a Doll-Making School," *Babyhood,* Dec. 1890, 13–14.

46. "Chase Sanitary Dolls," M. J. Chase Company circular, c. 1918.

47. Advertisement, "The Original Chase Stockinet Dolls," *LHJ,* Oct. 1911.

48. Olga Chase, "Twenty-Four Park Place," 8; Best & Company advertisement, *Children's Magazine,* Oct. 15, 1912.

49. "Pawtucket-Born Doll Find Way to All Parts of Globe," *Pawtucket Times,* Dec. 24, 1940; Robert Chase, "History of the M. J. Chase Co., Inc.," typescript, Margaret Woodbury Strong Museum Library. Mrs. M. L. Rayne, *What Can a Woman Do: Or, Her Position in the Business and Literary World* (Petersburgh, N.Y.: Eagle Publishing, 1893), 171. Bradshaw, *Doll House,* 51; Bruce, "The Chase Doll," 20; Barbara Melosh, *"The Physician's Hand": Work Culture and Conflict in American Nursing* (Philadelphia: Temple University Press, 1982), 52.

50. On scientific motherhood, see Barbara Ehrenreich and Deirdre English, *For Her Own Good: 150 Years of Experts' Advice to Women* (Garden City, N.Y.: Doubleday, 1979), 171; Lomax, Kagan, and Rosencrantz, *Science and Patterns of Child Care,* 19–44; Rima D. Apple, *Mothers and Medicine: A Social History of Infant Feeding, 1890–1950* (Madison, Wisc.: University of Wisconsin Press, 1987).

51. Mrs. George R. Ramsbottom, "Chase Stockinet Dolls," n.d., typescript, Rhode Island Historical Society. According to Marjorie A. Bradshaw, the first baby doll, modeled after a two-month-old infant, was made at the request of the Children's Hospital in Boston, (*Doll House,* 55).

52. "Chase Sanitary Dolls" circular; Busbey, quoted in Mary Lynn Stevens Heininger, "Children, Childhood and Change," in Heininger et al., *A Century of Childhood, 1820–1920* (Rochester, N.Y.: Margaret Woodbury Strong Museum, 1984), 28; "Life Size Doll is Model Baby for Embryo Nurses," *PT,* July, 1921, 92.

53. Jill Conway, "Women Reformers and American Culture, 1870–1930," *Journal of Social History* (Winter 1971–72): 164–177.

54. Ibid.; "Chase Funeral Tomorrow," *Evening Bulletin* (Providence, R.I.), Aug. 19, 1935; Bradshaw, *Doll House,* 22;

55. "Obituary for Mrs. Anna M. Wheaton," Chase family papers.

56. Ellen Key, *The Century of the Child* (New York: G. P. Putman, 1909).

CHAPTER FOUR
Marketing a Campbell Kids Culture

1. E. I. Horsman catalogue, 1915.
2. "What has the Future in Store?" *PT,* Jan. 1911, 51; "The Toy Men in Toy Town," in Dorothy S. Coleman and Elizabeth J. Coleman, *The Collector's Encyclopedia of Dolls,* 2 vols (New York: Crown, 1968; 1986), 1:544.
3. Jonas Frykman and Orvar Lofgren, *Culture Builders: A Historical Anthropology of Middle-Class Life* (New Brunswick, N.J.: Rutgers University Press, 1987), 78. Inez McClintock and Marshall McClintock, *Toys in America* (Washington, D.C.: Public Affairs Press, 1961), 357 for numerous examples of spin-offs. Barbara Whitton Jendrick, *Antique Advertising Paper Dolls in Full Color,* (New York: Dover, 1981). According to one source, "A typical vaudeville joke of the time went something like this: If Theodore Roosevelt is President of the United States with with his clothes *on,* what is he with he clothes *off?* Answer—Teddy Bare!" (McClintock, *Toys in America,* 359). Sources dispute whether Michtom owned a candy, stationery, or novelty store. He probably sold a little of everything.Simultaneous with Michtom, Margarete Steiff also produced a bear, which has led to a debate over the origin of the stuffed animals; see Peter Bull, *The Teddy Bear Book* (New York: Random House, 1969), 24; see item 1977.528.2, assumed to be one of the original Teddy Bears made by Michtom, in the Division of Political History, National Museum of American History, Smithsonian Institution, Washington, D.C. Sears catalogue, 1907, cited in McClintock, *Toys in America,* 317; 355.
4. The Ideal Toy & Novelty Co. of Brooklyn, N. Y., was incorporated with capital stock of $20,000 for the purposes of manufacturing and dealing in toys, dolls, and novelties in 1912 by Morris Michtom, Issac A. Rommer, and Aaron Cone (see *TN,* May 1912, 40); "Toy Men in Toy Town," *McClure's,* 1913 reprinted in *Collector's Encyclopedia,* 2:544; *World Book Encyclopedia,* vol. 2, 1957, s.v. "dolls."
5. "Freak Toy Productions," *TN* Feb. 1910, 14.
6. Dian Zillner, "Some Early Tentieth-Century Composition Dolls," *DR,* June–July 1988, 64–68. "Birth of the Baby Beautiful Doll," *PT,* May 1912, 97.
7. see illustration 1256 A, B in *Collector's Encyclopedia,* 1:72.
8. *PT,* May, 1909, 3; *PT,* Oct. 1908, 70.
9. Advertisement, *PT,* May 1909, 3.
10. Advertisement, *PT,* Sept. 1909, 12.
11. *PT,* Oct. 1908, 98; "Domestic Toys," *PT,* June 1909, 140; William R. Leach, "The Clown from Syracuse: The Life and Times of L. Frank Baum," in L. Frank Baum, *The Wonderful World of Oz* (Belmont, Calif.: Wadsworth, 1991), 28.
12. See Dorothy S. Coleman, Elizabeth A. Coleman, and Evelyn J. Coleman, *Col-*

lector's Book of Doll Clothes: Costumes in Miniature, 1700–1929 (New York: Crown, 1975).

13. "The Christmas Doll and its Dress," *LHJ*, Dec. 1914, 75; Julie Masterson Child and Linda Masterson, Grace Drayton's Roly-Poly 'Kids,' " in Albert Christian Revi, ed., *Spinning Wheel's Complete Book of Dolls,* (New York: Galahad, 1975), 47; Jurgen Cieslik and Marianne Cieslick, *German Doll Encyclopedia, 1800–1939* (Cumberland, Md.: Hobby House Press, 1985), 12.; The character dolls advertised by the German firm of Margueretta Steiff always appeared in boy-girl pairs like Farmer Boy and Farmer Girl. Steiff catalogue, p. 27.

14. Martha Banta, *Imaging Women: Idea and Ideas in Cultural History* (New York: Columbia University Press, 1987), 7; advertisement, *PT,* Jan. 1911, 106.

15. Advertisement, *PT,* July 1910, 3; In *LHournal* articles dolls continued to present blacks as plantation based. "Dolls that Children Can Make," *LHJ*, Dec. 15, 1910, 33.

16. Advertisement, *PT,* April 1909, 4; Steven Mintz and Susan Kellogg, *Domestic Revolutions: A Social History of American Family Life* (New York: Free Press, 1988), 114; I would suggest that E. U. Steiner's "Human Face Doll Campaign" in 1907 was part of an overall trend in the American and German doll industries to make dolls look more real. Nevertheless, Steiner's dolls were far closer to dolly-faced dolls than character dolls which followed them. For a picture of him with his dolls see: "New Faces for Dolldom," *PT,* March 1908, 74. "Imported Dolls of Every Variety have Arrived," *PT,* Jan. 1911, 124.

17. "The Birth of the Baby Beautiful Doll,: *PT,* June 1919, 97.

18. *PT,* March 1911, p. 94; Jan. 1911, p. 3, 106; Feb. 1911, p. 64; May 1909, 3.

19. As early as 1903 some dolls with smaller eyes and sideways glances had an intentionally flirty appearance, though these had been made in Germany and appear to have had a limited influence on the American industry.

20. "The Make-Believe World of Toys: Humorous Dollies and Merry Animals," *The Craftman* 27, 1914–1915, 288. Catalogue cover reprinted in Louise C. Amati, "Schoenhut Dolls: The Beginning of Commercial Dollmaking in America," *Hobbies,* Oct. 1984, 42. Schoenhut All-Wood Dolls, price list, 1923. Jan Foulke, "Schoenhut Dolls," *DR,* Feb.–Mar. 1987, 94. Harvey Green, "Scientific Thought and the Nature of Children in America, 1820–1920," in Mary Lynn Stevens Heininger et al., *A Century of Childhood, 1820–1920* (Rochester, N.Y.: Margaret Woodbury Strong Museum, 1984), 133.

21. John Higham, "The Reorientation of American Culture in the 1890s," in John Higham, ed., *Writing American History* (Bloomington: University of Indiana Press, 1970); Peter Filene, *Him/Her/Self: Sex Roles in Modern America* (New York: Harcourt, Brace Jovanovich, 1974); Elizabeth Pleck and Joseph Pleck, *The American Man* (Englewood Cliffs, N.J.: Prentice-Hall, 1980); Margaret Marsh,

"Suburban Men and Masculine Domesticity, 19870–1915," in Mark C. Carnes
and Clyde Griffen, eds., *Meanings of Manhood: Constructions of Masculinity
in Victorian America* (Chicago: University of Chicago Press, 1990), 111–128. *PT,*
Feb. 1911, 65. A. Steinhardt & Bros. also produced dolls of baseball players.
Jockey was probably used as a window display or for students of fine art. All
of the "Dolls Comic" advertised in the 1913 Steiff catalogue were male, and
many portray masculine roles like baseball player, butcher, tailor, hunter, and
messenger boy.

22. "A New Doll," *PT,* Feb. 1912, 80; Advertisement, March 1912, 6; *Collector's Encyclopedia,* 1:348. "Toy Man in Toy Town," cited in *Collector's Encyclopedia,*
2:544; advertisements, *PT,* Aug. 1910, 27; Jan. 1913, 8; *Collector's Encyclopedia,* 2:380. Albert Schoenhut filed his patent application in 1909 but it was not
granted until 1911; see *Collector's Encyclopedia,* 1:554. See also "Trade Notes
and Latest Market News," *PT,* Jan. 1911, 34; and *PT,* March 1911, 136. Women producers like Martha Chase and Ella Smith established doll hospitals within their
factories where broken or torn dolls could be sent. *Scientific American* reported
that thanks to the new substance, dolls "can be dropped upon the floor without
breaking" ("Manufacture of Toys & Dolls," *Scientific American,* Dec. 1902, 376).
To demonstrate the doll's strength, a man weighing nearly 200 pounds stood on
it, and even *he* couldn't crack it, reported *Playthings* (Feb. 1912, 166).

23. "Selling Toys to the Middle Classes," *PT,* Dec. 1909, 70. Mintz and Kellogg,
Domestic Revolutions, 114. Paula S. Flass, *The Damned and the Beautiful*
(Oxford: Oxford University Press, 1979).

24. Mary H. Morgan, *How to Dress a Doll* (Philadelphia: Henry Altemus Co., 1908),
3; Olive Hyde Foster, *Sewing for Little Girls* (New York: Duffield, 1911); Jane
Eayre Frayer, *Easy Steps in Sewing Or: Adventures Among the Thimble People*
(Chicago: John C. Winston, 1911); Flora Klickmann, ed., *The Little Girls' Sewing
Book* (New York: Frederick A. Stokes, 1916). Women's magazines continued
to include directions for making doll clothing, however; see Louise S. Hauck,
"Three Christmas Dolls," *WHC,* Aug. 1911, 22; "Making Dolls' Dresses," *PT,* Oct.
1911, 34.

25. For dolls, see advertisements, *PT,* Sept. 1910, 17; Oct. 1910, 95. Using soap
to keep the body clean as opposed to soaps used as cosmetics was a late
nineteenth-century invention (A. Steinhardt Bros. advertisement, *PT,* Aug. 1910,
27). *Collector's Encyclopedia,* 2:207.31 "The New Dolls," *PT,* Jan 1903, 1. The
manufacture of doll clothing was often separate from doll production, especially
so among male manufacturers. Often women entrepreneurs like Katherine
("Kitty") Rauser transformed it "from its Jenny Wren origins into a modern
business." As a young woman, Rauser left a job at Marshall Field in Chicago
and headed east. But she found that "Sentiment against a woman in business

way back in 1903" prevented her employment elsewhere. In 1904, she started to make dolls' clothes "without a penny and with my workshop, the borrowed dining room of a friend who had to loan me her machine to sew. But her capital of unlimited pluck and determination triumphed." Rauser became a leading manufacturer of doll clothing and by 1929 was known as the "First Lady of the Toy Industry." In a photograph of the "Toy Men of Chicago," the matronly Kitty Rauser sits amid a sea of dark business suits. As a mother or as a businesswoman, Rauser blended right in ("She's Setting Styles for American Dolldom," *TN*, Feb. 1913, 53). On dolls' dressmaking at the Amberg establishment see Coleman et al., *Collector's Book of Doll Clothes*, 474; *PT*, April 1911, 110.

26. This trend would continue. In 1916, Dutch dolls were modeled after the Old Dutch Cleanser images. In 1917, Georgene Averill would market dolls in Dutch costumes as well (see *Collector's Encyclopedia*, 2:373). Advertisement, *PT*, Jan. 1912, 2. *Collector's Encyclopedia*, 1:196. Harvey Green, "Scientific Thought," 133. "Domestic Toys," 118. The Mitred Box Co. also marketed a kimonoed infant doll in 1912, see advertisement, *PT*, Jan 1912, 3; cover, Jan. 1914.

27. *PT*, Jan. 1911, 108. Advertisement, *PT*, Jan. 1913, 8. *Collector's Encyclopedia*, 1:449. Interestingly enough, this doll was not a "character" doll but a jointed, undressed, bisque-headed one. See advertisement in *PT*, Jan. 1912, 80;also Feb. 1911, 33.

28. Lewis Hine Collection, lot 7481, photo number 2820, Feb. 1912, Library of Congress, Washington D.C.

29. For specific street locations of Italian neighborhoods where homeworkers lived, see *Second Report* of the Factory Investigating Commission," Jan. 15, 1913, 1:262, 111; "The East Side Toy Industry," *PT*, Oct. 1905, 51–53.

30. Lewis Hine Collection, lot 7481, print 2711A, Library of Congress, Washington, D.C.
Susan E. Hirsh, *Roots of the American Working-Class: The Industrialization of Crafts in Newark, 1800–1925* (Philadelphia: University of Pennsylvania Press, 1978), 15–16; Leslie Woodcock Tentler, *Wage-Earning Women: Industrial Work and Family Life in the United States, 1900–1930* (New York: Oxford University Press, 1979), 142–143.
As reported in "The New Tariff Bill," *PT*, April 1909, 55.

31. Jacob Riis, *How the Other Half Lives* (1890; New York: Scribner's, 1917); Kathy Peiss, *Cheap Amusements: Working Women and Leisure in Turn-of-the-Century New York* (Philadelphia: Temple University Press, 1986), 24; Virginia Yans McLoughlin, *Family and Community: Italian Immigrants in Buffalo, 1880–1930* (Ithaca, N.Y.: Cornell University Press, 1977); Alice Kessler-Harris, *Out to Work: A History of Wage-Earning Women in the United States* (New York: Oxford University Press, 1982); Elizabeth Ewen, *Immigrant Women in the Land of Dol-*

lars: Life and Culture on the Lower East Side, 1890–1925 (New York: Monthly Review Press, 1985).

32. *Preliminary Report of the Factory Investigating Committee,* (Albany, N.Y.: 1912), 90.

33. *Preliminary Report,* 90.

34. *Child Labor Bulletin,* Aug. 1913, 703.
    Second Report, 702.

35. Ruth Enalda Shallcross, *Industrial Homework: an Analysis of Homework Regulation, Here and Abroad* (New York: Industrial Affairs Publishing, 1939), 108. In 1913 the investigations of the National Child Labor Committee and the photojournalism of Lewis Hine has led to New York State legislation. A number of subcontractors circumvented the statute by relocating to New Jersey.
    Second Report, 101–102, 692.

36. *Preliminary Report,* 582.
    Barbara Ehrenreich and Deirdre English, *For Her Own Good: 150 Years of Experts' Advice* (Garden City, N.Y.: Doubleday, 1979), 157.
    "New York Doll Quarantine Possible," *TN,* Jan. 1913, 57.

37. "Dolly Dear," *Child Labor Bulletin,* Aug. 1913, 28–31.

38. Kate Simon, *Bronx Primitive;* Anzia Yezierska, *The Bread Givers.*

CHAPTER FIVE
New Women and Talismen

1. Kewpie soap was advertised with original Rose O'Neill jingles, such as "It's fun to take a bath, you see, with Kewpie soap to play with me."

2. On the other hand, those who have included her in encyclopedic bibliographies have described her as a romantic and eccentric given to baby talk; see *Notable American Women,* s.v. "Rose O'Neill," 650–651; *Dictionary of American Biography,* s.v. "Rose Cecil O'Neill," 573–574.

3. This portrait of the Kewpies emerges from my analysis of the themes, plots and characters in the over 100 Kewpie cartoons published between 1909 and 1920, O'Neill's unpublished autobiography, correspondence, published fiction and Kewpie dolls.

4. Rose O'Neill, *The Story of Rose O'Neill* (unpublished manuscript), 13. For published version, see Miriam Formanek-Brunell, ed., *The Autobiography of Rose O'Neill* (Missouri University Press, forthcoming). *Notable American Women,* 650; Ralph Alan McCanse, *Titans and Kewpies: The Life and Art of Rose O'Neill* (New York, Washington, Hollywood: Vantage Press, 1968), 34–35.

5. O'Neill, *Story of Rose O'Neill,* 37, 64, 13–15, 27. Greg G. Thielen, *Through Rose Colored Glasses: The Drawings and Illustrations of Rose Cecil O'Neill* (Springfield, Mo.: Springfield Art Museum, 1985), 5.

6. O'Neill, *Story of Rose O'Neill,* 5–6, 8, 18, 37, 78; McCanse, *Titans and Kewpies,* 34

7. O'Neill, *Story of Rose O'Neill,* 2, 4, 8, 10, 11, 36, 47, 77. Philadelphia art publisher George Gebbie encouraged his daughters, Grace and her sisters' artistic talents. As a teenager, Emma Clear had been inspired to study art after attending a sculpture exhibition at the Chicago World's Fair (Eleanor St. George, *The Dolls of Yesterday* [New York and London: Charles Scribner's Sons, 1948], 191).

   The peripatetic Mr. O'Neill traveled frequently on his own while "the rest of his family saw Rose daily . . . He finally settled down in Missouri, "at the bottom of this pit [and] built a little cabin" (Alexander King, "Profiled: Kewpie Doll," *New Yorker,* 24 Nov. 1934, 22, 24). See also Alexander King, *May This House be Safe from Tigers* (New York: Simon & Schuster, 1959). George Kummer, *Harry Leon Wilson* (Cleveland: The Press of Western Reserve Library, 1963): 36. *Notable American Woman,* 651; Ella W. Peattie, *The Twentieth Century Home,* cited in McCanse, *Kewpies and Titans,* 52. Rowena Fay (Godding) Ruggles, *The One Rose, Mother of the Immortal Kewpies: A Biography of Rose O'Neill and the Story of her Work* (Oakland, Calif.: n.p., 1964), 9–10.

8. Ruggles, *One Rose,* 10; O'Neill, *Story of Rose O'Neill,* 168. O'Neill also chainsmoked.

9. Ruggles, *One Rose,* 10; O'Neill, *Story of Rose O'Neill,* 81, 88, 91.

10. O'Neill, *Story of Rose O'Neill,* 9, 63, 65, 78, 101, 155; *Notable American Women,* 650. Alice O'Neill skipped "over a mountain with a wagon and mules" to see her husband every now and then.

11. Kummer, *Harry Leon Wilson,* 39, 41. Wilson was the author of *The Spenders, The Lions of the Lord* (which O'Neill illustrated), and *The Boss of Little Arcady.* He "was certainly no model husband . . . In the Spring of 1907, without telling Rose where he was going, he left her in Paris while he and George Tyler, the theatrical producer . . . toured Italy, Sicily, and Northern Africa in Tyler's automobile" (King, "Profiled: Kewpie Dolls," 24). *Dictionary of American Biography,* 573. O'Neill, *Story of Rose O'Neill,* 149.

12. Wernicke was the inventor of an unfolding or expanding bookcase. O'Neill, *Story of Rose O'Neill,* 133. Louisa Tarkington and O'Neill seemed to share a sensibility which personified the inanimate but did not always succeed in providing it with a sense of agency as also revealed in Tarkington's poem about a paperweight that O'Neill illustrated. Unlike the Wernicke or even the pencil in Tarkington's poem, however, the paperweight "must be content to sit/And never romp or play" (Louisa Tarkington, "The Envious Paperweight," *Harper's Bazaar*). McCanse, *Kewpies and Titans,* 117–118. Christopher Lasch, *Haven in a Heartless World: The Family Besieged* (New York: Basic Books, 1979), 10; King, "Profiled: Kewpie Dolls," 24.

13. O'Neill, *Story of Rose O'Neill,* 155, 317. Letter in possession of Paul O'Neill. The

Kewpie Doodle dog was inspired by Harry Leon Wilson's dog, Sprangle (O'Neill, *Story of Rose O'Neill,* 148). In Germany, Kathe Kruse modeled her dolls after her own children. Her four-year-old son, Friedebald, for example, modeled for Das Deutsche Kind doll. Maud Tousey Fangle's son, Lloyd, had posed for almost 1,500 of his mother's drawings by the time he was three years old.

14. O'Neill, *Story of Rose O'Neill,* 213–214, 241, 317. Carroll Smith-Rosenberg, *Disorderly Conduct: Visions of Gender in Victorian America* (New York and Oxford: Oxford University Press, 1985), 254–255. Rose O'Neill's Kewpie Shop was located at 646A Madison Avenue, New York City, according to Ruggles, *One Rose,* 23, 18. McCanse, *Titans and Kewpies,* 26.

    One German chambermaid referred to the O'Neills as "Kleines liebes gutes Schwesterchen," which O'Neill translated as "little lovely good sisterling" (O'Neill, *Story of Rose O'Neill,* 192).

    Mary McAboy's apple dolls were displayed in the headquarters for one women's suffrage chapter. Some women at the time patented suffrage dolls and trademarked egalitarian slogans for them. Lilian E. Whitteker made a "Little Suffragist" doll in 1914. Mabel Drake Nekarda trademarked, "Votes for Women," 55,504, April 4 1911 and "Suffragette Kid" in 1911; "Condition in Great Britain," *Toys & Novelties,* June 1909, 16 reported that Messrs. Whyte, Ridsdale & Co. of London were marketing a "Bobby" doll "escorting a fanatic to the station."

15. Schlereth, *Victorian America,* 186. O'Neill's doodles appealed to Edward Bok, editor of *Ladies' Home Journal;* "The Kewpies are Coming," *GH,* May 1914, 637. While in the early fall of 1915, the Kewpies who worried about their weight decided to walk instead of fly, it wasn't until *Good Housekeeping* changed its format a year later that the Kewpies puffed up considerably. When the illustrations had to fill a vertical sheet instead of a horizontal one, the Kewpies got rounder. "The Kewpies and the College," *GH,* Oct. 1916, 45–47. In fact, the early slimmer Kewpies looked more realistic slim than the later more rotund versions. By 1911 their neotenic proportions would become more caricatured. O'Neill, *Story of Rose O'Neill,* 3.

16. "The Kewpies Arrive," *GH,* June 1914, 762. "The Kewpies and Thanksgivings," *GH,* Nov. 1914, 568.

17. Reared as a Catholic, Rose O'Neill had received a parochial school education in Nebraska and New York, and Christian iconography had played a role in her life.

18. "The Kewpies and the Baby," *LHJ,* Feb. 1910, 29.

19. "Tom, Dick and Harry Meet the Kewpies," *GH,* June 1915, 634–637; "The Kewpies and Old Father Time," *GH,* Jan. 1915, 27; "The Kewpies and Samuel Gudge, *GH,* Sept. 1915, 307; "Dotty Darling and the Kewpies," *WHC,* March 1911, 24, reprinted in John Axe, *Kewpies—Dolls & Art* (Cumberland, Md.: Hobby House Press, 1987), 25; "The Kewpish Adventures of the Kewpidoodle," *GH,* Apr. 1915,

379; "The Kewpie and Little Petie," *GH,* July 1915, 40–43; "The Kewpies and Ducky Daddles," *GH,* July 1914, 45–47. In "How the Kewps Turned into Dolls," they dress up in dolls' clothes and give themselves to poor children (reprinted without citation in Axe, *Kewpies,* 28); "The Kewpies and the Young McShanes," *GH,* Sept. 1914, 361–33. "The Kewpies and Little Tibby's Tree," *GH,* Aug. 1914, 198–201.

20. The Kewpies bring a poorly-dressed girl to the country to have fun and grow flowers ("The Kewpies and their New Adventures," *WHC,* Oct. 1911, 26, reprinted in Axe, *Kewpies,* 15). "The Kindly Kewpies, *WHC,* Dec. 1911, 27, reprinted in John Axe, 27; "The Kewpies Kutouts: Little Assunta and her Kewpie Doll," *WHC,* July 1913, 28, reprinted in Axe, *Kewpies,* 30. "Kewpies and the Young McShanes," 362. "The Kewpie and Little Petie," *GH,* July 1915, 43.

21. The Information Kewp may have been based on her mother's Aunt Pamela, "a stickler for propriety and lady-like ways" (O'Neill, *Story of Rose O'Neill,* 43).

22. Postcard in private collection. The poster was based on the "Spirit of '76" by the artist Archibald M. Willard. The American revolutionary war theme had been first used by woman's rights advocates who fashioned the 1848 Declaration of Sentiments after the Declaration of Independence.

23. O'Neill, *Story of Rose O'Neill,* 164, 202, 165, 177–8.

24. O'Neill, *Story of Rose O'Neill,* 188, 191, 192; McCanse, *Kewpies and Titans,* 127. While in Germany, O'Neill invented a way of keeping the Kewpie's legs close together—unlike previous generations of dolls (193).

25. "Items of Interest in the Toy Trade," *Playthings,* Nov. 1929, 95. Jean Cantwell, "The Marvelously Creative Rose O'Neill," *DR,* Apr. 1983, 47. It was not until 1929 that Rose and Callista O'Neill (who was better with scissors and needle) created the prototype of soft-bodied "Kuddle Kewpies," manufactured by King Innovations (Mildred Adams, "The 'Kewpie' Lady," *The Woman Citizen,* Dec. 1925, 37–38). Although O'Neill's handmade Kewpie rag doll prototype had a flat and painted face, it also had an intentionally "wobbly disposition" (Cantwell, "Marvelously Creative," 77). Axe, *Kewpies,* 65.

26. Advertisement, *PT,* July 1913, 21; *WHC,* July 1913, n.p.

27. Representations of flight appeared widely in O'Neill's creative work. While her mother had been raised in a Protestant home, converted to Catholicism and sent her daughter to convent schools, it was birds and not angels that inspired Rose O'Neill. For example, instead of using an eraser, O'Neill would cover mistakes made in her personal correspondence with a bird's wing. O'Neill liked to watch birds from her third story studio in her rural Missouri home. O'Neill's own self-representation—her signature—consisted of stick figures with threadlike legs who wore rubber overshoes, carried umbrellas, expressed emotions and occasionally, also sported a pair of wings (O'Neill, *Story of Rose O'Neill,* 7). For

a discussion of what her signature looked like, see Rugglers, *One Rose,* 9, 12–14. For examples of birds in Kewpie cartoons, see The Kewpies and their New Adventures;" "Dotty Darling and the Kewpies;" O'Neill, *Story of Rose O'Neill,* 133, 196. In the 1920s, she would create Scootles, the baby tourist: "I sculptured her as a real baby," (299).

28. "Leg Emancipation," 6.

CHAPTER SIX

Forging the Modern American Doll Industry, 1914–1929

1. Dorothy S. Coleman and Evelyn J. Coleman, *The Collector's Encyclopedia of Dolls,* 2 vols. (New York: Crown, 1968, 1986), 1:402.

2. John Noble, Dolls, *Dolls* (New York: Walker, 1968), ch. 6. Janet Pragter Johl, *The Fascinating Story of Dolls* (Watkins Glen, N.Y.: Century House, 1970), 157.

3. "Hear Santa Claus is a War Prisoner," (Newark) *Evening News,* Aug. 11, 1914. "European War Stops Imports," *NYT,* Aug. 10, 1914, 4. "The Kewpie Lady," *Woman Citizen,* Dec. 1925, 13; "Hear Santa."

4. "Toy Industry's Growth," *NYT,* Nov. 14, 1920, 15. "New Era in Dolls," *World's Work,* Dec. 1916, 123–124. *Collector's Encyclopedia,* 1:317.
Unanimous consent of stockholders to increase capital stock, Dec. 20, 1918. 1518–98; certificate of increase of capital stock of Louis Amberg & Son, Dec. 14, 1927, 3179–140.
"Difficulties of Toymakers," *NYT,* 7; Harry A. Mount, "New American Toy Industry," *SA,* Dec. 25, 1920, 634. My view is that it was even higher. Certificate of Incorporation of Emkay Doll & Mfr. Co., March 13, 1918, 1455556–66. Both the capital stock and the firm's working capital were each placed at $10,000. "Difficulties of the Toymakers," 7.

5. Johl, *Fascinating Story,* 157; *Collector's Encyclopedia,* 1:317.

6. *TN,* May 1915, cited in *Collector's Encyclopedia,* 2:781, 1:173.
Collector's Encyclopedia, 2:565. Some believed that the glue process made dolls stronger than wood pulp heads, which broke, cracked, and were sensitive to humidity (1:19, 173).

7. "Bisque Dolls Now Made in America, *PT,* June 1919, 100. American producers of bisque were no match for the Japanese, who had taken advantage of the hiatus in German imports to produce bisque dolls of their own. By 1917, with their export and import firms fully coordinated, "the Japanese began to take the place of the Germans" in the export of dolls to England and the United States ("The Japanese Toy Trade," *PT,* Jan. 1919, 232). *Collector's Encyclopedia,* s.v. "Artcraft Toy Products Co.," "Republic Doll & Toy Corp.," "New Toy Co." The Bester Doll Mfr. Co. claimed that its composition "resembled bisque." Thus, despite the rhetoric about the superiority of composition dolls, bisque still appealed to

manufacturers, two of which were even named the American Bisque Doll Co. and the American Bisque Co.

8. In 1913, Amberg advertised that its composition dolls were not made with glue and therefore would not crack or peel.

   PT, 1924, quoted in *Collector's Encyclopedia,* 1:416, 2:781–782, 552.

9. "Manufacturing Policies that have Offset Europe's Cheap Labor," *PT,* Mar. 1928, 212.

   "Doll-Head Industry," 145.

   "Electricity Increases Doll Factory Output," *Electrical World,* Dec. 2, 1916, 1107–1108.

10. "Doll and Stuffed Toy Workers Strike," *PT,* June 1916, 59.

11. *TN,* Feb. 1916, reprinted in *Collector's Encyclopedia,* 11:782.

12. "Difficulties of the Toymakers," *NYT,* Dec. 3, 1916, 7, 7

    TN, Feb. 1916, reprinted in *Collector's Encyclopedia,* 2:782.

13. "Toy Makers Will Meet Competition," *NYT,* Dec. 2, 1917, 9:12; "Difficulties of the Toymakers," 7; "Doll and Stuffed Toy," 59.

14. Kathy Peiss, *Cheap Amusements: Working-Women and Leisure in Turn-of-the-Century New York* (Philadelphia: Temple University Press), ch. 4; "1,800 Dollmakers Strike," *NYT,* June 23, 1916, 14:2; "Our Doll Makers Now Go on Strike," *NYT,* June 24, 1916, 16.

15. "Our Doll Makers Now Go on Strike," *NYT,* June 24, 1916, 16; "Doll Strike Ended," *TN,* May 1920, 68.

16. "Electricity Increased Doll Factory Output," *Electrical World,* Dec. 2, 1916, 1107–1108.

17. "Doll and Stuffed Toy," 59.

    "Doll Strike Ended," 68.

    "The Doll Situation," *PT,* May 1920, p. 75;The next resurgence of union strength would be in 1927, when 17 doll and doll head factories were "wholly or partly unionized" and operatives at seven other factories went out on strike ("Strike Threatens," *PT,* Feb. 1927, 127–128). Employers feared striking operatives who attended mass meetings and were influenced by strike organizers among the paper box makers. For at least two months, doll union operatives conducted a drive of the recently formed Doll and Stuffed Toy Workers' Union and threatened a general strike for the next busy season the following summer and fall ("The Doll Strike," *PT,* April 1927, 71; "Doll Workers Return," *PT,* May 1927, 73). Though the workers returned, manufacturers feared that the general strike would cripple the industry which provided close to 90 percent of all domestically made dolls. "Doll Workers to Strike," *NYT,* May 1, 1927, 2:8. Buyers, who were urged to place their orders early, remained skeptical, however, and ascribed "the warnings of manufactures to a desire to stimulate early buying."

18. The committee that drafted the resolution included Joe L. Amberg. "Want Law to Bar All German Goods," *NYT,* Oct. 29, 1918, 15.
    Peter Gabriel Filene cites numerous examples from the *Saturday Evening Post,* other periodicals, and Elizabeth H. Pleck and Joseph H. Pleck, *The American Man* (Englewood Cliffs, N.J.: Prentice-Hall, Inc., 1980).

19. "Want Law to Bar All German Goods," 15.

20. "F. A. O. Schwarz: The Toystore," *Fortune,* Dec. 1940, 87; "Germany's Lost Toy Trade," *NYT,* Dec. 25, 1917, 14.

21. "Difficulties of the Toymakers," 7; advertisement, *St. Nicholas,* 1917–1918, 36.

22. *Collector's Encyclopedia,* 1:401.

23. "New Era in Dolls," *World's Week,* Dec. 1916, 123–124.

24. William C. Redfield, "The Heart Behind Our Power," *PT,* Feb. 1919, 134–138; "Germany's Plot to Gas the World's Trade," *PT,* May 1919, 94–98.

25. *PT* July 1920, 77. "Toy Makers Plan Drive," *NYT,* July 25, 1919, 3:2; advertisement, *LHJ,* Dec. 1919, 42;26 "A Great National Advertising Campaign," *PT,* Jan. 1919, 235; *PT,* Aug. 1920, 4; "American Toys are Doing Very Well," *NYT,* Dec. 19, 1920, 2:18.

26. Campaigns to encourage consumers to buy American toys did not prevent the German doll industry from resuming their undercutting prctices. According to a government report, by 1920dolls and doll parts exported to the United States were the same as in 1913 (Arthur Grey, *Postwar Conditions in the German Toy Industry,* [Washington D.C.: Government Printing Office, 1924], see table, 17). The German industry suffered from numerous problems in the postwar period—loss of the free labor of the apprenticeship system, higher praces for scarce raw materials, and rising freight rates—none of which were the American manufacturers' doings. Domestic manufacturers had taken in $10 million, making 1920 a good year. On the tariff see editorial, *PT,* April 1921, 72; "History of Toy Mfrs. Association from 1916 to 1941," in Toy Mfrs. of America archives; A. Cassey Morrison, "The Present European Situation and American Industry," *PT,* Dec. 1923, 231.

27. Charles E. Hawkes, "American Doll Manufacturers' Parade," *PT,* Dec. 1921, 108.

28. Frank Stricker, "Cookbooks and Lawbooks: The Hidden History of Career Women in Twentieth-Century America," in Nancy Cott and Elizabeth Pleck, eds., *A Heritage of Her Own* (New York: Simon & Schuster, 1982), 481.

29. Constance Eileen King, The *Collector's History of Dolls* (New York: Bonanza Books, 1977), 438; "Birth and Career of Skookum Told by Woman Originator," *Denver Post,* Dec. 4, 1921, 13. Susie Sexton, "The Story of the Doll Lady," *WHC,* Oct. 1919, 72.

30. "Women Manufacturers and Designers," n.p. file, in Margaret Woodbury Strong

Museum archives, Rochester, New York. Mrs. F. E. [Mary] McAboy, "The Origin of Skookum Indian Dolls," *PT,* Mar. 1920, 160.

31. *WHC,* Oct. 1919, 72. One might suspect that Hendren might have suffered from neurosthenia so common among late-Victorian middle-class women; see Dorothy M. Brown, *Setting a Course: American Women in the 1920s* (Boston: Twayne, 1987), 161. An important exception to the businessmen's model is the firm Etta, Inc., founded by Etta Kidd in 1926, which had a nearly all-female board of directors and hired only women to manufacture the dolls Kidd designed.

32. Certificate of incorporation, Berry and Ross, Inc., June 6, 1918, 1479–1485. The lawyers who executed the incorporation documents may have received shares of stock in exchange for their services, which was common among women inventors according to historian August Stanley (private correspondence). In 1919 Berry and Ross reduced the number of shares without reducing the amount of capital stock. At the same time, after placing an advertisement in the *Amsterdam News* calling for a special meeting of stockholders, Berry & Ross filed an increase of capital stock from $10,000 (in 2,000 shares of $5 par value) to $100,000 to consist of 10,000 shares at $10. Certificate of change of par value of shares of Berry & Ross, Inc., Nov. 18, 1919, 1636–1645. Certificate of incorporation of the Allison Novelty Co., Inc., Dec. 4, 1918, 1514–1578.

33. *TN,* 1928, reprinted in *Collector's Encyclopedia,* 2:131.

34. Estelle V. Allison, U.S. patent 46,241, Aug. 11, 1914; 49,916, Nov. 21, 1916; 51,490, Nov. 20, 1917. Allison also patented winged fairy doll designs, as well, see: U.S. design patents, 58,300, July 12, 1921; 58,298, July 12, 1921; 58,297, July 12, 1921.

35. Rose O'Neill and Callista Schuler, Bernice and Bertha Squire, and L. and B. Shinn were among the sisters listed on patents. "Leaders Among Toy Makers," 68; "Toy Makers Guild Elects New Officers," *TW,* Feb. 1929, photograph. "Mrs. Delavan Addresses Chamber of Commerce," *TN,* May 1920, 90; "Mrs. S. E. Delavan Honored," *TN,* April 1920, 100.

The manufacture of doll clothing was often separate from doll production itself, especially among male-owned firms. Often women entrepreneurs like Katherine ("Kitty") Rauser, who transformed it "from its Jenny Wren origins into a modern business." As a young woman, Rauser left a job at Marshall Field and headed east, but found that "sentiment against a woman in business way back in 1903" prevented her employment elsewhere. In 1904, she started to make dolls' clothes "without a penny and with my workshop, the borrowed dining room of a friend who had to loan me her machine to sew." "But her capital of unlimited pluck and determination triumphed." Rauser became a leading manufacturer of dolls clothing and by 1929 was known as the "First Lady of the Toy Industry." In a photograph of the "Toy Men of Chicago," the matronly Rauser sat amidst a sea of dark business suits. As mother or businesswoman, Rauser blended right in ("She's Setting Styles for American Dolldom," *TN,* Feb. 1913, 53).

36. "Mrs. S. E. Delavan Honored," *TN,* April 1920, 100; "Editress Embodies Spirit of Toy Trade," *TW,* Oct. 1927, 34.

37. Lois Banner, *Women in Modern America: A Brief History* (San Diego: Harcourt Brace, Jovanovich, 2nd. edition, 1984), 162. Mary Woloch, *Women and the American Experience* (New York: Alfred A. Knopf, 1984), 389.

38. H. A. Free, "Why Some Girls Succeed in Business," *PT,* April 1912, 90. Kathleen W. Jones, "Mother's Day: The Creation, Promotion, and Meaning of a New Holiday in the Progressive Era," *Texas Studies in Literature and Languages* 22 (Summer 1980): 176, 196. Estelle Friedman, "The New Woman: Changing View of Women in the 20s," *Journal of American History* 61 (Sept. 1974): 393. The perception of businesswomen as "undainty" is according to insurance sales-woman Edith Mae Cummings, quoted in Banner, *Women in Modern America,* 164. Georgene Hendren, Beatrice Behrman, and Leonore Bubenheim styled themselves "Madame." According to Behrman, a male buyer first suggested the title Mme. Alexander (interview with author, Sugarhill, Vermont, Summer 1986).

39. "Birth and Career of Skookum," 13.

40. Alice M. Chalmer, "Clever Little Woman Who Makes Life-Like Little Indian Dolls," *Sunset,* Feb. 1919, 48. *Collector's Encyclopedia,* 2:817. Berry & Ross made composition black dolls. Whitton, "Raleigh," 79–80. Quoted in *Collector's Encyclopedia,* 2:298.

41. "60 Years Ago," *Roanoke Leader,* Mar. 7, 1982, photocopy of original in col-lection of Mrs. John B. Stevenson. Ann Calvert, "The Indestructible Dolls of Roanoke, Alabama," *DR,* Aug.–Sept. 1983, 130.

42. McAboy, "Origin of Skookum," 160.

43. More often, husbands took control of companies with only limited support from their spouses, although in "How a Factory Grew Out of a Handkerchief," *Toy World* (March 1929) reported that Morrill accompanied his wife to stores where she found willing buyers for her handkerchief dolls. Initially, Benoliel gave "very limited" assistance to his wife, Eileen, who was anxious to manufacture the Skeezix dolls she designed (*TN,* 1928, reprinted in *Collector's Encyclopedia,* 2:132).

In addition to their husbands, career women depended upon other family members. Georgene Hendren's siblings and brother-in-law, Marguerete Steiff's brother, Grace Drayton's brother-in-law were all involved in dollmaking ven-tures.

44. "How a Factory." Stricker, "Cookbooks and Lawbooks," 478; Elaine Showalter, *These Modern Women: Autobiographical Essays from the Twenties,* (Old West-bury, N.Y.: Feminist Press: 1978).

45. Alice Kessler-Harris, *Out to Work: A History of Wage-Earning Women in the United States*, (New York: Oxford University Press, 1982), 228; William O'Neill, *Everyone Was Brave: The Rise and Fall of Feminism in America* (Chicago: Quadrangle, 1969), 264. Kessler-Harris, *Out to Work*, 228. Raleigh's sons recollection quoted in Whitton, "Raleigh Dolls," 80. *TN*, 1928, reprinted in *Collector's Encyclopedia*, 2:131. Johl, *Fascinating Story*, 166.

46. King, *Collector's Book*, 338, 438–441. "My first idea was to have the baby manufactured in rubber . . . with a face as soft and flesh like and as daintily tinted as a baby's face." The U.S. Rubber Co. considered the idea for some time and then rejected it saying they were curtailing their manufacture of toys" (quoted in Johl, *Fascinating*, 164).

47. "Mrs. J. P. Averill's Career," *NYT*, Nov. 3, 1940, 2:4. Although the late nineteenth-century dolls that talked and cried had jarred the sensibilities of America's first generation of women doll makers, it was Georgene Hendren who had introduced the first modern American mama doll, soon to be an industry staple. Now women inventors competed for their share of the mechanical doll market. Beulah Louise Henry, also known as "Lady Edison" according to the Women's News Service, patented more devices than any other woman in the country including a doll with changeable hair (*Women of 1924* [New York: Women of Today Press, 1924], 124). Now, only a small and divided contingent within the industry remained critical of the mechanical dolls produced. Beatrice Behrman never manufactured one because "to allow a doll to perform mechanically for a child would have the tendency to have her sit back [passively] and have others perform for her" (Patricia R. Smith, *Mme. Alexander, Collector's Dolls* [New York: Crown Publishers, 1978], 4). German dollmaker Kathe Kruse felt the same way, as did others. See Harriet M. Robinson, "Why Not Give Toys to Children Once a Month Instead of So Many at Christmas?" *TN*, Feb. 1928, 114. King, *Collector's History*, 470; Johl, *Fascinating*, 164. In her autobiography, Lenci explained that she designed her first doll after "having lost my little girl." Quoted in *Collector's Encyclopedia*, 2:701.

48. *NYT*, Nov. 8, 1925, 9; *Literary Digest*, Jan. 23, 1926, 25. *TN*, 1916, reprinted in *Collector's Encyclopedia*, 2:1105. Anne Wilson, "Christmas Dolls for the Kiddies," *WHC*, Dec. 1919, n.p. Rose O'Neill, unpublished autobiography, O'Neill family papers, 299.

49. Susan Porter Benson, *Counter Cultures: Saleswomen, Managers, and Customers in American Department Stores, 1890–1940* (Urbana and Chicago: University of Illinois Press, 1988), 51–60, 164. see also Grace Storey Putnam, unpublished autobiography, private collection, 398. Johl, *Fascinating*, 165. St. George, *Dolls of Yesterday*, 132.

50. King, *Collector's History*, 438.

51. When perturbed by the quality of work from one Japanese factory, Rose O'Neill attempted to break her contract. She succeed with one but not with the other.

52. *Collector's Encyclopedia,* 1151. Quoted in Whitton, "Raleigh Dolls," 80.

CHAPTER SEVEN
Children's Day

1. "C. W. Butler Entertains 5,000 Kiddies," *PT,* Mar. 1913, 74;"Dolls' Tea Party Scores," *PT,* Feb. 1912, 75; Richard Wightman Fox and T. J. Jackson Lears, eds., *The Culture of Consumption: Critical Essays in American History, 1880–1980* (New York: Pantheon, 1983).

2. Doll Oral History, Margaret Woodbury Strong Museum, Rochester, N.Y., typescript (hereafter, Strong Museum Doll Oral History): L. M. Wagner, p. 2; R. Ashburn, 3; F. Fancy, 5. Dorothy Howard, *Dorothy's World, 194.*

3. *Howard, Dorothy's World,* 195. Strong Museum Doll Oral History: R. Mauer, 7; M. Altman, 5; L. M. Wagner, 2–3; M. Mueller, 1; F. Ashburn, 4.

4. Genevieve Angione, *All-Bisque and Half-Bisque Dolls* (New York: Thomas Nelson & Sons, 1969), 220–221.

5. Catharine Brody, "A New York Childhood," *American Mercury* 14 (1928), 60, quoted in David Nasaw, *Children of the City: At Work & At Play* (Garden City, N.Y.: Doubleday, 1985), 106. Anna Kohler, "Children's Sense of Money," *Studies in Education* 1 (Mar. 1897): 323–331, cited by Victoria Bissell Brown, "Female Socialization among the Middle-Class of Los Angeles," in Elliott West and Paula Petrik, eds., *Small Worlds: Children and Adolescents in America* (Lawrence: University of Kansas Press, 1992), 240. Angione, *All-Bisque,* 222.

6. Betty Smith, *A Tree Grows in Brooklyn* (New York and London: Harper & Bros., 1947), 8. Ethel Spencer, *Spencers of Amberson Avenue: A Turn-of-the-Century Memoir* (Pittsburgh: University of Pittsburgh Press, 1984), 65;

7. "Offers Excellent Field for Feminine Sex," *TN,* Feb. 1911, 20, 221.

8. "Offers Excellent Field," 221–222.

9. Hunt, 9. Angione, *All-Bisque,* 222; "Offers Excellent Field," 221–222.

10. Zach McGhee, "A Study of the Play Life of Some South Carolina Children," *Pedagogical Seminary* 7, no. 4 (Dec. 1900): 464; Angione, *All-Bisque,* 224; Strong Museum Doll Oral History: F. Fancy, 13.

11. George E. Johnson, *Education through Recreation* (Cleveland, Ohio: Survey Committee of the Cleveland Foundation, 1916), 48–51, cited in Bernard Mergen, "Toys and the Culture of Childhood," in West and Petrik, eds., *Small Worlds,* 100. S. Comstock, "Your Girl at Play," *GH,* 64, Feb. 1914, 23–24; A. Parry, "Athletic Girl and Motherhood," *HB,* Aug. 1912, 380. "Recreation of Young City Girls," *Review of Reviews, American Monthly* 39, Jan. 1909, 115; Jane Addams, "Failure of the

Modern City to Provide for Young Girls," *Charities and Commons* Dec. 5, 1908, 365–368.

12. Angione, *All-Bisque,* 224. Strong Museum Doll Oral History: R. Brown, 5; Comstock, "Your Girl at Play," 24; Janet Gillespie, *With a Merry Heart* (New York: Harper & Row, 1976), 16–17.

13. Anna Fuller, "Tomboy," *Atlantic Monthly,* May 1910, 655–666, quoted in Comstock, "Your Girl at Play," 24; Jeannette L. Gilder, *The Autobiography of a Tomboy* (New York: Doubleday, Page & Co., 1900).

14. "The American Girl Overalls," advertisement, *Land of Sunshine,* April 12, 1900, n.p., cited by Brown, "Female Socialization," 249. Angione, *All-Bisque,* 221, 224.

15. Angione, *All-Bisque,* 224; Susanna Bryant Dakin, "The Scent of Violets," (typescript, 1966, Bancroft Library, University of California, Berkeley), 45–46, cited by Brown, "Female Socialization," 247. Johnson, *Education Through Recreation,* 48–51 cited in Mergen, "Toys and the Culture," 100. Gillespie, *Merry Heart,* 82–3. Strong Museum Doll Oral History: Wagner, 8; Mueller, 1;

16. Strong Museum Doll Oral History: Altman, 2; Fancy, 12. Mueller 6; R. Rugg, 17. Passage on Teddy Bears quoted by Laura Starr, *The Doll Book* (1908), and reprinted in Mary Hillier, *Teddy Bears: A Celebration* (New York: Beaufort Books, 1985), 37. See also Ada Sterling, "Dressed Dolls," *HB,* Nov. 1907, 125. Eda Lord, *Childplay* (New York: Simon & Schuster, 1961).

17. Strong Museum Doll Oral History: Mueller, 9; Cohn, 3–4; E. Merchey, 4. Elizabeth Ewen, *Immigrant Women in the Land of Dollars: Life and Culture on the Lower East Side, 1890–1925* (New York: Monthly Review Press, 1985), 112. Strong Museum Doll Oral History: E. Cohn, 3–4. Kate Simon, *Bronx Primitive: Portraits in a Childhood* (New York: Harper & Row, 1982), 28; Nasaw, *Children of the City,* 105–106. Rosalind Rosenberg, *Divided Lives: American Women in the Twentieth Century* (New York: Hill & Wang, 1992), 19.

18. Strong Museum Doll Oral History: E. Merchey, 4. Anzia Yezierska, *Bread Givers* (1925; reprint, New York: Persea, 1975), 20–21. *Child Labor Bulletin,* Aug. 1913, 25.

19. Helen Russell Wright, *Children of Wage-Earning Mothers,* U.S. Department of Labor, Children's Bureau, (Washington, D.C.: Government Printing Office, 1922), 21. Simon, *Bronx Primitive,* 28; Nasaw, *Children of the City,* 105–106. Strong Museum Doll Oral History: Cohn, 3–4. Elizabeth Stern, *Mother and I* (New York, 1917), 55–56, quoted in Nasaw, *Children of the Streets,* 106; see also Charlotte Baum, Paula Hyman, and Sonya Michel, *The Jewish Woman in America* (New York: Dial Press, 1976). Greenwich House, *Thirteenth Annual Report* (New York, 1913–1914), 18, quoted in Nasaw, *Children of the City,* 108.

20. Strong Museum Doll Oral History: J. Arbore Camelio, 3; E. Cohen, 3–4. Kathy Peiss, *Cheap Amusements: Working Women in Turn-of-the-Century New York*

(Philadelphia: Temple University Press, 1986), 58. Oral history of Marietta H. Interlandi, IC, 37, cited in Nasaw, *Children of the City,* 113.

21. David Nasaw, "Children and Commercial Culture," in West and Petrik, eds., *Small Worlds,* 23; Roy Rosenzweig, *Eight Hours for What We Will: Workers and Leisure in an Industrial City, 1870–1920* (Cambridge, 1983), 197. Jane Addams, *The Spirit of Youth and the City Streets* (New York: Macmillan, 1909), 80; Strong Museum Doll Oral History: Fancy, 12. Maurice Willows, "The Neckel Theatre," in National Children's Labor Committee, Seventh Annual Meeting, Annals (Philadelphia, 1911), 96, quoted in Nasaw, "Children and Consumer Culture, 18.

22. Anna Fuller, "Tomboy," *Atlantic Monthly* May 1910, 655–666; "Confessions of a Tomboy," *Delineator,* Feb. 7, 1921.

23. *PT,* Sept. 1928, 110.

24. Alice Kessler-Harris, *Out to Work: A History of Wage-Earning Women in the United States* (New York: Oxford University Press, 1982), 132. *NYT,* Dec. 12, 1920, 7:11.

25. "The Woman as a Purchaser," *PT,* Nov. 1911, 86. See the following issues of *PT:* Feb. 1911, 113–114; Jan. 1922, 225; Apr. 1921, 94; July 1921, 84. Cited in *PT,* Apr. 1921, 94. "Advice to Saleswomen," *PT,* May 1911, 82. "America's Wonderful Dolls," *PT,* Apr. 1919, 82. She was hired by an American manufacturer as "sole supervisor of the doll dresses and outfits." Susan Porter Benson, *Counter Cultures: Saleswomen, Managers, and Customers in American Department Stores, 1890–1940* (Urbana and Chicago: University of Illinois Press, 1988).

26. *PT,* July 1921, 80.

27. C. B. Larrabee, "Effanbee Campaign Gets Sales by Helping Parents Buy Toys," 125, *Printers Inc.,* Nov. 8, 1923, 18. Carl A. Naether, *Advertising to Women* (New York: Prentice-Hall, 1928), 27, cited in Glenna Matthews, *Just a Housewife: The Rise and Fall of Domesticity in America* (New York: Oxford University Press, 1987), 188. *TW,* July 1928, 65.

28. *PT,* Jan. 1919, 213. Simon, *Bronx Primitive,* 45.

29. Butler Bros., New York City, "Our Drummer" catalogues: 1889, 1890, 1903, 1916, 1924, 1925, 1928; Reprinted in Margaret Adams, *Collectible Dolls and Accessories of the Twenties and Thirties from Sears, Roebuck & Co. Catalogs* (New York: Dover, 1986), 15; Strong Museum Doll Oral History: S. Fagenbaum, 10; Howard, *Dorothy's World,* 9, 11.

30. A. A. Gridley, *PT,* Apr. 1927, 73; *PT,* May 1927, 76. *NYT,* Dec. 11, 1927, 2:12. *PT,* Jan. 1919, 213; *PT,* Feb. 1919, 123. Molly Haskell, *From Reverence to Rape: The Treatment of Women in the Movies* (New York: Holt, Rinehart & Winston, 1974); Margorie Rosen, *Popcorn Venus: Women, Movies and the American Dream* (London: Peter Owen, 1975).

31. *NYT,* Jan. 6, 1927, 10. Directors included a pastor, the executive secretary of the

Big Brothers and Big Sisters Federation, a nursery school director, a doctor, a lawyer, and a psychologist. *PT,* Dec. 1926, 268. *PT,* June 1927, 412. *NYT,* Jan. 6, 1927, 10; *PT,* Feb. 1927, 129; Margoree Candee, "A Glorious Magic City," *PT,* Feb. 1927, 130. "Children's Day, June 18," *PT,* Mar. 1926, 268. A. A. Gridley, "Chicago Shows Enthusiasm for Children's Day," *PT,* Jan. 1928, 429; Cal Lewis, "$1,500 Prizes for Children's Day Efforts," *PT,* Feb. 1928, 130.

32. William Leach, "Transformations in a Culture of Consumption: Women and Department Stores, 1890–1925," *Journal of American History* 71 (Sept. 1984): 322. *School and Society,* April 28, 1928, 500–501; *NYT,* March 27, 1929, 5.

33. Viviana Zelizer, *Pricing the Priceless Child* (New York: Basic Books, 1985), 23, 50. City Club, *Amusements and Recreation in Milwaukee* (Milwaukee, 1914), 10, and Rowland Haynes and Stanly Davies, *Public Provision for Recreation* (Cleveland, 1920), 23–24, cited in Nasaw, *Children of the City,* 37–8; Herbert L. May and Dorothy Pegen, *Leisure and its Uses: Some International Observations,* (New York: A. S. Barnes, 1928), 19–25; Dominick Cavallo, *Muscles and Morals* (Philadelphia: University of Pennsylvania Press, 1981).

34. James V. Mulholland, "Children's Day in New York Playgrounds," *PT,* Mar. 1927, 150. According to Robert McCready in an address delivered at the Summer Meeting of the Toy Mfrs. of the U.S.A., Lake Placid, New York and reprinted in *PT,* July 1927, 146.

35. Kathy Jones, " 'Straightening the Twig': William Healy and the Professionalization of American Child Psychiatry, 1899–1952," Ph.D. diss., Rutgers University, 1988. Ruth Schwartz Cowan, "Two Washes in the Morning and a Bridge Party at Night: The American Housewife Between the Wars," *Women Studies* 3 (1976): 147–72;

36. A. A. Gridley, "Chicago Shows Enthusiasm for Children's Day," *PT,* Apr. 1927, 73; Ernest R. Groves and William F. Ogburn, *American Marriage and Family Relationships* (New York: H. Holt & Co., 1925); "A New Understanding of Children," *PT,* June 1928, 93; "More Toys Will Curb Crime," Ibid., 103.; Ruth Schwartz Cowan, *More Work for Mother* (New York: Basic Books, 1983), 178–179. Robert S. Lynd and Helen Merrell Lynd, *Middletown* (New York: Harcourt, Brace and World, 1956). "Are You a 100% Mother," *WHC,* Jan. 1922, cited in Matthews, *Just a Housewife,* 182.

37. Jan Fuerst, "Children's Day," *PT,* May, 1927, 80.

38. "Resume of Results," *PT,* Sept. 1928, 88. Robert M. McCready, "Children's Day Makes a New Era in Toy Selling," *PT,* July 1927, 146. Robert H. McCready, "Children's Day Creates Enthusiasm," *PT,* Apr. 1927, 107. Robert H. McCready, "Children's Day Scored an Outstanding Success," *PT,* June 1927, 93. "Last Minute News on Children's Day—June 16," *PT,* May 1928, 93.

39. *NYT,* May 5, 1930, 15.

40. A. A. Gridley, *PT,* May 1927, 76. Marjoree Candee used the phrase "jazzization" to describe the purpose of Children's Day as did others, see: *PT,* Dec. 1926, 268; list of mayors who proclaimed Children's Day are listed in *PT,* June 1928, 74. "Reporting on Children's Day," *PT,* July 1932, 33.

41. James V. Mulholland, "How the Playgrounds of New York Celebrated Children's Day," *PT,* June 1929, 119; "50,000 Frolic here on Children's Day," *PT,* May 5, 1930; "Resume of Children's Day Results," *PT,* Sept. 1928, 86.

42. *PT,* Aug. 1928, 114.

43. "Prizes Awarded for Children's Day," *PT,* Apr. 1927, 107; *PT,* Feb. 1927, 80; "Prizes Awarded for Children's Day," *PT,* Apr. 1927, 107; "$1,500 Prizes for Children's Day Efforts," *PT,* Feb. 1928, 130.

44. *PT,* July 1927, 187; "A Prize-Winning Window for San Diego," *TW,* Oct. 1927, 30, 44. *PT,* July 1927, 187.

45. John B. Watson, *Psychological Care of Infant and Child* (New York: W. W. Norton, 1928); see Dorothy M. Brown, *Setting a Course: Women in the Twenties* (Boston: Twayne, 1987). Effanbee advertisement, *LHJ,* Dec. 1923, 154; C. B. Larrabee, "Effanbee Campaign," 19. *PT,* Oct. 1923, 80.

46. Matthews, *Just a Housewife,* 183. Dorothy Coleman et al., *The Collector's Book of Doll Clothes: Costumes in Miniature, 1700–1929* (New York: Crown Press, 1975), 568. "Antidote for Race Suicide," *PT,* Dec. 1927, 251, cited in Mergen, "Toys and the Culture," 112.

47. Advertisement, *PT,* Mar. 1927, reprinted in Dorothy Coleman et al., *Encyclopedia of Dolls,* 2 vols. (New York: Crown, 1968, 1986), 2:74. *PT,* June 1926, 21; *PT,* June 1923, 128. "Domestic Toys," *PT,* Jan. 1912, 118. Advertisement, *PT,* Jan. 1912, 7. Dorothy Coleman et al., *Collector's Encyclopedia,* 2 vols. (New York: Crown, 1968, 1986), 1:393, 2:728.

48. *PT,* Sept. 1926, 110. *PT,* Jan. 1929, 9. J. M. Barrie, *Peter Pan* (1911; reprinted ed., Toronto: Bantam, 1985), 144. *PT,* Mar. 1927, 148. Editorial in *PT,* Mar. 1927, 131; McCready, "Children's Day Strikes," 75.

49. Gridley, "Children's Day," 122. Robert H. McCready, "Children's Day Scored an Outstanding Success," 98. Cal Lewis, "Dressing Children's Day Windows," *PT,* Mar. 1928, 132.

50. "New Understanding of Children," *PT,* June 1928, 92.

51. *PT,* Mar. 1927, 148; John Fisk, "TV, Polysemy, and Popularity," *Critical Studies in Mass Communication* 3 (1986), 392. *PT,* Jan. 1928, 416. Strong Museum Doll Oral History: Wagner, 1.

52. Warren I. Susman, *Culture as History: The Transformation of American Society in the Twentieth Century* (New York: Pantheon, 1984). Strong Museum Doll Oral History: Mauer, 10–11; Rugg, 13. Gillespie, *With a Merry Heart,* 91.

EPILOGUE

1. Fleischaker & Baum Co. catalogue, "What Every Young Doll Mother Should Know," 1937.
2. Strong Museum Doll Oral History: S. Donaher, 3.
3. "Say It Ain't So, G. I. Joe," *Washington Post,* July 26, 1989, B1, cited by Bernard Mergen, "Made, Bought, and Stolen," in West and Petrik, eds., *Small Worlds,* 334.
4. Fleischaker & Baum, *My Doll's Magazine* (1931), "What Every Young Doll Mother Should Know," "Patty's Doll Club" (1932).
5. "Peter Rabbit Doll Made Her Fortune," *Forbes,* Oct. 1, 1928, 40; Marjorie Price, "Meet Mrs. Santa," *Independent Women,* Dec. 1940, 388; Mildred Adams, "The 'Kewpie' Lady," *Woman Citizen,* Dec. 1925, 37.

INDEX